AMERICAN PAINTED FURNITURE 1660-1880

AMERICAN PAINTED FURNITURE 1660-1880

DEAN A. FALES, JR.

ROBERT BISHOP
Illustrations and Design Editor

CYRIL I. NELSON
General Editor

BONANZA BOOKS

New York

Chest with drawer, oak, Northampton, Massachusetts, 1710–1720. W. 44¾″. Privately owned. See page 19.

Color plate, page 1: Dressing table, pine, etc., New England, 1820–1840. W. 36″. Collection of Mr. and Mrs. Peter H. Tillou. See page 194.

Color plate, page 2: Detail of painting on front of bellows illustrated on page 206. Museum of the City of New York.

This 1986 edition is published by Bonanza Books, distributed by Crown Publishers, Inc., 225 Park Avenue South, New York, New York 10003. All rights reserved under International and Pan-American Copyright Conventions.

Published by arrangement with E.P. Dutton, a division of New American Library

Printed and Bound in Hong Kong

Library of Congress Cataloging in Publication Data

Fales, Dean A.
    American painted furniture, 1660-1880.

    Reprint. Originally published: New York: E.P. Dutton, 1972.
    Includes index.
    1. Painted furniture—United States.   2. Painted country furniture—United States.   3. Decoration and ornament—United States.   I. Nelson, Cyril I.   I. Title.
NK2406.F3   1986   749.213   86-21555
ISBN 0-517-62531-8
h g f e d c b

PREFACE

In 1798 Thomas Dobson of Philadelphia brought out the first encyclopedia published in America. The work was a genteel, admitted lifting of the *Encyclopædia Britannica* in eighteen volumes with a supplement of three volumes covering American subjects. In Volume XIII painting is divided into eighteen categories. The sixteenth is "*Instruments of music, pieces of furniture,* and other inanimate objects: a trifling species, and in which able painters only accidentally employ their talents." Later, the painting of walls in houses and of furniture is described under a chapter on "Oeconomical Painting" as a type "educated to preserve and embellish."

While one might hope for a more glowing description of the painting of furniture, one could not ask for a more accurate one. Painting preserves and embellishes furniture, and it surely is economical. These three qualities are the main reasons for the great popularity of this pleasing lesser art. It could be performed by both amateurs and professionals, and its appeal was widespread. Since it is not constantly striving toward the heights of style, painted furniture can be an accurate reflection of the everyday tastes of regular people. Therefore it constitutes a most important contribution of these people; in the painted furniture of Norway and Switzerland, for example, can be seen more that is truly Norwegian and Swiss than in the finer, more formal pieces.

Now, hopefully, the same will be seen in the painted furniture of early America. The purpose of this book is to survey the development of this craft in the period 1660–1880 and to indicate for the first time the grand, sweeping variety of painted decoration in our furniture. Three basic types of decoration were used here: plain painting, imitative painting, and imaginative or fanciful painting. Stains were used as well as paints. A piece could be painted a single color, it could imitate a finer wood or marble, or it could be highly decorated in its own right. It could defy, emulate, or improve upon nature itself. As a whole, American painted furniture shows the coming together of people from other lands and the eventual emergence of a national style in the nineteenth century. There was always room for the individualist, and there was always room for humor, a quality not often associated with other types of furniture. In short, our painted furniture is a reflection of ourselves.

Only a few authors of general books on furniture have included chapters on American painted furniture. Harold Donaldson Eberlein and Abbot McClure did in their *The Practical Book of Period Furniture* in 1914, and then a half century elapsed until Charles F. Montgomery's fine *American Furniture: The Federal Period* in 1966 included a chapter on fancy furniture. The other branch of "Oeconomical Painting," wall painting, has been admirably covered in Nina Fletcher Little's *American Decorative Wall Painting* (1952); and varied writings of Esther Stevens Brazer, Jean Lipman, and others have admirably touched on specific phases of painted furniture. This book, then, was a joy to write, and full acknowledgments are listed on page 8. It is hoped this work will serve as a springboard for further deeper studies of countless clutches of local painted examples, each one of which adds its own distinctive flavor to the variety of the whole field.

Since the book is chronological in development, a few pieces with later decoration have been included in their earlier position as furniture, rather than in a later position according to their decoration. A single measurement is included, as is the most-used wood in a given piece. Since the emphasis is on the paints, colors are more fully described.

Little is said here on the restoration of damaged paint and decoration. It is the author's strong conviction that painted furniture should be treated like a panel painting (which it is), and extensive restoration work should be attempted only by a professional of the highest skills. Countless how-to-do-it books have been written on furniture decoration, but it should always be remembered that the piece repainted or restenciled is a fallen angel and one that no longer has a precise part as a historic object—at least in the history of early decoration.

Every collector has seen painted furniture in antiques shops with a small corner (usually on the front) carefully scraped to bare a patch of pine or other wood. This is highly informative to one unable to stoop over or to open a drawer, but it does little to help the piece itself. Since most furniture made of light woods in this country was originally painted or stained, each piece should be respectfully examined with care to determine its original finish, rather than ravaged to ascertain its woods. Thus it is with the greatest pleasure that this book is dedicated to those who have kept their knives in their pockets at all times. Through their care we are yet able to see how glorious and thoroughly pervasive was painted decoration on early American furniture.

New England led the country in decoration, a fact attested to by the number of surviving examples of all periods, rather than any regional geocentricity on the part of the author. While English influence was the strongest in early America, the Germans, Dutch, French, and Spanish left their marks on early painted work done here. From Maine to Mississippi and from New Jersey to New Mexico, ornamental painters plied their craft of embellishing and preserving, always with economy. Their efforts surely brought a sense of pleasure and brightness to their own world, just as they have brought it to ours.

DEAN A. FALES, JR.

Kennebunkport, Maine

FOREWORD

What, then, do I look for when considering a new addition to my small, specialized collection? Basic integrity of the painted surface (has it been previously touched up or drastically overcleaned?); vitality of design (is it pleasing to the senses and/or exciting to the eye?); date of decoration (is it the first finish or was it a later addition to an earlier piece?); a reliable statement of previous ownership (which, hopefully, may indicate the history or provenance).

The pine blanket chest illustrated here (H. 38¾"; W. 36½") was a happy addition in 1965. In many ways an unusual example, it probably dates from the first quarter of the eighteenth century and presumably originated in Massachusetts. The moldings are of single-arch type, and the lower drawers (the upper are simulated) are constructed with one wide dovetail reinforced with large rose-headed nails. Original pin hinges remain with the plain lift top, which is molded only on its front edge. The center escutcheons and one brass plate were found still in place, and from the latter the missing pulls were copied by hand. The overall decoration is laid on a reddish-brown background and consists of black running vines terminating in three-petaled flowers also in black. The other blossoms are picked out in a worn but still lively shade of deep coral pink. The ends are ornamented in a simple though typical manner: hollow circles with scalloped edges, which measure nearly two-and-one-half inches in diameter, are spaced at random and enclose large dots of the same coral shade. The meandering floral pattern exhibits an affinity with contemporary needlework, and I have always suspected that the decoration, so unlike the motifs of perky birds, stylized trees, crescents, etc., usual to the period, could well be an example of home talent rather than the work of a professional artisan.

In our day of machine production hand craftsmanship of any kind is becoming increasingly rare. I find that my satisfaction in the warmth and subtlety of the old hand-mixed pigments does not diminish, nor does my conviction that in saving the old finishes, and recording them in print, we are preserving for the future a few significant scraps of America's fast-vanishing heritage of painted decoration.

Nina Fletcher Little

The beginning of my long acquaintance with New England painted furniture developed from my curiosity concerning the architectural use of paint in New England houses. Investigation of the paneling in several rooms of our own 1735 farmhouse revealed that the woodwork was originally painted to simulate the appearance of cedar, mahogany, and marble. My subsequent search for compatible furniture and accessories resulted in the gradual assembling of an informal group of decorated pieces that now contains representative examples from the late seventeenth to the mid-nineteenth centuries.

During the exciting collecting days of the pre-Depression era, restorationists suggested the use of white paint for all so-called colonial interiors, and also recommended a return to natural wood for furniture of corresponding periods. The fact that the majority of light-wood pieces had originally been intended to receive a painted finish was not then generally recognized, and refinishing (with its obvious need to scrape, sand, stain, and shellac) was therefore pursued as a matter of course by all but the most knowing connoisseurs. In this way much documentation of paint colors was irrevocably lost, leaving far fewer examples for study today. Now, in the 1970s, I note with interest that "restoration" is coming full circle. Whereas I once observed old painted surfaces being scraped to the bare wood, I presently see pieces long since refinished now being expertly repainted in a belated effort to return them to some semblance of their original appearance!

FOREWORD

When, in the thirties, my husband and I first became interested in, then excited about, then collectors of American folk art, we thought only about primitive paintings for our old Connecticut farmhouse. However, in the course of antiquing trips, which became a full-time vacation avocation, the painted folk carvings just couldn't be ignored even though we had no idea of where to put them. We ended this progressive collecting mania with, besides the paintings, several hundred ships' figureheads, cigar-store figures, weathervanes, toys, decoys, and various house, garden, and circus carvings that took over most of our living space. Fortunately, this sort of collectors' disease is highly contagious, and the late Stephen C. Clark, a truly great collector of contemporary art, acquired our entire collection for the New York State Historical Association at Cooperstown. Free at last to inhabit our house alone, after fifteen years of living closely with (and as full-time curators of) our folk art, we vowed never to *collect* anything again. We have (technically) kept our vow, but there was a strange vacuum in our lives that we immediately began to fill by interesting ourselves in contemporary sculpture. As we fell in love again, this time with the works of David Smith, Alexander Calder, Louise Nevelson, and quite a few others, we bought some of them for our garden and fields, then a few for the Whitney Museum, and . . . But we were *not* collecting. Nor were we thinking of collecting when we found that the eighteenth- and nineteenth-century decorated furniture that we saw in antique shops (we still *looked* at folk art of all kinds) was just as fascinating as the paintings and carvings, and that some of it seemed extraordinarily in the spirit of twentieth-century avant-garde art. We recognized the freewheeling action of the Abstract Expressionists in the bold swirls of color on painted chests, the precisionists' super-realism in the imitation wood graining. We ended up by outfitting our entire house with decorated furniture and accessories, and *this* kind of folk art is *not* a collection, but an admitted obsession!

The small table shown here (H. 29″; W. 26″) was made and ornamented in the early nineteenth century by a rural carpenter who, naïvely and charmingly, imitated in its construction a drop-leaf table (although nothing actually drops) and in its decoration elaborate inlays of birch, satinwood, and other veneers (some very realistically painted, others quite freely). This table, which we found some years ago in Connecticut, can almost be viewed as a sampler of the country furniture-decorator's art. The various kinds of graining painted on the surface of this one small table are combined with much the same attitude with which young ladies embroidered their samplers a century or two ago: to show the greatest possible range and skill in the execution of a chosen piece of work. Whoever painted this table in a variety of rich colors (reds and yellows and greens), and in a variety of suave brushstrokes (from the broad sweep of the swirls on the tabletop to the stylized birch polka dots on the drawer), was performing with prideful verve. The result is a charming piece of early American painted furniture—both delicate and bold, amusing and impressive, with a lively personality all its own.

Some time ago, Alice Winchester, Editor of The Magazine *Antiques*, assembled a picture-article for *Art in America* (the magazine I edited for thirty years) that was titled "Antiques for the Avant-Garde." Our little trompe-l'oeil "drop-leaf" table, which is often admired by many of the advanced artists who visit us, is a worthy addition to this new category of antiques.

Jean Lipman

ACKNOWLEDGMENTS

Grateful acknowledgment is made to the following persons and institutions for so generously providing material published in this book: Abby Aldrich Rockefeller Folk Art Collection, Williamsburg, Virginia; Albany Institute of History and Art, Albany, New York; Miss Mary Allis; American Antiquarian Society, Worcester, Massachusetts; American Clock & Watch Museum, Bristol, Connecticut; The American Philosophical Society Library, Philadelphia, Pennsylvania; The Art Institute of Chicago, Chicago, Illinois; The Baltimore Museum of Art, Baltimore, Maryland; The Bayou Bend Collection, The Museum of Fine Arts, Houston, Texas; Beauvoir, Jefferson Davis Shrine, Biloxi, Mississippi; Mr. and Mrs. Jerome Blum; The Bostonian Society, Boston, Massachusetts; The Brooklyn Museum, Brooklyn, New York; Mr. and Mrs. Charles L. Bybee; Charles H. and Mary Grace Carpenter; Mr. and Mrs. William F. Carr; Russell Carrell; Lillian Blankley Cogan; The Colonial Williamsburg Foundation, Williamsburg, Virginia; The Connecticut Historical Society, Hartford, Connecticut; Cooper–Hewitt Museum of Decorative Arts and Design, New York; Craig and Tarlton, Inc., Raleigh, North Carolina; Gary R. Davenport; The Detroit Institute of Arts, Detroit, Michigan; Mr. and Mrs. Paul R. Eckley; Essex Institute, Salem, Massachusetts; Jack F. Fenstermacher; Forbes Library, Northampton, Massachusetts; Edgar William and Bernice Chrysler Garbisch; Ginsburg & Levy, Inc., New York; Mr. and Mrs. John Gordon; Dr. and Mrs. William Greenspon; Greenfield Village and Henry Ford Museum, Dearborn, Michigan; Stewart E. Gregory; Mr. and Mrs. Charles V. Hagler; The Hammond–Harwood House, Annapolis, Maryland; Mr. and Mrs. Robert C. Hartlein; Mr. and Mrs. W. Denning Harvey; The Henry Francis du Pont Winterthur Museum, Winterthur, Delaware; Herbert W. Hemphill, Jr.; Peter Hill, Washington, D.C.; Historic Deerfield, Inc., Deerfield, Massachusetts; The Hudson Shop, Red Bank, New Jersey; Mr. and Mrs. Christopher Huntington; Mrs. Barbara Johnson; Mr. and Mrs. Harvey Kahn; Joe Kindig, Jr., York, Pennsylvania; The Library Company of Philadelphia, Philadelphia, Pennsylvania; Library of Congress, Washington, D.C.; Mr. and Mrs. Howard W. Lipman; Mr. and Mrs. Bertram K. Little; The Litchfield Historical Society, Litchfield, Connecticut; Lyman Allyn Museum, New London, Connecticut; Mrs. Douglas MacNeil; Mr. and Mrs. Quinto Maganini; The Magazine *Antiques*, New York; Maryland Historical Society, Baltimore, Maryland; The Metropolitan Museum of Art, New York; Mr. and Mrs. Samuel L. Meulendyke; Monmouth County Historical Association, Freehold, New Jersey; Mr. and Mrs. Charles F. Montgomery; The Mount Vernon Ladies' Association of the Union, Mount Vernon, Virginia; Munson–Williams–Proctor Institute, Utica, New York; Museum of Fine Arts, Boston, Massachusetts; Museum of New Mexico, Santa Fe, New Mexico; Museum of the City of New York, New York; The National Society of the Colonial Dames of America in the Commonwealth of Massachusetts, Boston, Massachusetts; Elise Macy Nelson; The Newark Museum, Newark, New Jersey; New Hampshire Historical Society, Concord, New Hampshire; New Haven Colony Historical Society, New Haven, Connecticut; Newport Historical Society, Newport, Rhode Island; The New-York Historical Society, New York; New York State Historical Association, Cooperstown, New York; The New York Public Library, New York; North Andover Historical Society, North Andover, Massachusetts; Old Gaol Museum, York, Maine; Old Dartmouth Historical Society Whaling Museum, New Bedford, Massachusetts; Old Sturbridge Village, Sturbridge, Massachusetts; The Peabody Museum of Salem, Salem, Massachusetts; William Penn Memorial Museum, Harrisburg, Pennsylvania; Philadelphia Museum of Art, Philadelphia, Pennsylvania; Pocumtuck Valley Memorial Association, Deerfield, Massachusetts; Mr. and Mrs. David Pottinger; Allen Prescott; Francis M. Reynolds; Israel Sack, Inc., New York; The Seamen's Bank for Savings, New York; The Shaker Museum, Old Chatham, New York; Shelburne Museum, Inc., Shelburne, Vermont; Mr. and Mrs. Walter E. Simmons; Sleepy Hollow Restorations, Tarrytown, New York; Mr. and Mrs. Langley Smart; Smithsonian Institution, Washington, D.C.; The Society for the Preservation of New England Antiquities, Boston, Massachusetts; Mr. and Mrs. Frank O. Spinney; Mr. and Mrs. Edward L. Steckler; Mr. and Mrs. Vernon C. Stoneman; Stratford Hall, Stratford, Virginia; Mr. and Mrs. Mitchel Taradash; Mr. and Mrs. Peter H. Tillou; University Art Gallery, Rutgers—The State University of New Jersey, New Brunswick, New Jersey; Wadsworth Atheneum, Hartford, Connecticut; William L. Warren; Samuel H. Wax; Mrs. C. McGregory Wells; White House Historical Association, Washington, D.C.; Richard Withington; Mrs. M. Richard Wyman; Yale University Art Gallery, New Haven, Connecticut; Several Anonymous Private Collectors.

The following individuals have kindly provided valuable assistance: Gray D. Boone; Peter A. G. Brown; Joseph T. Butler; Richard M. Candee; Henry Coger; William Voss Elder III; Nancy Goyne Evans; Miss Etta Faulkner; Miss Jennifer Furkel; Avis and Rockwell Gardiner; Jane C. Giffen; Miss Mary Glaze; Miss Frances Gruber; Katharine B. Hagler; Roland B. Hammond; David A. Hanks; Henry J. Harlow; Thompson R. Harlow; Calvin S. Hathaway; Eugenia Calvert Holland; Robert W. Lovett; Peter O. Marlow; Edgar de N. Mayhew; Henry P. Maynard; Mrs. Richard S. Munford; Milo M. Naeve; Charles S. Parsons; Mrs. Gilbert R. Payson; Robert L. Raley; Richard H. Randall, Jr.; Mr. and Mrs. Norbert H. Savage; Karol G. Schmiegel; Raymond V. Shepherd, Jr.; Miss Patricia E. Smith; J. Peter Spang III; Miss Margaret D. Stearns; Miss Katherine B. Susman; Miss Pamela M. Tosi; Miss Celestina Ucciferri; David B. Warren; and John Wright.

Valued suggestions have been made by Miss Alice Winchester, Charles F. Montgomery, Frank O. Spinney, and the late Henry N. Flynt.

Grateful thanks are due Howard W. and Jean Lipman and Bertram K. and Nina Fletcher Little. Their collecting and scholarship have brought a high level of responsible appreciation to American painted furniture, making this book possible.

Finally, to the Assayer of the Kennebunk Beach Chowder and Marching Club go the author's everlasting thanks for so perfectly broadening his spectrum.

D. A. F., Jr.

CONTENTS

See page 26.

See page 39.

See page 19.

1. Chest, oak, manner of Thomas Dennis, Portsmouth, New Hampshire, or Ipswich, Massachusetts, 1660–1680. W. 44⅜″. Museum of Fine Arts, Boston.

2. Chest with drawer, oak and pine, probably Plymouth, Massachusetts, 1675–1695. W. 53⅝″. Museum of Fine Arts, Boston.

I. EARLY COLONIAL

The Seventeenth Century

Woods, like people, have always needed to be covered to be protected. On furniture, exterior surfaces could be waxed, oiled, varnished, or painted. In the seventeenth century, paints, including stains and glazes, had become widely available in Europe. Painted furniture, easily decorated and also inexpensive, became popular. American furniture styles in the last half of the seventeenth century were constantly on the move. Extravaganzas of floral carving slowly gave way to simpler, geometrical decoration in products of the joiner. The turner added his split spindles and bosses. However, the move was on, from Jacobean floridity through Cromwellian conservatism and finally to Baroque flamboyance, and painted decoration played a significant and exciting part in these changes.

Most of the early oak furniture made in the Colonies was stained or painted originally. Stains were easily available, made normally from vegetable coloring matter dissolved in oil. Pigments for paints were mostly imported from England and ground in oil prior to use. They were made from metals and earths. Colors were highly unstable at times, and the binders could easily become unbound, before the arrival of professionally trained painter-stainers by the 1680s. However, the finishes that could survive such foes as poor manufacture and the wear and tear of centuries had one more ordeal to undergo—that of friendship. The first wave of American antiques collectors, who flourished in the "golden-oak" period, thought nothing of removing original finishes from their favorite pieces of seventeenth century furniture.

In spite of both love and neglect, a few key examples of early furniture have survived with their decoration basically intact. Found in Portsmouth, New Hampshire, in 1891, a chest (1) features flat, abstracted leaf forms typical of our earliest pieces. Scrolls and palmettes are on the rails, while embryonic fleurs-de-lis, a favorite early device, descend the stiles. The motion of the carving is accented and unified by red, black, blue, and white paint.

Thomas Dennis, who worked in Portsmouth in the 1660s and in Ipswich, Massachusetts, from 1668 until his death in 1706, was one of the early joiners working in the Colonies and could have made two of the chests shown here (1, 3). Figure 3 bears the initials of his near-neighbors John and Margaret Staniford and is dated 1678. It is our earliest fully developed chest of drawers. The carving has retreated to a single drawer front, and the surface is varied by moldings, panels, and split spindles. Its painted decoration, in red, white, and black, makes it the most significant example of early painted furniture in America.[1] In the final chest (2) geometrics have all but eliminated carving, yet black and red paints and stains provide lively contrasts.

3. Chest of drawers, oak, probably made by Thomas Dennis, Ipswich, Massachusetts, dated 1678. W. 44¾". The Henry Francis du Pont Winterthur Museum.

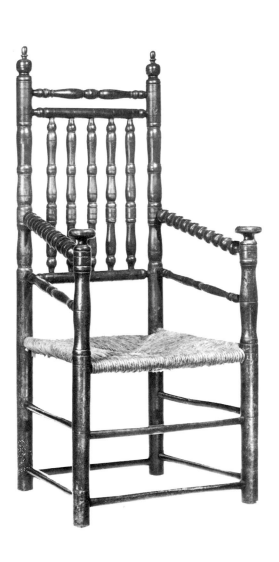

4. Armchair, maple, New England, last half of the seventeenth century. Painted red. H. 53½". The Henry Ford Museum.

5. Chest (with drawer)-on-frame, oak and pine, Massachusetts, last quarter of the seventeenth century. Painted black. W. 28". The Metropolitan Museum of Art.

The best paints for furniture decorating were those ground in oil. Distemper paints, ground in water with size, were also used. The latter were less expensive and less favored, since they were not so permanent. It was not until the 1860s that cans of premixed paints were available in stores. The most-used early colors were black (made from lampblack and bituminous earths) and red (made from cinnabar, red lead, or iron oxides). White, from white lead, was the old standby and could vary from pure white to a stone color. Blues and greens were available from minerals and verdigris; and in Bos-

ton a "halfe headed bedsted wᵗʰ blew pillars" and a "livery Cupboard coloured blue" were listed in a 1651 inventory, as was a "Green desk for a woman" in 1654.[2] All four examples on these two pages made use of early uniform turnings in their decoration. The Carver armchair and table were painted red. The terms "Indian red" and "Spanish brown" were used to describe high-quality reds originally from the East Indies and Spain. The chest above was painted black, and the one at the right (7), denuded by later enthusiasm, has ebonized bosses, balusters, and panels to contrast with the oak.

6. Table, drop-leaf, maple, oak, and pine, New England, 1675–1695. Red paint. W. 36½″. The Metropolitan Museum of Art.

7. Chest (with drawer)-on-frame, oak and maple, Essex County, Massachusetts, c. 1690. Black accents. W. 30½″. The Art Institute of Chicago.

13

By far the most flavorful collector of seventeenth-century objects—and one of the first—was the Reverend William Bentley (1759–1819) of Salem. He was pastor of the East Church from 1783 until his death, but he is best-known today for his peripatetic four-volume diary, the most revealing and rewarding one written in Federal America. Constantly, Dr. Bentley could snoop and snipe about to perfection, and his innate antiquarian proclivities are fully vented throughout his writings in descriptions of early objects of all sorts.

This fine slat-back armchair, with extremely well-turned finials, was recorded by Bentley in June 1793:

Ordered the Chair received from the family of English in memory of 1692 to be painted green, & on the back 1692, upper slat; middle slat, *M. English;* lower slat, *Ap. 22,* the time of her mittimus; on the front upper slat, *It shall be told of her.*

The chair exists today with its color and inscriptions intact as a memorial to Mary English and her husband, Philip, who were accused of being witches in 1692.

8. Armchair, oak, Salem, Massachusetts,
last half of the seventeenth century.
Painted green. H. 48″. Essex Institute.

9. The Bostonian Society.

Bentley missed little of antiquarian interest in the Salem-Boston area, but he failed to record this fascinating sign that was displayed on a building on Hanover Street in Boston until 1933. The sign, nearly a yard square, displays the arms of the Painter-Stainers Company of London, founded in the sixteenth century. Thomas Child, who was born about 1658 in Middlesex, England, became a freeman of the Company in 1679; and he came to the Boston area before 1688, when he married Katherine Masters. The upper part of the arms had been broken off, and Child added a section with his and his wife's initials. He changed the date 1697 to 1701, the year he purchased property in Boston from the estate of Thomas Marshall, a former shoemaker and selectman.[3]

Until his death in 1706 Child carried on the varied functions of a painter-stainer. His training would have included the refining of oils, grinding of colors, making brushes, staining furniture and woodwork, painting houses, and also the drawing of figures and landscapes. In Boston he painted window frames, shutters, and even an hourglass for King's Chapel. He painted the fence and exterior of the "Latten Schoolmaster's House," as well as primed the inside. He painted twenty gun carriages for Castle William, and he painted a funeral hatchment for the estate of Samuel Shrimpton. Around 1700 he acquired a stone trough about twelve feet long, with a large ball of stone for the grinding of pigments. After his death a fragment of this stone and the ball were set up as "The Boston Stone," indicating the center of the city. It exists today downtown.

Child was one of the first of the many painter-stainers who did so much to add color everywhere in the eighteenth century. It was rumored that he also did portraits—some after death—and when Child died, Samuel Sewall wrote in his diary, November 10, 1706:

This morning Tom Child the Painter died.

"Tom Child had often painted Death,
But never to the Life, before:
Doing it now, he's out of Breath;
He paints it once, and paints no more."

10. Bible box, pine, New England, 1680–1710. Painted blue-green. W. 27″. The Detroit Institute of Arts, Gift of Mr. and Mrs. Edsel B. Ford.

11. Folding table, oak and maple, Essex County, Massachusetts, 1675–1690. W. 36″. The Metropolitan Museum of Art.

12. Court cupboard, oak and maple, Essex County, Massachusetts, dated 1680. W. 50″. Winterthur Museum.

Two major constituents make up paints—the pigment and the vehicle. Vehicles must contain binders, solvents, and dryers. If any one of these fails to act properly, the longevity of the paint is doomed from the start. Pigments can change color or the paint can revert to dust. Colors like "lead" color, which change over the years and practically disappear, are referred to as "fugitive colors." Most of the early finishes have also fled, and it should be borne in mind that they were highly glossy until relatively modern times.

In the four examples shown here, only the box at the left and a single drawer of the cupboard at the right retain earlier Jacobean carving. The tulip carving on the Bible box, which is painted a strong blue-green, is a delightful echo of the earlier tradition. The fleur-de-lis carving on the cupboard drawer is similar to that on a drawer of the Staniford chest of drawers (see figure 3, pages 10–11).

The bold turnings on the legs of the table at the left relate to the baluster turnings on the two cupboards. One of the legs swings to hold the folding top, which is round when opened. The bottom of the table is painted red with fuzzy black designs, and the top was repainted at a later date with gray and white impressionistic marbleizing.

Early cupboards were "kings of the jungle" in the seventeenth century. Those with open bases, such as figure 12, are referred to in this country as "court cupboards," while those which are enclosed to the bottom are called "press cupboards" (13). Both of these would also be called "splayed cupboards," since their upper sections are angled rather than straight. Figure 12 has a buxom overhang in the upper section reminiscent of early houses. Its balusters and spindles are painted black. On the cupboard at the right, behind the applied decoration, which is painted black, can be seen lingerings of red and black paints or stains. The bottom drawer certainly would have been a strong candidate for painted scroll decoration like that on the Staniford chest.

Most of the earliest American furniture known was made in Massachusetts. As the seventeenth century drew to a close, however, craftsmen from other Colonies started making their own individual and regional preferences felt.

13. Press cupboard, oak and maple, Essex County, Massachusetts, 1675–1690.
W. 48½". Museum of Fine Arts, Boston.

Up the Connecticut River

14

14. Press cupboard, oak, etc., probably Wethersfield, Connecticut, associated with Peter Blin, 1675–1700. Carved decoration with tulips, roses, thistles, and hearts. W. 49¼". Yale University Art Gallery, Gift of Charles Wyllys Betts.
15. Chest with drawers, oak, Hartford County, Connecticut, dated 1704. W. 48". The Art Institute of Chicago.

16. (Opposite). Chest with drawer, oak, Hadley–Hatfield area, Massachusetts, 1680–1710. W. 48". Privately owned.
17. Chest with drawer, oak, Northampton, Massachusetts, 1710–1720. W. 44¾". Privately owned.
18. Chest with drawers, oak, Hadley–Hatfield area, Massachusetts, 1675–1710. W. 42". Forbes Library.

By the end of the seventeenth century Boston and New York had become the principal centers of the Colonies, with Philadelphia still to be heard from. Connecticut had a location that permitted a view of the latest styles, yet she also had a geography (and population) that preferred to develop its own. Furniture in the English mode had been made in the colony around the middle of the seventeenth century, but by the 1680s that wondrous spirit of strong accomplishment, coupled with occasional stylistic irreverence, gave the productions of Connecticut a spirited delight that was to continue throughout the next century. While the Connecticut River flowed south, there was an upstream direction of influences on local joiners and turners that was felt in west-central Massachusetts and along what was to be the border between New Hampshire and Vermont.

Decorative motifs introduced in the Connecticut River Valley remained a long time. Tulips, Tudor roses, scrolls, and leafy vines won favor with joiners from near Hartford northward to Deerfield, Massachusetts.

15

Over forty case pieces with distinctive carving make up the sunflower type. Stylized roses and tulips are their hallmarks. The cupboard (14) is painted a deep red ground, with applied ornamentation in black. Black lines on yellowed white moldings appear above and below the upper doors. One chest of this type has been ascribed to Peter Blin, a joiner of Wethersfield, near Hartford.[4] Figure 15 is important in the study of painted furniture. The carving, not too well executed, has disappeared from the center panel, as have the bosses and some of the split spindles on the lower front and sides. It was made to be decorated, and the yellow, red, and black paint provides a transition from earlier carved surfaces on chests to the flat facades of the eighteenth century. Dovetails fasten the drawers, instead of the earlier rabbet-and-nail method usual in sunflower chests.

The terms "sunflower" and "Hadley" are relatively modern. Examples of the so-called Hadley type were made in the Connecticut River Valley in the areas of Hadley–Hatfield and Northampton in Massachusetts, and in Connecticut from Enfield downriver to Hartford County. Extremely flat tulip and leaf carving are the hallmarks of these chests, with pinwheels and hearts occasionally used. The entire surface is usually treated with a scratch-carving technique with squiggly scrolls that give the surface a feeling of embroidery. Variations occur often in the decoration. Around 150 of these chests and boxes are known, made from 1670 to about 1730. Many were made for young ladies as hope chests, while a few were initialed as wedding chests. Some makers are known—or at least suspected—such as John Pease of Enfield, John and Ichabod Allis and Samuel Belding, Jr., of Hadley and Hatfield, and John Hawks of Hatfield and Deerfield. Since other joiners or carpenters could have produced chests along this fifty-mile stretch of the valley, definite attributions to particular makers can be risky indeed.

Hadley chests were painted or stained when made, the colors unifying the incredibly worked-over details of their facades. The rails and stiles of 16 have aged to a deep maroon, the drawers and panels being black. It is representative of the Hadley type, with tulips and scrolled leaves gamboling stiffly over the front. Hearts on the panels and vertical stiles are repeated on the bottom rail with lunettes. The decoration does not run over onto the stiles, as it does on 18. The "MM" chest is notable for its early paint (see color plate page 9). The stiles and rails are black, with the exception of the red rail below the red central panel. The top drawer is dark brown, and the lower drawer and two outside panels are lightly stained natural, as is much of the stippled background. The "ESTHER LYMAN" chest (17) is unusual in having the full name of its owner, who was born in Northampton in 1698 and married Benjamin Talcott in 1724. Its fleurs-de-lis, scrolls, and panels differ from usual Hadley chests, and its red and black colors survive (see color plate page 4).[5]

16

17

18

19

20a. Detail showing left panel on top drawer of chest page 22.

At the turn of the century a highly spirited group of cased pieces with painted polychrome decoration was made in the Hadley area. Three are shown here and on the next two pages. Like the carved chests, they could be hope chests for young ladies—or, in the case of 21, a hope cupboard! The "SW" chest (19) and top of the cupboard have earlier recessed panels, but around the drawers the surfaces are all flat. The chest of drawers (20) and cupboard make use of heavy moldings, which are not on the "SW" chest. The turned legs on 20 are a later feature, and the balusters of the cupboard lack the heft of earlier turned work.

Made to be decorated, these examples form an effective transition from earlier carved work, on which painting could be a supplemental and unifying force in the decoration, to plainer forms on which painted decoration was meant to be featured in its own right. Blues and reds of varying shades were used as colors, as well as yellow, black, and white. Since the Baroque had not yet curved its way up the Connecticut Valley, earlier types of decoration were translated into paint. The sunflower or Tudor rose became a segmented circle. Tulips disappeared and leafy vines became much smaller and highly stylized. The inverted hearts of the earlier Hadley chests were continued, and simple diamonds and bull's-eyes were used to produce a colorful and delightful well-ordered series of doodles.

The "SW" chest at the right has a modest history representative of many important pieces in the older historical societies. George Sheldon, Deerfield's colorful antiquarian, purchased it in 1870 from Jonathan A. Saxton, who said the chest had been owned in the White family and had come over on the *Mayflower!* Although its travels were not so extensive as once hoped, the chest combines the early type of joinery with gloriously naïve geometrical painting. The outer two panels contain what appears to be almost a dart-board type of decoration.

The compartmented rectangles with invected corners on the drawers are done with greater boldness on the chest and press cupboard on the next two pages. The chest of drawers (20), found in Vermont, combines red, black, maroon, and yellow in the geometric designs. The background color is cream, probably from white lead acting up as usual, and the compartments are painted black. The turned legs are unusual and a bit skimpy for the mass of the case. However, this practice was evidently a local preference, since other early framed chests—alas, mostly refinished—are found in the Hadley–Deerfield area with small turned legs which are continuations of the stiles. The similarity of the decoration on both the chest of drawers and the cupboard is striking. The press cupboard, made and so clearly inscribed for Hannah Barnard of Hadley, is an example of the persistence of successful forms in rural areas. Born in 1684, Hannah Barnard married John Marsh in 1715 and died in childbirth within two years. The date of the cupboard, then, can be assumed to cover the years of her eligibility, from around 1700 to 1715. Since it is so well documented, this press cupboard is a key in the dating of this select group of painted pieces. In them, paint had replaced carving, and inventiveness and expediency joined together to produce an effect which, though outdated, was one of true resplendence.

19. Chest with drawers, Hadley area, Massachusetts, 1695–1720. W. 42".
Pocumtuck Valley Memorial Association.

20. Chest of drawers, oak, Hadley area, Massachusetts, early eighteenth century. Cream field; black panel outlines; polychrome decoration. W. 43½″. Winterthur Museum.

21. Press cupboard, oak, Hadley area, Massachusetts, c. 1700–1715. Owned by Hannah Barnard Marsh (1684–1717). Black lettering; polychrome decoration. W. 50″. The Henry Ford Museum.

Along the Connecticut Shore

22a

The Connecticut coastline, east of New Haven from Guilford to Saybrook, at the mouth of the Connecticut River, was the starting point of several groups of well-decorated chests early in the 1700s. The most interesting of these is typified by the chest of drawers on these pages, with roses, fleurs-de-lis, thistles, and crowns featured in the decoration. These motifs, found in the British royal arms, had been popular for generations and are found in printers' devices (see 23) as early as the 1611 King James Bible headpiece for the book of Job.[6] Their usage, coupled with early vases, birds, undulating vines, and pinks and other flowers, results in a group of chests with very sophisticated decoration. Some, like the chest on frame (26) and the high chest of drawers (29), were in the new William and Mary style with turned legs, while others, like the chest of drawers (22) and the chest with drawer (28), were joined in the older manner. The ends of the chest of drawers (22a) bear a large dotted tulip. Yellow, red, pink, and white are used on a black painted ground over a red stain primer. Birds occur on the ends also (see 26 and 28).

One feature shared by these chests is their woods. Instead of oak of the early period, native tulip is used largely as the primary wood. The makers were able to use easily available, local soft woods, which, by a mere priming, were well suited for decoration at a very low cost.

Charles Gillam of Saybrook may have made some of these Guilford–Saybrook chests. His inventory in 1727 listed ochre, umber, "a painted chest with drawers," "a parcel of collours," partially completed furniture, and cabinetmaking tools. Others also made painted furniture, since more than one type of chest is found along the shore area. Decorative-arts historians will long ponder the inspiration of these fine chests. Whether the motivation was provided by marquetry, heraldry, embroidery, "Turkey carpits," printers' devices, burled woods, or by actual English examples, the result is a distinctive American contribution to furniture design and decoration.

By the end of the seventeenth century a new force, the William and Mary style, had been felt in the larger seaports of the Colonies. A new wood (walnut), new methods of construction, and new elements from trumpet turnings to burled veneers had been introduced, and the curves and reverse curves of the Baroque flourished.

Not so in the smaller towns. The tried and true methods of construction and decoration continued, with only an occasional admission of the new styles. Painted furniture, mostly a rural product until the 1790s, shared in these cautions.

22. Chest of drawers, tulip and oak, Guilford–Saybrook area, Connecticut, 1700–1720. W. 44¼″. 22a. Detail showing decoration on side of chest. Wadsworth Atheneum.

23. Chapter heading from [John Worlidge], *Systema Agriculturae*, London, 1675. Winterthur Museum.

24a

24. Chest with drawers, tulip, Connecticut Shore, dated 1724. W. 42½″. 24a. Detail showing central devices painted in upper section of chest. Winterthur Museum.

25. Chest with drawers, tulip, Connecticut Shore, dated 1726. W. 29⅞". Winterthur Museum.

The chests with drawers on these two pages have painted decoration that differs from the normal Guilford–Saybrook type. They were made in the same shore area, both using tulip extensively as the primary wood. The one to the left (24) has excellent decoration, with black strips at the top and base containing delicate vine and floral scrolls. The unusual paneled drawers and edges of the case are also outlined in black. The lighter background is yellow ochre; and birds, scrolls, and flowers are done in white, green, black, and red (see color plate page 9). The sides are decorated in the same colors on a reddish-brown ground, with black half-circles at the base. The central devices in the upper section, ascending from a bird to a door and a window, then through crosshatching to a baluster, are most fanciful. It is dated 1724.[7] The less startling, smaller chest (above) has similar reddish-brown sides and front panels. The other areas have a black ground; and the decoration, in white only, with scrolls and abstract flowers, seems almost a preview of stenciled decoration of the next century. It is dated July 9, 1726. Both chests have brass pulls on the drawers.

26. Chest-on-frame, tulip, Guilford–Saybrook area, Connecticut, 1700–1725. Black ground. W. 30¼″. The Metropolitan Museum of Art.

27. Chest, tulip, Guilford–Saybrook area, Connecticut, 1700–1725. Reddish-brown ground. W. 47″. Privately owned.

28. Chest with drawer, tulip and oak, Guilford–Saybrook area, Connecticut, 1700–1720. Dark-green ground, with pheasants painted on ends, and dotted zigzags on rails and stiles. W. 47½″. The four chests on these two pages show the variety of forms and ground colors used with this forceful decoration. The Henry Ford Museum.

29. High chest of drawers, tulip, ash, and pine, Guilford–Saybrook area, Connecticut, 1700–1725. W. 40⅛″. This high chest is the most impressive example of the Guilford–Saybrook productions. Wintherthur Museum.

31. Chest with drawer, pine and maple, probably
Guilford–Saybrook area, Connecticut, 1700–1725. Black
ground. W. 17½″. Privately owned.

30. Side chair, maple, poplar, and ash, western Connecticut Shore, eighteenth century. H. 43″. Painted black.
Collection of Lillian Blankley Cogan.

32. Chest with drawers, Connecticut Shore, 1700–1730. Red ground. Two tulips on each end. Decoration extends over both top false drawers, an unusual feature in Connecticut. W. 37¼". Privately owned.

33. Bible box, pine, Connecticut, 1710–1740. Red ground, with black, cream, and orange-red decoration. Not related to Guilford–Saybrook examples. W. 24". Privately owned.

The Eighteenth Century

34. Wadsworth Atheneum.

Furniture is the most basic of the decorative arts and draws a great measure of its inspiration from the most basic of the fine arts, architecture. Certain forms, such as settles and cupboards, are architectural in nature; and most of the principles of design and proportion that govern furniture have come from that major art. In the period 1700–1750 one of the biggest developments in architecture in the Colonies was the more extensive use of paints. Buildings were painted more often on the outside, and decorative painting was especially suited to the newer paneling. In 1705 the House of Burgesses in Williamsburg voted to have the "wanscote and other Wooden work" of their meeting-house "painted like marble." [8] The imitative techniques of graining and marbleizing became popular.

In 1753 George Tilley, a Boston shopkeeper, advertised his house to be sold. One room was "painted Green, another Blue, one Cedar and one Marble; the other four a Lead colour." [9] The fireplace wall above, at the Wadsworth Atheneum, is a striking example of early marbleizing and is from an upstairs room of the house built by Joseph Pitkin in East Hartford, Connecticut, in 1723. Another change in the eighteenth century was the greater availability of painters' colors. In Boston they had been advertised as early as 1710; but by 1738 John Marrett was able to offer in the May 9th *New England Journal* over thirty colors for sale, including white and red lead, Spanish white, Spanish brown, spruce yellow, vermilion, ruddle, Indian red, smalt, and umber "for Oyl or Water."

36. The William and Mary Parlor, c. 1725, contains eastern New England furnishings of the first half of the eighteenth century. Winterthur Museum.

The most important early book on the painting of furniture was *A Treatise of Japaning and Varnishing,* by John Stalker and George Parker, printed in Oxford, England, in 1688. In addition to instructions on japanning, it contains much information on paints and painting. One chapter is entitled "To Imitate and Counterfeit Tortoise-shell and Marble" and describes methods for their imitations. The paneling in the room above is from the Thomas Goble house in Lincoln, Massachusetts, and was marbleized and grained when it was installed about 1725. The colors are red, gray, and white; and the cedar graining runs vertically and horizontally on the panels, which are contained by marbleized surrounds and moldings. The furniture is in the new William and Mary style, which became widespread in the Colonies in the early 1700s. The chair next to the fireplace is grained to imitate walnut, the banister-back armchair is painted black, and the small chest under the window is decorated (see page 39). Of all the imitative techniques, graining was by far the most popular and long-lived, lasting beyond the middle of the nineteenth century. Grains of any woods could be imitated, and the result, when done well, as in the high chest of drawers at the left, could be stylish and economical.

35. High chest of drawers, tulip, southern New England, 1700–1735. Brown graining. W. 37″ Old Sturbridge Village.

The furniture shown here represents the best in the first half of the eighteenth century in northern New England. The looking glass (39), from the house of Sir William Pepperrell in Kittery, Maine, is one of the few instances of imitation of tortoiseshell work done in the Colonies. It is painted red and black. The other pieces here are all plain painted. The easy chair, with its embryonic Queen Anne legs and colorful woven Bargello-work upholstery, is painted black. The sprightly splay-leg, oval-top table was painted a reddish-brown, while the armchair at the right is brown. All three have carved Spanish feet. The armchair (40) is one of a group associated with the Gaines family of Ipswich and Portsmouth. An account book of John and Thomas Gaines, Ipswich, 1707–1762, lists brown and black chairs.[10] Transitional Queen Anne side chairs quite similar to 40 were made in 1728 by the younger John Gaines of Portsmouth for his own family.

37. Easy chair, maple, Portsmouth area, New Hampshire, 1725–1750. H. 50½". New Hampshire Historical Society.

39. Looking glass, pine, New England, early eighteenth century. H. 46¾″. Winterthur Museum.

38. Table, maple and pine, Portsmouth area, New Hampshire, 1720–1750. W. 34″. Old Gaol Museum.

40. Armchair, cherry and maple, associated with Gaines family, Ipswich, Massachusetts, and Portsmouth, New Hampshire, 1725–1745. H. 43″. Winterthur Museum.

41, 41a, 41b. Chest of drawers, pine, probably eastern Massachusetts, 1710–1750. W. 38½″. Shelburne Museum, Inc.

41a   41b

The two colors used over and over on both plain-painted and decorated furniture of the eighteenth century were black and red. Along with white lead, they were by far the easiest pigments to procure, and fortunately they were well suited for furniture paints. These basic colors, plus a hint of yellow, are found in a small group of chests with very distinctive decoration. Probably made in some rural area of eastern Massachusetts, they are later than they first appear, and their sampler-like decoration adds much to their "japanned" quality. On this chest (41) the red-on-black decoration features shell forms at the center base of all the drawers, diagonal stairs on the lowest drawer and two brick buildings with cupolas on the drawer above. Fanciful flowers and leaves are on the drawers, the smaller ones at the top having curious sprouts with spade tips. The decoration is confined to each drawer, with the shell forms and colors providing unity to the facade. Another chest is known that is practically identical to this one, except it has a single drawer across the top.[11] A third example featuring buildings on one of the drawers is a high chest of drawers (43) on page 38. With some restoration, especially

along the base, its decoration is similar to the chest on the opposite page. The stairway has a landing, and the windows of the buildings contain diamond-shaped panes of glass, rather than the square panes of the other two chests. Details such as windows were a whim of the painter, and little significance should be attached to the dating of these pieces by their use of casement or double-hung window sashes. The exact dates of these chests are unknown, but they were all probably made within a relatively brief time span sometime well into the eighteenth century.

A variant of this type can be seen in 42. The diagonal stairs, shells, and plant life remain, but two birds have supplanted the buildings.[12] This chest has five banks of drawers, a record for the type. A single-drawer blanket chest, with three simulated drawers, in the Sheldon-Hawks house at Deerfield, is birdless, with only the shells and flowers. These chests were once referred to optimistically as "Harvard chests," but a comparison with the 1726 William Burgis view of "the Colleges in Cambridge" confirms the fact that the buildings on the chests, while charming and fanciful, are hardly academic.

42. Chest of drawers, pine, probably eastern Massachusetts, 1710–1750. Black, with red, white, and yellow decoration. W. 38″. Privately owned.

43. High chest of drawers, pine and maple, probably eastern Massachusetts, 1710–1750. Black, with red-and-white decoration. W. 39″. North Andover Historical Society.

46. Chest with drawers, pine, Taunton,
Massachusetts, dated 1742. W. 24″.
Winterthur Museum.

44. Small chest with drawer, pine,
Taunton, Massachusetts, 1725–1730.
W. 17″. Privately owned

45. Chest with drawer, pine, Taunton,
Massachusetts, 1725–1730. W. 38½″.
Collection of Mr. and Mrs. Mitchel
Taradash.

Among the most charming types of decorated
chests are those made in Taunton, Massachusetts. Esther Stevens Fraser Brazer, one of the
first modern students of early American decoration, published her discoveries on them in
1933.[13] A key piece was a small decorated chest,
dated 1729 and inscribed "TaunTon/R C:/1729."
Robert Crosman (1707–1799), a drum maker of
Taunton, is considered most likely to be the
maker of these chests, which number barely
over a dozen. Some are dated between 1729 and
1742. Made of white pine, they are simple
chests, the side boards continuing down to the
floor and cut out to form the feet. Trees, vines,
and birds are part of their decorative vocabulary, as is the rusty blackish-brown ground on
which vermilion and white form the designs.
The blanket chest and small chest with drawer
at the left are early examples of this type, while
the one above is the latest, most highly developed example known, with double-arched
drawer moldings (see color plate page 9). The
designs spread over the entire front of the chest,
without regard to drawer divisions, with the
greatest delicacy.

A delightful arboreal interlude is provided by the chest on these two pages. The chest itself is later than those we have seen, with lipped drawers, lighter moldings, and engraved brasses that became popular after 1720. However, the great charm of the piece is its decoration, which was added about 1825. It is done in the manner of itinerant wall painters and bears similarities to work done by the most fascinating and facile of these nomadic decorators, Rufus Porter (1792–1884).[14] Trained as a house-and-sign painter in Maine, Porter moved to Massachusetts and went all over northern New England from 1823 to 1843 painting wall decorations in many houses. He published *A Select Collection of Valuable and Curious Arts, and Interesting Experiments* in 1825, and it contains his instructions for fresco painting. Here, and in later articles in *Scientific American,* Porter theorized on his art. He felt landscape painting should go beyond nature itself and show better forms, conceived in the mind of the artist. The trees on the chest tie in directly with his theories and are very similar to early landscapes he painted about 1824 in the ballroom of the Coburn Tavern, East Pepperell, Massachusetts. While the thirteen trees on the upper panel are well done, the tree at lowest right suggests exoticism or exhaustion!

47a

47b

47, 47a, 47b. Chest with drawers, pine, New England, 1720–1760. Decoration added c. 1825. Top and base are gray-green, with trees in red and ochre on a cream background. Two rows of trees on sides. W. 37¾″. Collection of Mr. and Mrs. Mitchel Taradash.

48

49

50

The chests on these two pages provide a review of early eighteenth-century decorative motifs in New England. The chest with drawers at the upper left (48) is a stylish one, with crisp moldings. The black foliated scrolls are done with verve on the red background and are highly reminiscent of seaweed marquetry decoration on English chests. It combines boldness with delicacy in a most urbane and satisfying manner. It was made in eastern Massachusetts.[15]

Not every decorated chest was the work of a professional painter. The two other chests at the left are obvious examples of "at home" decoration. The same term might be applied to the construction of 49. This chest with drawer is made of pine, with very simple moldings, rather weakly defined front ball feet, and rear legs made from slightly shaped tree branches! The colors are the simplest—white and ochre on a black background. The drawer divisions are delineated by a series of dashes which enclose meandering floral vines that grow in different directions on alternating drawer divisions. On the ends, commas or apostrophes complete the rather humble, yet forthright decoration of this chest, which was probably made south of Boston, toward the Rhode Island border.

The chest of drawers at the left (50) boasts slightly better cabinetmaking, yet its painting is on the simple side, with only red and white designs on a dark-brown ground. The upper two drawers have an envelope sort of decoration, while the lower two feature leafy vines, all within rectangular compartments. The top of the chest has quarter circles painted on the four corners and a diamond at the center.

While the decoration of both 49 and 50 lacks the snap and quality of better-finished work, these chests have a charm of their own and provide us a truer appearance of rural eighteenth-century chests than they ever could if they had been stripped down to their pine and refinished. Practically every chest made of pine or other soft woods in the Colonies was made originally to be at least plain painted, if not decorated.

The diversity of Connecticut decoration can

48. Chest with drawers, pine, ash, oak, and maple, Massachusetts, 1710–1725. W. 39½". Winterthur Museum.
49. Chest with drawer, pine and maple, southern Massachusetts, 1710–1740. W. 40". Museum of Fine Arts, Boston.
50. Chest of drawers, pine, probably Massachusetts, 1710–1740. W. 37¼". The Henry Ford Museum.

be seen on the three examples shown on page 43. The chest of drawers at the top (51) is the earliest chest on these two pages, with heavy, half-round horizontal moldings on the case and recessed, molded panels on the drawers. Paints of only two colors, a lighter and a darker brown, make an interesting, highly stylized design of thistles, flowers, and leafy vines on the drawer fronts. This decoration uses the thistle in a different manner than on the Guilford–Saybrook chests (see pages 25, 28, and 29).

Figure 52 is one of an interesting small group that features three-petaled flowers that terminate in fleurs-de-lis. On a black ground, red, white, and yellow ochre make up the decoration, which continues on the ends of the chest. A border of wavy lines frames the edges of the front and surrounds the keyhole. On a similar chest dots were used for this border.[16] Three chests, with similar decoration, have been associated with the Milford or Woodbury areas of Connecticut. This chest, however, was owned by the Shepherd family of Montague, Massachusetts, in the Connecticut River Valley. In the old catalogue of the Pocumtuck Valley Memorial Association, it was described as a "Lily chest. . . . An old and odd affair." It also shows in an old photograph entitled "The Dash Churn," which features a woman churning, in George Francis Dow's *Every Day Life in the Massachusetts Bay Colony*. It would appear, then, that this chest had come up the valley at a relatively early date. Its drawer is raised up above the base, and the molding along the base at the front becomes a woodless stripe of red along the sides.

The final chest (53), also with the cut-out ends, has a scalloped, bracketed front skirt and has double-arch drawer moldings which make a triple division in the upper, simulated drawer. Black tulips are on the rust ground on the sides and upper drawer divisions, while the two working drawers have dotted peregrinations charmingly wandering over their surfaces. The skirt and top and bottom moldings are dark yellow-green.

51. Chest of drawers, tulip, probably Connecticut, 1700–1725. W. 49¼". Shelburne Museum, Inc.
52. Chest with drawer, pine, Connecticut, 1700–1735. W. 36". Pocumtuck Valley Memorial Association.
53. Chest with drawers, pine and poplar, Connecticut, 1710–1740. W. 45½". New Haven Colony Historical Society.

51

52

53

54. Chest of drawers, pine, New England, 1710–1730. W. 36½". Privately owned.

54a. Detail showing side of 54.

Painted graining could be strictly imitative or it could be highly fanciful, creating an illusive air in its decoration. This striking chest of drawers (54 and 54a) is hardly a strictly imitative rendition of tortoiseshell or richly burled veneers! Indian red (reddish-brown) and ochre are the only colors used to achieve this startling decoration. As in most graining, the lighter color was applied to the wood first, which was usually primed with the same color. Then the darker red was carefully applied with well-defined brushstrokes. The decoration of the long drawers is divided into two compartments and suggests the burled veneers and inlays of finer furniture. This suggestion is typical of eighteenth-century graining, which was more indicative than exact. Cedar graining, which was lighter than mahogany, and mahogany graining were the two popular types in the 1700s, as was also marbleizing. It was not until early in the nineteenth century that exact copies of numerous woods became widespread. Even lowly knots progressed from swirling abstractions to literal simulations. In 1816 William Bentley mentioned interiors painted for Dudley Woodbridge before 1750 by John Holliman, a painter-stainer and gravestone cutter of Salem and Boston. He described the parlor paneling: "The ground is variegated white & black shaded. The pannels brown framed in white. Above in the chamber the ground white & red variegated shades, frame and pannel as below. One beam till lately covered by a closet exhibits all the beauty of this man's colouring." [17]

55. Chest with drawer, pine, Hampton, New Hampshire,
1710–1740. W. 43½″. Privately owned.

One of the lesser-known local clutches of early painted furniture
was made in the Hampton area of New Hampshire in the first
half of the 1700s. The attribution of a few chests, boxes, and deliciously outdated press cupboards stems from the discovery of a
chest dated 1719 and signed by Samuel Lane (1698–1776), a
joiner and carpenter of Hampton Falls.[18] The chest featured unsophisticated decoration, some in an enamel-like white paint, a
use of four-way, geometrical designs, a stylized branching tree,
and a rounded cusp at the center of each of the cut-out sides.
Other pieces from the same area make use of geometrical decoration, with crescents, apostrophes, and circles quite crudely
drawn. A key piece in defining the locale (but not necessarily
the maker) is the press cupboard at the right (56). Made of
curled maple, its decoration is in black paint. Freewheeling vines
enclose a tree at the center of the front, and the entire surface is
covered with black squiggles. The sides have looser vines, with
a bird in the center. It is initialed "SR," for Sarah Rowell of
Hampton Falls. The sides have the pointed pendant that is on
other Hampton pieces. The chest (55), initialed "AB," is of pine,
with a red ground and decorated in pink and black. The tree is
limper than that on the cupboard, but the flowers and leaves
have much the same feeling, especially in the geometric circular
blooms. The shaping of the front skirts on both pieces is quite
similar.

56. Press cupboard, maple and pine, Hampton area, New Hampshire,
1700–1740. W. 35″. Yale University Art Gallery, The Mabel Brady Garvan
Collection.

The Legacy of Nieu Netherland

The fall of Nieu Amsterdam to the British in 1664 ended a half century of Dutch colonizing in America. While rulers changed, influences did not. The Dutch, Flemish, and Huguenots worked beside English settlers; and influences from the Continent spread to Long Island, New Jersey, and western Connecticut. After the founding of the Dutch West India Company in 1621, emigration to the colony, Nieu Netherland, was greatly encouraged. Nieu Amsterdam was its capital, and the broad Hudson River became its avenue of settlement. Patroons bringing fifty new settlers were granted manorial and proprietary rights to sixteen miles of frontage on the Hudson, with "all the land behind." Settlements grew up along the valley to Fort Orange (Albany), which had been settled in the 1620s. As the century progressed, the large landowners surrounded themselves with the best furnishings.

Most of the early remaining buildings and objects date after the English capture of New York in 1664. In many of them, however, Dutch influences can be seen—frequently as details grafted onto English forms. These influences lasted into the nineteenth century in rural areas.

Upriver two-thirds of the way to Albany is Leeds, in Greene County. A detail of an overmantel painting shows a farmhouse there which was built in 1729 for Martin Van Bergen. He and his family stand in front of their Dutch-style stone house, with the Catskills in the background. The painting was removed from the house when it was torn down in 1862. Below is a portrait of Susanna Truax of Schenectady, done in 1730, when she was four years old. She is partaking of a sweet by a scroll-footed tea table that holds chinaware and a bullet-shaped silver teapot. These and her clothing bespeak some glitter in Susanna's middle-class world.

57. (Above). Detail of panel showing Van Bergen's farmhouse, Greene County, New York, c. 1735. Overall length 90″. New York State Historical Association.

58. (Right). Portrait of Susanna Truax (1726–1805), by "Gansevoort limner," Schenectady, New York, dated 1730. H. 37⅞″. Collection of Edgar William and Bernice Chrysler Garbisch.

In painted furniture by far the most important early form with strong Dutch influences was the *kas*, or cupboard. Dutch examples had been imported to the colony in the seventeenth century, but the examples made here simplified the imposing form and substituted grisaille decoration for carving.[19]

59. *Kas*, pine, New York, 1690–1720. Found in Saugerties, New York. Grisaille and polychrome decoration: cherubim, pears, apples, and grapes. W. 43″. Collection of Mr. and Mrs. Mitchel Taradash, on loan to Van Cortlandt Manor, Sleepy Hollow Restorations.

60. *Kas*, pine and oak, New York, 1690–1720. From Woodbury, Long Island. Grisaille decoration; characteristic fruit, with pomegranate on left door. W. 57¾″. The Metropolitan Museum of Art.

61. *Kas*, gum, New York, 1690–1720. From Middletown, New Jersey. Grisaille decoration. Most sophisticated of those shown here. W. 53″. Monmouth County Historical Association.

Kerhonkson is a small town tucked in Ulster County about twenty miles west of the Hudson. Near there, in 1762, Johannes Hardenbergh built a Dutch-style farmhouse, two rooms from which are at Winterthur. In the bedroom above can be seen furnishings from the Hudson Valley area. The *kas* is similar to 61 on the previous page, and its decoration is a fascinating translation of Dutch baroque carving into Colonial paint. The trophy-like panoplies of fruit on these *kasten* represent the earliest still-life painting in the Colonies. The monochromatic grays making up the grisaille decoration were sometimes enlivened by a sparing use of other colors. Continental in form, *kasten* were also made by German settlers in Pennsylvania and New Jersey, usually of unpainted, darker woods.

A Delft garniture perches on this *kas*, and beyond, next to the bed, is a small stand with trestle feet painted reddish brown. The bed is freestanding, dressed in crewelwork. In some earlier interiors the beds were built right into the paneling in Dutch fashion. At the left is a Queen Anne chair grained to resemble walnut. This type of chair, with bold trumpet-turned legs and offset pad feet, was especially favored in the Hudson Valley into the early nineteenth century.

On plain-painted furniture, red and black were used, as in New England. However, in the Hudson Valley, a distinctive orange-red paint was used, as was greenish blue, which often has faded to a gray today. The *kas* from Dutchess County (63) was originally a brick red, repainted green. The arched doors are like Queen Anne looking glasses, and the peculiar "Dutch kick" to the feet seems a two-dimensional memory of the ball feet of earlier examples. The table (64) is red, and its plenitude of supporting stretchers meet magically at the center. Other similar tables, sprouting abundant bracings while retaining an air of delicacy, have been found in the Hudson Valley and constitute a most unusual and picturesque local type. Another local form is seen in the paneled chest with ball feet (65), one of a small group from the Oyster Bay area. It shows Dutch influences and is painted a typical New York blue.[20]

63. *Kas*, pine, probably Dutchess County, New York, 1715–1750. Painted green over brick-red. W. 59″. Winterthur Museum.

64. Table, pine, Hudson River Valley, eighteenth century. Painted red. L. 41½″. Van Cortlandt Manor, Sleepy Hollow Restorations.

65. Chest with drawer, Long Island, 1700–1740. Blue-green paint. Photograph courtesy Ginsburg & Levy, Inc.

51

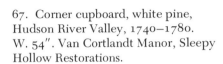

67. Corner cupboard, white pine, Hudson River Valley, 1740–1780. W. 54″. Van Cortlandt Manor, Sleepy Hollow Restorations.

66. Side chair, beech, probably English, 1700–1720. H. 46⅛″. Van Cortlandt Manor, Sleepy Hollow Restorations.

The staunch corner cupboard above, containing imported earthenware used in Hudson River Valley homes in the eighteenth century, is painted with two colors typical of the area. Its exterior is blue-green, while the interior is painted with an orange-red, frequently called "Dutch red" in recent times. Its doors have flat panels with simple beading and resemble window shutters on houses in the valley. By the middle of the eighteenth century a wide range of painters' colors was available in New York City, with "White-Lead, Red-Lead, Spanish Brown, English, French, Spruce and Stone Oker, Indian and Venetian Red, Ivory, Frankford and Lamp-Black, umber Cullin's Earth, Smalt's Prusian Blue, Vermillion, Verdigrase, the whole ground in Powder or in Oil" listed in 1754 by Gerardus Duyckinck, Jr., the japanner and painter.

The cane-back side chair (66) was owned by the Van Rensselaer family in Claverack, near Hudson. It is made of beech and painted black. With England controlling the importation of caning from the East Indies, little cane was shipped directly to the Colonies. However, quantities of completed cane-back chairs, invariably of beech, were sent here in droves around 1700 to satisfy the Colonists' desire for the newest style. Some were highly elaborate, while others, like this one, were much simpler, with turnings and the carving on the top rail resembling that on certain banister-back chairs made in New England.[21]

68. Box, pine, New York State, 1700–1740. W. 11$\frac{15}{16}$". Van Cortlandt Manor, Sleepy Hollow Restorations.

69. Box, pine, New York State, 1700–1740. W. 14". Van Cortlandt Manor, Sleepy Hollow Restorations.

70. Chest, oak, etc., Hudson River Valley, dated 1765. W. 53". Van Cortlandt Manor, Sleepy Hollow Restorations.

71. Slat-back armchair, maple and ash, probably New York, 1690–1725. H. 40". The Art Institute of Chicago.

The small box above (68) is painted green with the flowers and birds in yellow, green, and brown. It is similar to 69, which has tulips and sunflowers in white and pink on a gray-green ground, and was found near Stone Ridge, south of Kingston. From the Johannes Bruyn House, also near Kingston, came the unusual chest (70) which is initialed "I.W" and dated 1765. Painted in "oyster" patterns, its front and sides have a brown-and-white ground, with touches of blue. Rectangular and heart-shaped outlines of white contain blue-mottled decoration. Its trestle feet give the chest an early appearance. It is interesting to compare this chest with those made by the Pennsylvania Germans. Germans had settled in upper New York State early in the eighteenth century, and there are several decorated chests from the vicinity of Schoharie (later in the century) that resemble to some extent the better-known pieces made in Pennsylvania. Both types spring from a Continental heritage. Several highly decorated stools with Dutch inscriptions have been found in the Hudson River Valley, but—alas—it now appears they were made in Holland and brought here at an early date.[22] Some magnificent early slat-back armchairs have been located in the Hudson Valley area. Some have very bold, winglike slats. Figure 71 is a good example, with strong turnings and spool-turned supports under the flattened arms. It is painted black over earlier red.

73. Side chair, maple, northeastern New England, 1700–1720. H. 45½" Privately owned.

72. Chest (with drawer)-on-frame, oak and pine, eastern Massachusetts, 1700–1720. W. 30¼". The Brooklyn Museum.

Patterns and Plain Paints

The examples on these and the following two pages are a review of colors and styles of the early eighteenth century. The chest-on-frame at far left (72), owned by the Hancock family, is one of the few left with much of its old decoration remaining. Black, red, and white are used to great effect. Traces of black vines remain on the stiles. The vase-and-ring turnings on the stretchers are crisply executed. The side chair (73) is made of red maple and is one of a handful of cane chairs that may safely be considered American-made. Black was finely brushed over red-brown, and the result is a dark graining of great subtlety. The two pieces below were plain painted. The slat-back armchair (74) is of a striking vermilion color. It is extremely stylish for this form, with variety in its turned posts, excellent finials, fine sausage-turned supports under the arms, ball-and-ring front stretchers, and gentle points at the upper centers of the slats. One of the most restful old colors is blue-green, which covers the unusual chest-on-chest below (75). It was owned by the Perkins family of Newburyport, Massachusetts. The twenty-four small drawers in the top section contained herbs, powders, and other apothecarial accouterments. The lower part has three long drawers, the upper one slanting back much in the manner of a desk lid. The thirty-two teardrop brasses on the drawers must constitute a record of sorts in American William and Mary furniture!

74. Armchair, maple and ash, probably New England, 1720–1760. H. 50″. The Brooklyn Museum.

75. Doctor's or apothecary's chest, pine, probably Newburyport, Massachusetts, 1700–1730. W. 36½″. Historic Deerfield, Inc.

76. Pewter cupboard or dresser, pine, Hudson River Valley, eighteenth century. W. 65″. Van Cortlandt Manor, Sleepy Hollow Restorations.

The cupboard and table on these pages are painted red, while the armchair is black. We have seen that oil paints were the best. Distemper painting substituted a glue size and hot water for the oil and was not so successful in its binding properties. After 1800 another vehicle could be used. That was milk, and casein paints, which had gone out of favor in the fifteenth century, when oil-based paints were invented, were again used. Thus, the "old buttermilk" formulas that have been bandied about seem more fiction than fact in the Colonial period. Brick dust, the fancied comrade of buttermilk, was ground and used as a pigment with tar or resins as an exterior paint in the eighteenth century, but no documentation has been found to link brick dust and buttermilk. Red lead, iron oxides,

other red earths, and vermilion would have provided the Colonial painter ample opportunities to see red when he wished.[23]

The pewter cupboard has large fielded panels in the lower section that closely relate to architecture. The table has a round top and shaped trestle feet which are connected by a central molded stretcher. Both these pieces are forms which continued to be made throughout the eighteenth century—and even into the 1800s. Made of native curled maple, the armchair has turned-and-split banisters that conform to the pattern of the outer stiles, but the scroll carving of the cresting rail is most unusual. The slip seat and gentle turnings of the arm supports reflect the newer Queen Anne style, as does the overall "softened" quality of the chair.[24]

78. Armchair, curled maple painted black, American, 1710–1740. H. 55½″. The Henry Ford Museum.

77. Hutch table, pine and oak, probably New England, 1695–1725. Diameter 46¾″. Van Cortlandt Manor, Sleepy Hollow Restorations.

II. LATE COLONIAL

79. Japanned high chest of drawers, maple, Boston, 1710–1740. W. 39½″.
The Metropolitan Museum of Art.

80. (Opposite). Japanned looking glass, pine, New York, 1730–1760. From Van
Keuren family. H. 44⅜″. The Henry Ford Museum.

Japanning

The remoteness and exoticism of the Orient have always had a strong lure for the West. In the decorative arts of the Colonies this influence could be direct, through Chinese porcelains; one step removed, through books and Indian calicoes; or delightfully obfuscated, through translation by English and Dutch craftsmen, whose delftware, furniture, and prints were imported here with increasing frequency from the mid-seventeenth century on.

In furniture the exquisite lacquered examples of the East defied emulation. Lacking the proper materials and conditions, not to mention an able patience so necessary in Oriental work, Europeans were forced to invent other means by which to achieve the desired effect. Since the "lac tree," a member of the sumac family, grew only in China, Japan, and Malaya, this crucial ingredient had to be replaced by a substitute. The English covered the wood with a mixture of whiting and size to fill in the coarse-grained oak or deal. Then the wood was covered by one or more coats of opaque varnish composed of gum-lac or seed-lac, a resinous substance left by an insect, the *Coccus lacca,* on trees. The ground colors fashionable in 1688 were "Black Japan, Red Japan, Chestnut Color, Blew Japan, Olive Color, Yellow, Green, Counterfeit Tortoiseshell." The raised portions were built up with a mixture of gum arabic, whiting, and oc-

80

casionally sawdust. After the designs were shaped, a final decoration of metal dusts, ranging from tin to copper, brass, silver, and gold, was applied. This method was called "Japan-work" or "Indian work" in 1688 by John Stalker and George Parker in the first popular work on this technique, *A Treatise of Japaning and Varnishing,* published in Oxford.

Japanned furniture became a quiet rage in many eighteenth-century Colonial homes from New Hampshire to South Carolina. A great number of pieces were imported early in the 1700s,[25] and Boston and New York had their own japanners by 1712 and 1735 respectively. This early type of japanned furniture was made in these cities until around 1770.

Colonial japanners simplified the English process in two ways. They used fine-grained woods for their case pieces, eliminating any need of a gesso-like base on the wood; and they merely applied a clear varnish over the coats of paint, obviating the laborious and costly mixing of seed-lac varnish with ground colors. Black or tortoiseshell were the normal base colors, and the decoration was usually raised up on city-made examples. Whimsical animals, flowers, people, and birds play in a scaleless world on the drawer fronts of the early Boston high chest at the left; while Chinese figures and flowers bask serenely on the frame above.

79a. Detail showing front of second full drawer of chest opposite.

81

82

83

The four round vignettes above are designs for powder-box lids from *A Treatise of Japaning and Varnishing*. The book was so popular in England that in 1689, the year after publication, the third edition had already appeared. Twenty-four pages of plates were crowded with "Oriental scenes"—some Dutch in inspiration—and the authors' language was more picturesque than the scenes they depicted. They claimed their patterns were true imitations of the Japanese, adding, "Perhaps we have helpt them a little in their proportions, where they were lame or defective, and made them more pleasant yet altogether as Antick." Later,

> Lay all your Colours and Blacks exquisitely even and smooth; and where ever mole-hills and knobs, asperities and roughness in colours or varnish offer to appear, with your Rush sweep them off, and tell them their room is more acceptable to you than their company. If this ill usage will not terrifie them, or make them avoid your work, give them no better entertainment than you did before, but maintain your former severity, and with your Rush whip them off, as often as they molest you.[26]

Their opinion of teachers of japanning was not too high—"those wiffling, impotent fellows who pretend to teach young Ladies that Art, in which they themselves have need to be instructed."

Other books of instruction for japanning were issued in England in the eighteenth century, but none had the zest or impact of the first.

The Boston area was the most important center of japanning in the Colonies, with more than a

83 and 86. Two panels from the Vernon House, Newport, Rhode Island, c. 1720–1728. Black ground, with red, yellow, black, white, and green decoration. H. 59″. Photographs courtesy Mr. and Mrs. Quinto Maganini.

84

85

dozen artisans plying the trade between 1712 and
1771. Thomas Johnston (1708–1767) was also an en-
graver, organ builder, and jack-of-all-trades. His
trade card, engraved in 1732, advertised that he
sold japanned "Looking-Glasses, Chests of Draws,
Chamber & Dressing Tables, Tea Tables, Write-
ing Desks, Book-Cases, Clock-Cases, &c." At least
two of his sons continued in the trade. In New
York the only two known japanners represent another family enterprise, with Gerardus Duyckinck,
Senior and Junior, working between 1735 and 1772.
Other japanning was done east of Boston and in
Connecticut, but Boston and New York were the
centers. Japanner Stephen Whiting of Boston advertised in 1767 that he "does more at present to-
wards manufacturing Looking Glasses than any-
one in the Province, or perhaps on the Continent."

Existing examples of American japanning vary
a great deal in technique and quality. Raised figures were used on the best pieces, while simple
paint and powders provided the decoration on
the less grand works. No early "schoolgirl" examples of American japanning have yet been
found.

A unique sample of American japanned wall
decoration is found in the Vernon House in Newport, Rhode Island. Two walls contain Oriental
panels framed by marbleized simulated bolection
moldings, probably done by the painter William
Gibbs between 1720 and 1728 while he lived in the
house.[27] The panels have neither raised figures nor
metal dust, but thick, pigmented varnishes were
used throughout.

81, 82, 84, and 85. Details from Stalker and Parker,
A Treatise of Japaning and Varnishing, Oxford, 1688.
The New York Public Library, Art and Architecture
Division.

86

87. Chest of drawers, pine, from Stoughton family,
East Windsor Hill, Connecticut, 1720–1735.
W. 43″. The Metropolitan Museum of Art.

The influence of the urban japanner upon the rural painter can be
seen in these two painted chests from the Windsor, Connecticut, area.
The painter of the chest of drawers above (87) used an olive-brown
ground, the decoration consisting merely of black, red, and cream.
Dogs play, strange buildings rise, and flowers grow, while a lady on
the upper left drawer fans herself under a tree, perhaps exhausted
from watching her male companion chase butterflies on the drawer
below. All this is mild, however, when compared to the fancies of the
high chest at the right (88). Here, giraffes and gazelles stand in awe
of the verdant flora, while an Indian shoots an arrow and a falconer
kneels poised to set free his bird. The high chest is painted black over
a red ground and decorated only in cream. The cabinetmaker, it
should be noted, could turn a mean cabriole leg! A group of these
painted pieces from the Windsor area, all probably made after 1720,
show how effectively and spiritedly japanning could be simulated
with a simple palette.

89. This looking glass from Massachusetts is more formally decorated, with flat, Chinese figures and flowers in gilt on a black-lacquered pine frame. 1740–1760. H. 41¼". Old Sturbridge Village.

88. High chest of drawers, maple and pine, Windsor area, Connecticut, dated 1736. W. 41⅜". Winterthur Museum.

90. Tall clock, oak, by Bartholomew Barwell, New York, advertising 1749–1760. H. 96". The Brooklyn Museum.

In the *Boston News-Letter* of April 9/16, 1716, William Gent advertised: "Lately come from London, a Parcel of very fine Clocks, They go a Week, and repeat the Hour when pull'd; in Japan cases or Wall-nut." Other japanned clocks were imported to the Colonies during the eighteenth century, and examples are known with works by James Atkinson, Edward Faulkner, Richard Motley, and Thomas Wagstaffe. They set high standards for American japanners, also conveniently serving as prototypes.

In New York japanned clock cases were often made of oak, with whiting applied to fill in the grain of the wood much in the English manner. All three New York examples shown here (90, 92, 93) have oak cases. They also have raised figures, with the decoration in gold, red, and dark ochre. A range of backgrounds is seen on them, the one at the left having tortoiseshell, 92 having black, and the clock at the far right, dark olive-green. These colors, and a few looking glasses with dark-blue and pomegranate grounds, represent the spectrum of background colors used in New York. Since Gerardus Duyckinck, Senior and Junior, were the only japanners advertising in the city from 1735 on, it is likely that one of them decorated these cases. Bartholomew Barwell, the clockmaker of 90 and 92, came to New York in 1749 from Bath, England, and perhaps he brought a preference for japanned clock cases with him.

Two of the clocks shown here have rocking-ship dials. The clock at the center (91, 91a) was made by Gawen Brown of Boston. Like Barwell, Brown came from England by 1749. The raised japanned decoration on the pine case is on a black-over-red tortoiseshell ground, and the gilt chinoiserie decoration was well executed, probably by Thomas Johnston, since Brown advertised in 1749:

> This is to give Notice to the Public that Gawen Brown Clock and Watchmaker lately from London, keeps his shop at Mr. Johnson's, Japanner, in Brattle-Street, Boston, near Mr. Cooper's Meeting House, where he makes and sells all sorts of plain, repeating, and astronomical Clocks, with Cases plain, black walnut, mahogany or Japann'd.[28]

Another clock by Benjamin Bagnall had a Johnston trade card on its door, and two japanned clocks have William Claggett works (Boston and Newport).

91a

91, 91a. Tall clock, pine, by Gawen Brown, Boston, c. 1749. Japanned probably by Thomas Johnston. H. 94½″. Winterthur Museum.

92. Tall clock, oak, by Bartholomew Barwell, New York, 1749–1760. From Maserole family. H. 92″. Museum of the City of New York.

93. Tall clock, oak, New York, mid-eighteenth century. From De Bevoise family. H. 91″. Museum of the City of New York.

91

92

93

94, 94a. Side chair, Massachusetts, 1725–1760, with
decoration added c. 1810. H. 40″. The Bayou Bend
Collection, The Museum of Fine Arts, Houston.

94a

95

In England the earlier method of japanning was re-vived in a simpli-fied form around 1750. Priming was not used, and the colors were laid on with gum water rather than varnish. This was the technique used by many of the followers of Robert Adam. Later, by the time of Hepplewhite and Shera-ton, more simplifications had taken place, and most japanners used a varnish-over-paint tech-nique that was very similar to that done by Co-lonial American japanners two generations earlier. From a study of Chinese lacquered dressing glasses and boxes imported to America from the 1790s on, it appears that a simplifica-tion in the technique of lacquering took place there, too.[29]

The Massachusetts Queen Anne side chairs on these pages are two of six known walnut chairs painted black with later gilt japanning. According to tradition, they descended in the Winthrop–Blanchard family and were decorated in China about 1795. The gilt decoration, how-ever, ties in with the later japanning done here from the 1790s on, so the chairs never knew the joys of an ocean voyage. The arms are those of Samuel P. Gardner, whose grandniece Eliza Blanchard, whom he raised, married Robert C. Winthrop in 1832.[30]

An advertisement of the Baltimore ornamen-tal painters Brakley and O'Meara aptly an-nounced in the April 13, 1792, *Maryland Jour-nal:*

> and Heraldry, either cyphered or blazoned, with Coats of Arms, correct. —As they are acquainted with Achievements, of many Families of English, Irish, and Scotch Descent, they will be able to as-sist in that Part, without Information from the Herald's Office.

The scrolls and grape leaves on the stiles and legs echo border designs of Chinese porcelains.

96

95. Bookplate of Samuel Pickering Gardner, Boston merchant, on paper watermarked 1809. Privately owned.
96. Side chair, Massachusetts, 1725–1760, with dec-oration added c. 1810. H. 40″. Historic Deerfield, Inc.

97

97 and 98. High chest of drawers and dressing table, maple and pine, Boston, 1735–1750. W. 40½″ and 33½″, respectively. The Metropolitan Museum of Art.

Boston craftsmen combined to produce the best japanned furniture in the Colonies. The companion pieces on this page were owned in the Pickman family of Salem, and the magnificent high chest opposite (99) was made by John Pimm of Boston for Commodore Joshua Loring, who eloped, by the way, in 1740, a date that might be as helpful to our dating of the piece as it was to him.[31] All three have tortoiseshell backgrounds, made by streaking vermilion with lampblack, and raised gilt figures. They combine classic balance of form with exoticism of decoration in a majestic manner.

Japanned furniture had been imported to Massachusetts in the 1690s. Boston and New York became the centers of import and manufacture. Fewer references exist in Philadelphia, but Plunket Fleeson offered a "neat japan'd chest of drawers to be sold Cheap" in 1742; and in Letitia (Penn) Aubrey's inventory in 1746 are two "Japan Corner Cupboards." An "India Cabinet frame" was sold in Charleston, South Carolina, in the effects of Sarah Saxby in 1747. Both North and South felt shimmers of the East.

98

99. High chest of drawers, maple and pine, made by John Pimm, japanner unknown, Boston, 1740–1750. W. 41″. Winterthur Museum.

Queen Anne and Chippendale

100. High chest of drawers, maple and pine, northeastern New England, 1740–1765. The original decoration of fanciful burls is black on dark ochre. W. 38″. Privately owned.

101

With the occasional exceptions of japanned furniture and some city-made bread-and-butter pieces, American painted furniture largely continued its rural ways until after the Revolution. There are a number of examples in the Queen Anne style, both plain painted and decorated. When the Chippendale style came into favor after the middle of the century, however, carving became king—even in the country—and decorative painting on furniture waned. Plain painting continued, naturally, and in urban areas a new artisan arose—the gilder, who became a force in purveying decoration and materials after the 1750s.

The free-form swirling burls are brushed on the high chest of drawers on the opposite page with sureness and accuracy. The surface of the piece is full of motion and contrasts with the more literal nineteenth-century graining on the dressing table below. The small looking glass at the left (101) is painted Indian red with brownish-black squiggly decoration. Glasses of this type have been attributed to the Boston japanner Nehemiah Partridge, without foundation.[32] The other looking glass (102) is painted black, with red and yellow stylized leaves. Both of these looking glasses retain their original cutout crestings.

102

101. Looking glass, pine, eastern Massachusetts, 1720–1750. H. 12″. Essex Institute.

102. Looking glass, pine, Massachusetts, 1730–1750. H. 13⅝″. The Colonial Williamsburg Foundation.

103. Dressing table, cherry, New Hampshire, 1740–1765. The nineteenth-century graining is red and black. Found in Amherst, New Hampshire. W. 33¾″. Privately owned.

104. Side chair, maple, New England, 1730–1780. Black, with nineteenth-century gold decoration. H. 41¾". Shelburne Museum, Inc.

105. Side chair, cherry, etc., probably Connecticut, 1730–1760. Painted black. H. 43½". Van Cortlandt Manor, Sleepy Hollow Restorations.

106. Armchair, maple, etc., Hudson River Valley, New York, 1730–1800. Red-and-black graining. H. 46½". Van Cortlandt Manor, Sleepy Hollow Restorations.

107. Side chair, maple, probably Essex County, Massachusetts, 1740–1780. Ochre and dark-brown graining. H. 39½". Winterthur Museum.

So-called country chairs, many of which were actually plainer productions of town and city chairmakers, are as spirited as any early furniture. Styles and motifs mingle with impure impunity, and the results can often crackle with an individuality that can be as charming as it is outdated. Most of these chairs were plain painted originally, although many were grained (106, 107, and 110). Occasionally some of them were perked up by a nineteenth-century decorative painter, and 104 shows this later gold striping "fancying up" an earlier chair. The delicate grape decoration on 108 could have been applied later, or the chair itself might be a Federal lingering of a Chippendale form. Its decoration recalls that on the Gardner side chairs shown on pages 66 and 67.

The chairs on this page all have Queen Anne vase-shaped splats. One has earlier Spanish feet (104), and another has a Chippendale cresting rail (107). The spool turnings between the knees and seat of 105 are a characteristic found frequently in Connecticut. The graining on 106 is heavily done in red and black and simulates mahogany. This chair is a typical Hudson Valley type that was made from the 1730s until the early nineteenth century (see figure 152, page 91). The ochre-and-brown graining on 107 is done with great skill and delicacy. The chair and its decoration give the impression of a restrained elegance at its best.

108. Side chair, maple, New England, 1770–c. 1800. Black, with gold decoration. H. 36¾". Collection of Stewart E. Gregory.

109. Side chair, maple, Essex County, Massachusetts, 1780–1800. Painted red. H. 37¾". Old Sturbridge Village.

110. Side chair, maple, New England, 1780–1800. Reddish-brown graining over red-orange base. H. 36½". Collection of Dr. and Mrs. William Greenspon.

Chippendale variants are featured on this page. Figures 108 and 109 are simplifications of stylish pierced splat- and ladder-back types, while the ribbon back (110) is a simple, effective restatement of the latter type. It is grained in dull orange and reddish-brown over an extremely brilliant red-orange undercoat, producing a vibrant effect that enhances its wiggly lines.

Of all "country" chairs one of the most intriguing is attributed to Major John Dunlap of Bedford, New Hampshire (111). It is painted a dark bluish green and was made between 1775 and 1790. Its elements practically defy description; but the exaggerated ears, shells on the crest and skirt, and cutout scrolls in the splat that are echoed in the scalloping of the skirt are but a few of the parts that make up such a hopelessly wonderful, rural whole. John Dunlap and his brother Samuel were the stars of a family galaxy working in New Hampshire and other northern states in the late eighteenth and early nineteenth centuries.[33] Squat, bandy-legged high chests of drawers are probably the best-known pieces made by the earlier Dunlaps (see figure 129, page 82). Most were painted originally in red, blue-green, or orange—and, occasionally, all three. Major John's account book lists recipes for staining wood orange, green, and mahogany. Chairs are noted in black, "culered," and white (perhaps bare, to be painted by the owner).

111. Side chair, maple, attributed to John Dunlap (1746–1792), Bedford, New Hampshire. Dark blue-green. H. 45". Winterthur Museum.

112. Mixing table, maple, eastern Massachusetts, 1720–
1760. Painted black, with blue-and-white tiles. W. 29″.
The Henry Ford Museum.

113. Tea table, maple, New Hampshire, 1740–1775.
Black paint on base; gray marbleized top. W. 30¼″.
Privately owned.

114. Tea table, birch and maple, coastal New Hampshire, 1740–1760. Painted red. W. 31½". The Colonial Williamsburg Foundation.

115. Corner or roundabout chair, maple, New England, 1750–1780. Painted black. H. 28". Van Cortlandt Manor, Sleepy Hollow Restorations.

In 1730 Robert Furber of London noted in announcing his famous *Twelve Months of Flowers* that his prints could be of use to painters, carvers, and japanners for "Furniture for the Closet." While botanical illustrations had influence on European painted furniture around the middle of the eighteenth century, American productions of that period favored plain paint, with occasional graining or marbleizing featured.

Fancy marble-top tables were emulated in several ways. Delft tiles could be inserted on a dark painted base (112).[34] An even more "economical" result could be achieved by painted marbleizing on a tray top, in this case on a simple, yet highly effective base with straight turned legs (113). Plain red paint was used on an exquisitely proportioned table traditionally made by a member of the Trefethern family of Rye, New Hampshire (114). The corner chair also translates high fashion into tasteful simplicity.

117. Tea table, cherry, probably Connecticut, 1750–1780. Greenish-brown, with red decoration. W. 32½″. The Metropolitan Museum of Art.

Direct architectural influences may be seen in the raised, simple-fielded panels of both the green cupboard at the left (116) and the black settle at the right (120). The settle's original red paint is underneath, and it was traditionally owned by the Trumbull family of Lebanon, Connecticut.

The tilt-top tea table above is painted a greenish-brown ground and has stippling in red on its octagonal top and pedestal base. The curled-maple Newport table (119) has black paint on its base and top edges, and its porringer top and curved skirt with their cyma curves add immeasurably to its quiet elegance.

While most early painted pieces are from New England, painted furniture was made throughout the Colonies. In Pennsylvania plain painting was preferred by English settlers over the fanciful decorations of the Germans.[35] Christopher Marshall listed nearly forty imported pigments in the June 25, 1747, *Pennsylvania Gazette*. The blanket chest shown here (118) was made in the Maryland-Virginia-North Carolina area, and its bubbly marbleizing in white with two shades of gray suggests early book endpapers. In 1788 George Ladner of Edenton, North Carolina, advertised "Mahogany-Graining to its perfection; also Marbling after the Italian Method."

116. Cupboard, pine, New England, 1750–1790. Painted green. W. 47¼″. The Colonial Williamsburg Foundation.

118. Chest with drawers, tulip, southern,
1760–1790. Gray and white marbleizing. W. 49⅝".
The Colonial Williamsburg Foundation.

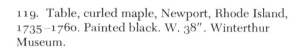

119. Table, curled maple, Newport, Rhode Island,
1735–1760. Painted black. W. 38". Winterthur
Museum.

120. Settle, pine, etc., Connecticut, 1720–1780.
Black over old red. L. 72". Privately owned.

121

Repose of a temporary or more permanent nature was much on the minds of eighteenth-century people. Prudence Punderson of Preston, Connecticut, wrought this silk needlework mortality picture, depicting herself in three stages of existence: an infant, a mature woman doing needlework, and an unseen corpse in her coffin. Done between 1776 and 1783 in threads of yellow, white, green, tans, browns, and black, the picture is one of the few documents of Colonial American interiors, showing such varied features as window hangings and the covering of looking glasses after death. Coffins and cradles were frequently painted. The cradle below is grained in red and yellow, its interior painted blue-gray over red. Its domed top is most unusual, as is its history. Owned by the Wheatland–Peabody families of Salem, it was also traditionally used by Sir William Pepperrell, Roger Sherman, and Senator Benjamin Goodhue! In the field of temporary repose, beds were one of the most common plain-painted forms in the eighteenth century, with green the most-used color from Boston to Philadelphia. At Mount Vernon in 1787 green paint was used to paint bedsteads.[36]

122

121. (Opposite). Silk mortality picture by Prudence Punderson, Preston, Connecticut, 1776–1783. 16½″ x 12½″. The Connecticut Historical Society.
122. (Opposite). Cradle, pine, Massachusetts, 1710–1760. L. 38¼″. Essex Institute.

123. Table, maple, Westport area, Connecticut, 1730–1770. Painted blue-green. W. 34⅝″. Privately owned.
124. High chest of drawers, maple, etc., probably Guilford, Connecticut, 1740–1760. W. 34½″. New Haven Colony Historical Society.

124

123

The two Connecticut pieces on this page show very well both methods of painting furniture around the middle of the eighteenth century. The high chest features loose, almost abstract decoration in black, carefully brushed over ochre, with a red base underneath. Swirling knots are suggested in the upper section, with that on the upper drawer going off in another direction from its three compatriots below, as if the board were reversed. Wiggly lines hint at fancy burled woods all across the facade, the entire effect being accomplished with much simplicity and economy of decoration. The table is a pleasingly simple statement of the Queen Anne style, with its squared feet echoed in a straight skirt. Its plain-painted finish, however, delightfully complements its lines and makes a singing entity that eager refinishing would have reduced to a banal state of undress.

125. Press for air pump, pine, made by John Harrison, 1739, and
painted by John Winter, 1740, for The Library Company of Philadelphia.
Originally painted deep gray, with black moldings and gilt; interior
red over cream. H. 130½″. The Library Company of Philadelphia.

126. H. 45½". Winterthur Museum.

127. H. 55½". Winterthur Museum.

One of the earliest truly sophisticated examples of painted furniture is a press (125), or case, for an air pump presented to the Library Company of Philadelphia by John Penn in 1738. It was constructed in the following year by John Harrison, a member of the Carpenters' Company who had done joiner work on the State House. In 1740 John Winter charged £3.10 for "painting, varnishing & gilding the Air-Pump Case." Winter was a painter "from London," who advertised in 1739 that he did "Landskip and Coach-Painting, Coats of Arms, Signs, Shewboards, Gilding, Writing in Gold and common Colours and Ornaments of all kinds very reasonable." [37] Its deep gray color, with a black base molding and red interior, was a perfect foil for the early Palladian-revival carved moldings that embellish the facade. Nearly eleven feet in height, this press was a gigantic preview of things to come in both architecture and furniture in Philadelphia. By the middle of the century, so-called Georgian paneling and the first flourishes of Chippendale furniture were felt in Philadelphia, New York, and Boston. City dwellers could have houses and furniture of high elaboration. With the advent of the rococo, the artisan classes experienced a separation of labors, with carvers and gilders plying their spe-

128. H. 16½". Winterthur Museum.

cialties to complement the work of the cabinetmaker. The painter-stainers of earlier periods became more specialized and less general in their activities. In smaller towns such as Salem, however, Samuel Blyth could still operate in the older manner, paying a bill to the silversmith Edward Lang in 1773 by painting window frames, two pictures, a "chequerboard," a door, and a chimney. The general jack-of-all-trades, however, became more and more relegated to the country. With carving king from the middle of the century until after the Revolution, decorative painting on furniture almost vanished. Paint could be used to accentuate trim on fine mahogany pieces occasionally,[38] and the carvers and gilders used gilt and gray (or white) at times to enhance their work. Figure 126 is one of a pair of pine looking glasses made in Boston after the middle of the century. The frame is painted light gray and the carving gilded. Figure 127 shows more of the lightness and naturalism of the rococo. It was made by James Reynolds of Philadelphia for John Cadwalader in 1770 and is painted white and gold.[39] The small wall bracket, like the Cadwalader looking glass, is made of yellow pine, in this instance stained to resemble mahogany. Almost dripping with rococo frilleries, it is based on a 1758 London design.[40]

81

130. Portrait of Ann Proctor of Baltimore, Maryland, by Charles Willson Peale, 1789. 22″ x 18″. The Hammond–Harwood House.

129. Double chest-on-frame, maple, attributed to Major John Dunlap, Bedford, New Hampshire, 1777–1792. Had reddish-brown stain originally. Grained in yellow-ochre and brown, c. 1830. W. 41″. Privately owned.

131. Dressing table, pine, Salem, Massachusetts, 1785–1790. Marbleized top; red-and-black mahogany graining on skirt and legs. W. 42″. Essex Institute.

What carving did not do to discourage painting on furniture the Townshend Act did, for it levied high duties on all paints entering the Colonies from 1767 to 1770. Some native pigments had been developed, but they could not take the place of those that were imported. However, within these limitations painted furniture continued to be produced in the Chippendale style. A very handsome chamber table (131), marbleized and mahoganized, was lent by Daniel Oliver of Salem to Joshua Ward on October 29, 1789 as a dressing table for George Washington's use. A handful of early Masonic chairs has survived, and 132, with an elaborate painted back and gilded balls on the front feet, is one of the best. It brings to mind a pair of mahogany side chairs attributed to Thomas Elfe of Charleston, South Carolina, with gilded elements in their splats and top rails.[41] Urban furniture could still be plain, as we see in the gray-green slat-back armchair (130) holding Ann Proctor, her parrot, and her doll. A staggering Dunlap double chest-on-frame (129) received an enthusiastic updating, with wooden knobs and graining added to the original reddish-brown color still seen at the left of the base (see also page 73). The kettle stand at the right has an upstanding primness worthy of its New Hampshire heritage.

133. Kettle stand, marble and maple, probably New Hampshire, 1775–1800. Reddish-brown-and-black "tortoiseshell" paint. H. 29″. Winterthur Museum.

132. Armchair, mahogany, Boston or Salem, 1760–1785. Painted and gilded decoration on front and back feet. H. 50″. Photograph courtesy Joe Kindig, Jr.

134. (Opposite). Detail of painting of William Denning of New York and his family, by William Williams, 1772. Dimensions of entire painting: 34½" x 51". Collection of Mr. and Mrs. W. Denning Harvey.

135. Early type of low-back Windsor armchair, 1750–1780. Painted green; owned in Glen–Sanders family, Scotia, New York. W. 27⅛". The Colonial Williamsburg Foundation.

136. Portrait of Roger Sherman (1721–1793) by Ralph Earl (1751–1801). H. 64⅝". Yale University Art Gallery.

Early Windsors

The American Windsor chair was one of the most exciting native expressions in Colonial furniture. The seeds of the form had come from England, they germinated in Philadelphia during the Queen Anne period, and they came to full bloom in New York and other towns around the time of the Revolution. The American Windsor developed into forms of universal delicacy that became as-suitable for the parlor as for the kitchen or even the garden. They were all made of different woods. Hardwoods were needed for the legs and stretchers, softwoods were used for the shaped and scooped seats, and springy woods were demanded for shaped tops and spindles. With such a discordant variety of light woods used, Windsors were meant to be painted. Green was the most popular color until the end of the century; and red,

blue, yellow, black, white, and mahogany colors were also used, as were two-toned combinations. In the painting at the left, William Denning is shown sitting in a green low-back armchair in his garden in downtown New York, while Roger Sherman of Connecticut (above) is on a dark-green Windsor with a red seat. Most Windsors before the Revolution were armchairs, and the green example above exhibits many Philadelphia characteristics. A French visitor to Philadelphia in 1798 described the "simple" mahogany furniture owned there. He continued, "Other classes have walnut furniture and wooden chairs painted green like garden furniture in France." Before 1790 Philadelphia, the style setter, had shipped over 6,000 Windsors to other Colonies, the West Indies, and abroad.[42]

137

138

139

140

137. Sack-back Windsor armchair, chestnut, maple, and oak, stamped by Amos Denison Allen, Norwich, Connecticut, 1796–1805. H. 37¼″. Winterthur Museum.
138. Portrait of Ephraim Starr (1745–1809) of Middletown, Connecticut, by Simon Fitch, 1802. H. 59″. Wadsworth Atheneum.
139. Braced high-back Windsor armchair, tulip, etc., Pennsylvania, 1760–1790. Painted black. H. 40½″. The Art Institute of Chicago.
140. Braced continuous-bow Windsor armchair, chestnut, maple, and oak, stamped by Ebenezer Tracy, Lisbon, Connecticut, 1780–1803. H. 38¼″. Winterthur Museum.

141. The Commons Room at Winterthur shows a variety of Windsors, including a triple-back settee from Connecticut, two low-backs, and a high-back armchair from Pennsylvania, and two New England bow-back side chairs at the left. Winterthur Museum.

142. H. 42½".

143. H. 35½".

144. H. 38".

145. H. 35½".

A 1763 advertisement for Philadelphia Windsors referred to them as "high back'd," "low back'd," and "sack back'd." These are the three major types of early Windsors. At the left (137 and 140) are two sack-backs, one of the most popular of all the types. Figure 137 has well-defined baluster turnings on its base. Its paint is a case history for all Windsors, since mobile chairs could not keep their old paints so easily as stationary chests. Its colors, from outside to inside, are dark brown, mustard, orange-red, several layers of white and gray, muddy brown, grass green, and finally gray-green, which still may not be the original coat! Such is the fragility of mortality of old paint. Figure 139 is a high-back armchair (now called "comb-back"), and fan-backs developed from this form about 1780. The long, straight sleeve on the lower legs and ball feet (sometimes slightly pointed) were favored by Pennsylvania makers (see also 135 and 142). The Tracy armchair (140) features arms and back of one continuous piece of oak, a practice of New York and southern New England makers after the Revolution. Similarly good turnings were done in Rhode Island, with a pronounced taper frequently appearing at the bottom of the leg. The Tracy chair is now painted brown but was probably a chalky blue-green originally. Regional characteristics can be great aids to the student of furniture. In Windsors, however, one must always bear in mind that migration, emulation, and transportation can join together to provide as many exceptions as there are rules. For instance, 143 is a fan-back side chair, owned by the Sowle family of South Dartmouth, Massachusetts. It is painted green with a red seat and is very similar to a chair branded by Francis Trumble of Philadelphia between 1775 and 1795.[43] It is owned now by the Newport Historical Society. It is interesting to compare this fan-back with one made later in Connecticut (144), now at the Yale University Art Gallery. It is a truly delightful eccentric, with exaggerated turnings and top rail. It is painted black with a pineapple on the top, asterisks on the ears, and stripes on the turnings in gold. Figure 142 is another delight: a black, late eighteenth-century auricular sack-back (The Philadelphia Museum of Art, Titus C. Geesey Collection). Figure 145, at Shelburne Museum, is painted red and black. It is a later, less vigorous expression of the high-back form, yet with much poise.

87

146. Drawing of fan chair by Charles Willson Peale,
Philadelphia, 1786. American Philosophical Society
Library.

147. Windsor fan chair (or eagle's-wing chair), owned
by Dr. Eneas Munson, Sr., of New Haven, Connecticut,
c. 1785–1790. Painted dark brown; fan gilded and
decorated with painted feathers. H. 77″. New Haven
Colony Historical Society.

148. Windsor triple round-top settee, maple, oak, and hickory, probably Connecticut, 1765–1795. Painted dark brown. W. 81¾". Winterthur Museum.

149. Bow-back Windsor side chair, ash, maple, and pine, stamped by James Chapman Tuttle, Salem, Massachusetts, 1795–1805. Painted red. H. 38½". Privately owned.

Windsor furniture included stools, tables, cradles, and stands, as well as chairs. All were painted originally. In early account books, "white chairs" could refer to plain unfinished chairs, which would be painted by the purchaser. In 1796 John Letchworth of Philadelphia charged William Meredith for forty oval-back Windsors; twenty were painted white and twenty, green. He also made Windsors with unpainted mahogany arms. Combinations of paints have been noted. In New York eight yellow-and-green Windsors were listed in the small parlor of Charles Ward Apthorp of Westchester in 1797; and John De Witt & Co. of New York City advertised "Windsor Chairs japann'd and neatly flowered" from 1795 to 1799.[44]

The amazing fan chair at the left (147) was a hoped-for solution to two problems, heat and flies. John Cram, an inventor and instrument maker of Philadelphia, was its apparent creator. A sack-back armchair was used in the Connecticut version.[45]

On this page are variants of "round top" Windsors. The graceful settee is notable, and the bow-back (149) is a rather stiff, later version of the sack-back. In 1796 James Chapman Tuttle advertised in the *Salem Gazette* that he made "Philadelphia or Windsor chairs and Settees . . . well painted with different colors as the buyer chooses." He made fan-backs and upholstered Windsors, too.

150. Continuous-bow Windsor armchair, maple, hickory, etc., stamped by J. M. Hasbrouck, Kingston, New York, 1775–1787. Painted black. H. 36¼". The Art Institute of Chicago.

Windsors (and other plank-seat chairs) sometimes carry their maker's name in a stamp or
brand on the underside of the seat. The seats
themselves could add much to the color of a
Windsor. They could be painted in contrasting
colors, or they could be upholstered in colored
leathers or fabrics. Martha Washington wrought
reddish-brown-and-yellow needlework cushions
for bow-back side chairs in the Little Parlor at
Mount Vernon. They resembled 155, which has
quieter bamboo turnings that came into vogue
at the end of the eighteenth century.[46]

The Chestney advertisement (152) demonstrates the durability of popular slat-back and
yoke-back chairs, as well as a modish Windsor,
in Albany.

In 1795 the Boston merchant Joseph Barrell,
furnishing his mansion, Pleasant Hill, wrote to
his New York agent, John Atkinson:

> Also 18 of the handsomest windsor chairs fit
> for Dining and my Hall. I would have them with
> arms, rather less in the seat than larger than com-
> mon, as they will thereby accommodate more at
> table. I would have them painted of light blue
> grey colour, the same as my summer dining room.
> Let them be strong and neat.[47]

151. This high-back writing armchair was made
in Connecticut probably in 1780, as indicated by
S. E. White of Rutland, Vermont, when he repainted the chair in 1897. It is one of the highest
developed Windsor forms. H. 46¼″. Winterthur
Museum.

By James Cheftney,
No. 72, Market-ftreet, ALBANY,
Where may be had,
All kinds of rufh-bottomed and
Windfor Chairs,
on moderate terms.   Chairs made to any
pattern on the fhorteft notice.

152. From *Albany Gazette*, June 11, 1798. Albany Institute of History and Art.

153. Slat-back armchair, New England, 1790–1830. Red paint, with black-and-yellow decoration. H. 45″. Privately owned.

154. Side chair, maple painted black, probably Albany, New York, 1730–1800. H. 39½″. Albany Institute of History and Art.

155. Bow-back Windsor side chair, poplar and maple, painted green, probably Philadelphia, 1790–1800. H. 36″. The Mount Vernon Ladies' Association of the Union.

III. FEDERAL

156. Mantel and two side chairs from the Elias Hasket Derby mansion in Salem, Massachusetts. The gilded girandole with its convex glass became popular after 1800. The French wallpaper shows rustic Italian scenes. The Metropolitan Museum of Art.

157. (Opposite). Final working drawing for the Derby mansion by Samuel McIntire, 1795. Essex Institute.

Federal Furniture

157

The Classic revival of the eighteenth century wafted wreathes, urns, swags, paterae, tablets, busts, and other decorative devices to America from ancient Italy by way of England. At the instigation of Robert Adam, the new style had swept England by the 1760s, and design books of all sorts heralded the new architecture and decoration. In furniture the more important works were George Hepplewhite's *The Cabinet-Maker and Upholsterer's Guide,* published in London in 1788, the year in which our Constitution was adopted, and Thomas Sheraton's *The Cabinet-Maker and Upholsterer's Drawing Book,* which appeared in 1793. These books introduced new delicacy and balance into American furniture of the Federal period, which dates from 1788 to the second decade of the 1800s. Elaborate painted and decorated furniture had become popular in England once more, and it influenced a number of high-style American productions in town and country alike.

In 1796 Elias Hasket Derby, the famous Salem shipowner and merchant, ordered twenty-four oval-back chairs for his new mansion from his Philadelphia agents, Joseph Anthony & Co. Two of these are shown on the opposite page. They are based on a Hepplewhite design and are of the highest quality. They are painted white, their splats consisting of four green plumes tied together by dark-green bowknots. Floral sprays meander over the top rail and depend from bowknots on the legs, and bold gilt scrolls join the back with the seat.

The chairs and mantelpiece are but a taste of the glorious mansion built by Derby and his wife, Elizabeth. They enlisted the talents of Charles Bulfinch of Boston, Samuel McIntire, Salem's renowned designer and carver, and the leading local carpenter, Daniel Bancroft. The mansion was built between 1795 and 1798. Both Derbys died within a year of its completion, and, sadly, the house was demolished in 1811.

158a. Detail showing painting by John R. Penniman on top of commode.

158. In Federal furniture painted decoration could be used sparingly as an embellishment to provide contrast with the natural patterns of choice woods and veneers. This commode (mahogany and satinwood; W. 50") one of the supreme achievements of American cabinetmaking, combines the four primary methods of furniture decoration—carving, veneering, inlaying, and painting. It was made for the Derbys' daughter, Elizabeth, in 1809 by Thomas Seymour of Boston. The original bill exists with the commode at the Museum of Fine Arts, Boston, and it identifies John R. Penniman as the painter of the "shels on Top." The commode cost $80, and the shells $10. The shells, reading clockwise from the left, are a panther cowrie, a moon snail, a variety of *Murex*, a peanut shell, a *Bursa rana*, and a large harp shell in the center. In an 1827 auction of Penniman's belongings appeared a "Sportsman's Basket containing a great variety of Marine Shells." [48]

159. A worthy companion to the commode is this handsome dressing chest (mahogany and satinwood; W. 45″) at the Essex Institute in Salem. It was also owned originally by Elizabeth Derby, and it well could be the "Elligant Dressing Table" listed on the same Seymour bill, with carved legs and skirt by Thomas Whitman. Painting is sublimated to scrolls and stripings on the looking-glass supports. Like the commode, its main effect is won by singing woods. One bit of paint used by the Seymours that has found wide renown is the blue-green color used inside the upper sections of their secretaries. Other makers also used the same color, and in the teens in Salem a robin's-egg-blue lining paper was used in drawers.

161. Side chair, maple painted black, with polychrome and gilt decoration, probably Philadelphia, 1801. H. 38½". The Metropolitan Museum of Art.

160. Perspective glass in obelisk memorial, white pine painted black and white, carving attributed to Samuel McIntire, Salem, Massachusetts, c. 1800–1810. H. 75½". Museum of Fine Arts, Boston.

Perspective glasses provided eighteenth-century viewers the opportunity to scan prints with magnification and an illusion of depth. Usually they were simple table stands, although two are known that were incorporated in tambour-door Salem desks. At the left is a perspective glass mounted in a delightfully classical obelisk that is painted black, with white moldings and a carved profile bust and urn attributed to Samuel McIntire.

Traditionally, the glass, like the chair above, was owned by the Derby family.[49] The chair, a variant of the white oval-backs owned by Derby (as seen in the room setting on page 92), is painted black, with highly delicate grape and floral decoration on the back. It is likely one of the set of "6 Gold & green chairs" and "6 Gold & black do." ordered by John Derby, Elias' brother, from John Stillé, Jr., and Company, of Philadelphia, in 1801. Two other types of these chairs are known.

At the right is Elias Hasket Derby, the famous merchant. With his wife, Elizabeth Crowninshield Derby, he became a patron and inspirer of the finest craftsmen and artists in America. He had one brown and one blue eye, but his vision was perfect.

162. Portrait of Elias Hasket Derby (1739–1799),
oil on canvas, painted after his death by James
Frothingham of Boston. 41½″ x 32¼″.
The Peabody Museum of Salem.

163a

163

163, 163a. This card table makes use of much stylish Adamesque detail. It has a yellow ground, with a musical trophy in the center of the skirt. Two covered urns and rosettes in green and sepia flank the center. The outside top has a finely executed swag of flowers, with a floral border. When opened, the top is green, with ivory edging. Stripings on the legs simulate inlay. An 1801 Connecticut cabinetmaker described the "Laying on of your Colering, for outdore work it must be mixed with linsid oil, but for indoor work it may be mixed with Strong Beer or milk." He said starch would help the sheen of the varnish, as would applying it warm and in the sun.[50] Made of maple and white pine between 1785 and 1810, this stunning circular card table was found in Middletown, Connecticut. W. 38″. Winterthur Museum.

164

The Boston side table above (164) approaches the very best English classical furniture in elegance. The rich veneers of mahogany on the top and bird's-eye maple on the skirt are even further enhanced by applied gilt-composition decorations that resemble the finest ormolu mounts. The borders of the skirt and legs are also painted red. The quality of decoration and construction is superb. W. 52½″. Winterthur Museum.

Plain-painted and grained pieces were made throughout the Federal period. The account book of William Gray, a Salem painter of the late eighteenth century, records these forms:

painting a bedsted green—1790, 1793
   ″   4 chairs blew—1792
   ″   a stool seder color—1793
   ″   large table mahogany—1794
   ″   a table mahog^y & marble—1797
   ″   desk & secretary mahogany—1797
   ″   large table seder color—1797
   ″   a table chocolate color—1797.

In the manner of earlier painter-stainers, Gray also painted signs, houses, gates, ships, and fire buckets. He also did gilding, and once he even cut and made a coat![51]

The early nineteenth-century New England candlestand (165) features imitative mahogany graining, with painted inlay and crossbanding on the maple top. H. 27½″. The Henry Ford Museum.

165

167. Clock case (detail), mahogany,
New York, 1800–1810. H. 96″.
Photograph courtesy Israel Sack, Inc.

166. Pole screen, mahogany,
American, 1800–1810. H. 52¼″.
Winterthur Museum.

By the early nineteenth century great quantities of colors and finishes were being manufactured in America. Herman Vosburgh & Company of New York advertised in 1804:

the following Hard Varnishes and Patent Mineral Yellow, of their own Manufacture, warranted equal to any ever imported, and 50 per cent cheaper:—

Copal Varnishes	Japan Varnishes
Amber do	Shellecca do
Spirit of Wine do	Gold and Silver Sizes

Transparent Green do. for Metals—[also Red and Blue]
Black Japan Varnishes, for horsemen's caps, holsters, &c.
Do. for marble monuments and tomb-stones
Do. for violins and drums Do. of any color for printing on leather, paper, &c. Gold Lacker for Metals. Together with every other article in the Paint and Color line sold Wholesale, Retail and for Exportation.[52]

Floral decoration was used as a minor accent—but with great effect—on the tympanum of a New York clock case (167) and on the satinwood dashboard of a piano (168). The pole screen (166) has a delicately painted panel with a leafy border and a bowknot swinging a lurching basket of fruit into tree stumps.

168. Piano (detail), John Geib, New
York, 1804–1814. Winterthur Museum.

170. Box decorated by Hannah Crowninshield (1789–1834), maple and mahogany, Salem, Massachusetts, 1810–1815. W. 12″. The Peabody Museum of Salem.

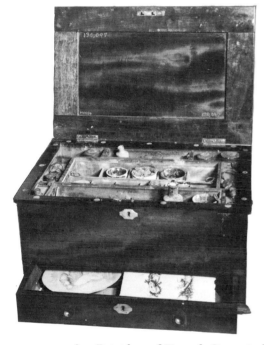

169. Paint box of Hannah Crowninshield, mahogany, English or American, c. 1800. W. 18″. The Peabody Museum of Salem.

Hannah was the daughter of Captain Benjamin and Mary Lambert Crowninshield of Salem. They lived on Essex Street in the Crowninshield-Bentley house, now owned by the Essex Institute. The Reverend William Bentley was their star boarder, and he encouraged the children to become proficient in the arts (see also page 170). Hannah was his favorite, and when Bentley sent samples of their penmanship to his friend Thomas Jefferson in 1808, the President replied, "I have certainly never seen anything in either way equally perfect, & I esteem them as models which will not, I believe, be exceeded." [53] Hannah executed watercolor portraits and scenes; decorated a box as a wedding present for her sister Maria in 1814; and successfully restored the seventeenth-century portrait of Captain George Corwin of Salem, which, according to Bentley, had been daubed and almost ruined by Michele Felice Corné, the decorative painter brought to Salem by Elias Hasket Derby. At the left is Hannah's paint box, with several small watercolor trophies in the drawer. Above (170) is a maple and mahogany box decorated by her, with her mother's initials on the front. Two swans are on the top, and trophies of music and the arts on the sides, done much in the manner of academy art (see pages 176–183).

Fancy chairs were available quite early in New York. In 1797 William Challen, "Fancy Chairmaker from London," advertised "all sorts of dyed, japanned, wangee and bamboo chairs, settees, etc. and every article in the fancy chair line." [54] This stunning settee and side chair are part of a large set owned by Joseph C. Yates and Anna Elizabeth De Lancey Yates of Albany. They were married on December 1, 1800, and Yates became Governor of New York in 1822. The settee and chair are painted white, with white lead ground in oil and turpentine and a bit of color added to prevent yellowing; the floral decoration is gilt. The Gothic arches in the back were popular in carved mahogany chairs made in New York right after 1800 by Slover and Taylor and other cabinetmakers and described in *The New-York Book of Prices for Cabinet and Chair Work . . .* in 1802. Here the carving on the back and legs has been omitted in deference to paint.

171 and 172. Settee and side chair, cherry and birch, probably New York City, 1800–1810. Settee, 75″ wide; chair, 35½″ high. Winterthur Museum.

173. Bed. H. 96½". Winterthur Museum.

Many of the highest-style examples of American Federal furniture have white as the background color. The elegant white-and-gold bed (173) was owned in Albany by the Yates family, its history being the same as that of the settee and chair on pages 102 and 103. The stop-fluted footposts, with stylized leaf carving and reeding, are of high quality. The bed is made of maple and birch, with a pine headboard, and was made probably in New York City shortly after 1800. It is dressed in period French silks.

The basin stand (174) is painted with dark-red and sage-green decoration and outlinings. The bowed front, scalloped backboards, and flaring legs serve as a perfect foil for the strong decoration. It was made in New England between 1800 and 1810, the woods being birch, basswood, and white pine.

The dressing table (175) has composition gilt beading applied around its edges and in a swag on the drawer front. Tables of this sort were often called "toilet," "toighlight," or—even more charmingly—"twilite" tables. The wood is white pine, and it was made in eastern Massachusetts just after 1800. The festoon is of green French satin.

The secretary (176) is an unusual painted rendering of a form often seen in dark woods in New England. Stripes of blue-gray and mulberry, and little sprigs on the legs, relieve the white ground. It was made most likely in eastern Massachusetts between 1800 and 1810, white pine again being its only wood. It was owned by the Cutts family, a prominent tribe in Saco, Maine. An old paper in a drawer shows it belonged to Richard Cutts and his wife, Anne Payne Cutts, a sister of Dolley Madison. Interestingly, the glorious, labeled John Seymour desk at Winterthur was also a Cutts piece.[55]

It should be noted that, like the Yates furniture, each of these examples was probably part of a larger painted set.

174. Basin stand. H. 35⅜". Winterthur Museum.

175. Dressing table. W. 36½". Winterthur Museum.

176. Secretary-desk. W. 41". Privately owned.

177. Dressing chest, white and gold, eastern Massachusetts, 1810–1820. W. 39″. Privately owned.

The dressing chest with attached looking glass (177) is a later version of the Derby example on page 95. This form was favored in the Boston–Salem area for a brief period. Painted white with gilt stripings on the turnings and drawer edges, this chest has exaggerated lotus forms at the junctures of the scrolls on the looking-glass supports and a lonely bellflower at the top of the crest of the swinging glass. An unusual feature is the pull-out workbag in the base molding, a device usually associated with worktables of the Federal period.[56] The bed, in the Asa Stebbins house at Old Deerfield, has delicate turnings on the footposts that characterize the best in New England Sheraton furniture. An outstanding feature is the delicacy of the painted decoration on the white posts. Grapes and acorns in dark blue and tans twine primly down the posts, and the footposts feature red columbines (178a). The leaves are shaded in green-gold, while borders in two shades of gray, gilt, and black striping complete the decoration.

178a

178, 178a. Bed, cherry and birch, New England, early nineteenth century. H. 74″. Historic Deerfield, Inc.

180. Armchair, ash, one of a set of
twelve, Philadelphia, 1790–1800.
H. 35½″. Philadelphia Museum of Art.

179. Armchair, Philadelphia, 1795–
1800. H. 37⅝″. The Bayou Bend
Collection, The Museum of Fine Arts,
Houston.

181. Sofa, ash, matches 180. W. 73½".
Philadelphia Museum of Art.

The best painted chairs of Federal America were made in
Philadelphia. Like the Derby family side chairs shown on
pages 92 and 96, figure 179 is in the Hepplewhite mold.
Owned by the Chew family, it is painted pale yellow, with
the bellflower and ribbon decoration in pale blue, dark blue,
and white. The arms and arm supports are mahogany.

While French ties with Federal America were strong, it
was in Philadelphia that the first really solid pangs of
French influence were felt after the American Revolution.
William Long, a cabinetmaker and carver "late of London,"
offered "French Sophas in the modern taste" and "Cabriole
and French Chairs" as early as 1787.[57] Figures 180 and 181
are a part of a large set of a dozen armchairs and a sofa
which were owned in the Burd family of Philadelphia.
They are in the Louis XVI style, painted off-white with
gilding on the laurel leaves, the edges, and the reeded legs,
and upholstered in soft blue-green French lampas. Figure
182 is a highly elaborate cabriole (upholstered back) armchair. Carved reeding and applied composition acorns and
oak leaves, shimmering in gold, stand in relief against the
gleaming white background. The upholstery is a green
French taboret with moiré and satin stripes of about 1800,
the date of the chair itself. It unites both French and English influences handsomely.

182. Armchair, ash, Philadelphia,
c. 1800. H. 36½". Winterthur Museum.

183. This side chair, traditionally owned in Salem by Nathaniel Silsbee and thought to have been made by John Seymour, was made in the Boston area about 1800. Black background, with the splats in greens and browns, the flowers in shades of pink, and with yellow striping. H. 36″. Privately owned.

184 and 185. This matching side chair (one of a pair) and settee were made of chestnut in New York about 1800. The background color is black, and the thin, vertical members of the splats are also painted brown to simulate grooving. The central vase portions of the splats have ornamental borders of painted paterae and swags of pearls, with polychrome roses and flowers extending into the top rails. The stiles and legs are painted with nearly identical sprays of flowers in white and green. All three examples shown on these two pages resemble early Sheraton designs and English prototypes closely, and they are most unusual in American painted furniture. The side chair (184) is 34½″ high, and the settee (185) is 56″ wide. Both, The Metropolitan Museum of Art.

184

185

186. Side chair, beech, oak, and birch, branded "s. GRAGG/BOSTON/PATENT," 1808–1815. H. 34⅜". Winterthur Museum.

One of the fascinations about American furniture is its informal adherence to the dictates of high style. Federal furniture can become a delightful imbroglio of elements that both confound the purist and result in spectacular, satisfying hybrids. In Boston, Samuel Gragg, a chairmaker working from 1808 to 1830, tried his innovative daring on a type of chair that combined the most up-to-date Grecian influences in its base with a lingering arrangement of the vertical members of the back (186). The peacock-plume decoration had been used before on Derby family chairs, but the bentwood construction, achieved by steam, had never been carried out with such freedom earlier. Windsor-chair makers had steamed bows, but they were well supported by many spindles. Here Gragg relied on the wood itself, and the stiles, seat frames, and legs are one sinuous strip of beech, with the vertical bars of the back curving down to become part of the seat. The chair has a pale-yellow background.

Since Gragg worked the woods to their limits, few of his chairs have escaped damage over the years. Parts of only three or four sets of these highly unusual chairs have survived.[58] Figure 188 is from a signed set of two armchairs, eight side chairs, and a quadruple-back settee. With noncontinuous round front legs terminating in goat's-hoof feet, it is a variant of the chair on the opposite page. It is also made of white oak, beech, and birch and is painted a yellowish-tan color with decoration in tan, brown, and green. It is at the Art Institute of Chicago, the gift of Mr. and Mrs. Charles F. Montgomery.

Figure 187 is an unmarked side chair, probably made by Gragg, at the Museum of Fine Arts, Boston. Here the top rail and legs resemble those on more conventional fancy Sheraton chairs, while the back is laminated in the Gragg manner. The chair is painted cream, with brown striping and the eagle in gold. Perhaps more stable, the chairs on this page lack the oozing delights of figure 186.

187. H. 32".

188. H. 34½".

189. The technique of painted decoration on light wood was used to great advantage on this sprightly and deliciously delicate worktable signed by Vose and Coates of Boston between 1808 and 1818. Shells, corals, and seaweeds swirl about the top; and nine dependent shells—not bellflowers!—are at the tops of the legs, which, with the stretchers, are laminated in a manner similar to that used in the chairs by Samuel Gragg shown on the two previous pages. W. 17″. Winterthur Museum.

190. Another Boston worktable of the same period as 189 is this most refined example. A polychrome bouquet of flowers is painted on the top, which is framed by a strip of highly figured mahogany and lunette inlay that extends over the edges. The drawer fronts have more abstract leafage and scrolls, and painted pillars are on the corners of the case. Curled-maple legs set off the table, which bears many similarities to the Seymours' work. W. 20". Collection of Mr. and Mrs. Vernon C. Stoneman.

192. Label of John Doggett (1780–1857), Roxbury, Massachusetts, c. 1805–1820. Labeled looking glasses, frames, and a dressing glass are known. Privately owned.

191. Silhouette of John Doggett, cut by "Master Hubard" (William James Hubard, 1807–1862), Boston, c. 1824–1826. Photograph courtesy The Magazine *Antiques*.

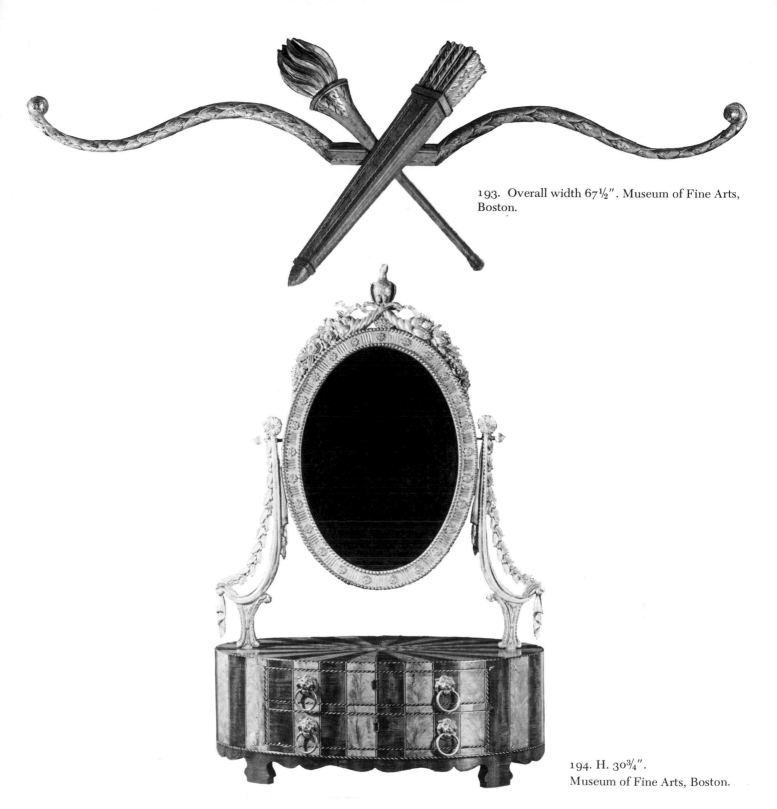

193. Overall width 67½″. Museum of Fine Arts, Boston.

194. H. 30¾″.
Museum of Fine Arts, Boston.

John Doggett (191), shown in silhouette on the opposite page, was one of a group of expert craftsmen working in Roxbury, Massachusetts, in the early 1800s. He made cases for Simon Willard's tall clocks, as well as gilt and painted tablets, balls, and eagles for the new Willard banjo clocks. Doggett's main fame was gained as a gilder of both carved and composition ornaments. His accounts show that he supplied glass, gilt balls, other materials, and looking glasses to frame makers and dealers from Maine to Louisiana. In his own area he had a considerable reputation and was responsible for many fine pieces made for the Derbys.

In 1808 Doggett billed Elizabeth Derby (the daughter of Elias) for gilding a bed cornice with "Bows Darts Quiver Arrows" made by William Lemon (193). Sheraton and Hepplewhite showed these motifs on a cornice and chair back. Other painted and gilded Massachusetts cornices are known. Since Mme. Derby was divorced in 1806, one can only ponder the use of these marriage symbols of Cupid's bow, quiver and arrows, and Hymen's torch. The elegant dressing glass (194) relates to the commode (page 94) and may be the one for which Doggett charged Mme. Derby "frame & Eagle for Dressing Glass" in 1809.[59]

The huge gilded looking glass on this page (195) is nearly seven feet high and was owned by Elizabeth Derby at Oak Hill, in Peabody, Massachusetts. In May 1809 Doggett charged Mme. Derby (as she preferred to be called after her divorce from Nathaniel West) $110 for "1 Oval Looking Glass with carved ornaments." [60] The carving is magnificently done. Moldings with freestanding balls surround the glass. At the top an eagle rises from a pedestal under which a chain grasps scrolled leaves. The base pendant features two doves nestled in grape leaves and fruit. The gilding is done to perfection. Among other craftsmen who worked for John Doggett were Thomas Whitman, who had done the carving for the famous Seymour commode made for Mme. Derby (page 94). John Penniman, who painted the shells on its top, also did ornamental painting for Doggett, as did Spencer Nolen and Aaron Willard, Jr. The looking glass is in the Karolik Collection at the Museum of Fine Arts, Boston.

Overlaying wood with gold leaf has always been tricky for the gilder. Two methods were used, water gilding and oil gilding. The former could be burnished to a high luster and was used on the best furniture. Gilding in oil lacked the brilliance of water gilding but was resistant to dampness and both cheaper and simpler to apply. In the 1790s American gilders frequently advertised as working in "Oil or Burnished Gold." [61] The great majority of elaborate looking glasses used here prior to the second quarter of the nineteenth century were imported.[62] America simply did not have the means of manufacturing glass of the quality or size made in England or France. Thus, either the glass or the whole looking glass was brought from abroad. After 1800 a new type was introduced. Called a "mirror," it was defined by Sheraton in his 1803 *Cabinet Dictionary* as "a circular convex glass in a gilt frame, silvered on the concave side." Very few of these were made in America.

197. Girandole mirror, pine, gilded, American or English, 1800–1815. Sheraton comments on the "agreeable effect" of mirrors pinpointing the rays of light in a room. H. 39″. The Henry Ford Museum.

196. Looking glass with sconces, pine, gilded, American or English, 1800–1810. Glass panel in upper section painted red, blue, black, and gold. H. 50½″. The Metropolitan Museum of Art.

198. Detail. W. 28″. Photograph courtesy Ginsburg & Levy, Inc. Stratford Hall.

199. Detail. Wintherthur Museum.

200. Detail. The Metropolitan Museum of Art.

201. Dressing glass, mahogany, New England, 1800–1815. W. 23¾″. Winterthur Museum.

Reverse painting on glass became popular in Federal America for professional and amateur alike. Gold leaf and oil colors were used, and subject matter ranged from flowers and geometric devices to allegory, mythology, hero worship, and scenic views. Looking glasses and wall clocks were the favored vehicles for glass painting. With the exception of 201, where a crusty New Englander set a fragment with a maritime scene (probably from a damaged looking glass) into a new dressing box trimmed with ivory finials and pulls, the other examples here are from tablets of looking glasses made in the Albany–New York City area early in the nineteenth century. Figures 199 and 202 are in polychrome, while the rest are done in white and gold, with outlining in black on occasion. The scene on 198 is based on a representation done in 1796 by Alexander Robertson of Brooklyn, New York, from the Hobuck Ferry House in Hoboken. At the left Washington is based upon one of Gilbert Stuart's likenesses.[63] Figure 202 depicts mourners at the tomb of George and Martha Washington, whose busts are on the tomb in front of Mount Vernon, which is suggested also in 203. Figure 200 shows Liberty seated.

Painting on Glass

202. Detail. Winterthur Museum.

203. H. 60½″. The Henry Ford Museum.

204. Chimney glass, pine, gilt, New York, c. 1805. W. 75½". Winterthur Museum.

Frames of early nineteenth-century looking glasses were often referred to in advertisements as "twisted," "pillared," and "double-pillared." A New York City carver and gilder, John Dixey, offered "a few very elegant" chimney glasses for sale in 1804. He noted, "As they are the first articles of this kind finished agreeably to the present prevailing fashion in Europe, it is hoped they will merit the attention of persons of taste." [64] The two elaborate examples shown here have Albany area histories and were probably made there or in New York City. The chimney glass (204) was owned by Governor and Mrs. Joseph Yates (see pages 102–105) and is made of wood, wire, glass, and burnished gold. Narrow glass panels above and around the oval looking glass are pale blue, gold, and white, as is the scenic tablet under the eagle. Figure 205 was owned by the Lansing family. The glass panels at the sides have gold grapes and leaves on a light-blue ground. There are also six small landscape vignettes. One at the top left depicts Albany's Old Dutch Church, which was torn down in 1806 and was shown in an engraving (205a) by Henry W. Snyder from a drawing by Philip Hooker, the Albany architect. [65]

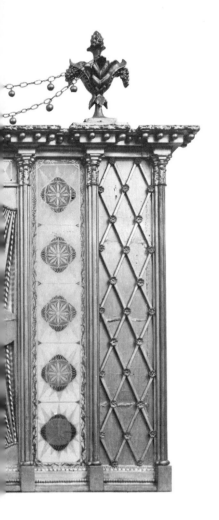

205a

205. Looking glass, pine, gilt, New York,
c. 1806–1810. H. 86½″. Albany Institute
of History and Art.
205a. Engraving of Old Dutch Church,
New York, published by John Low, New York,
1806. Albany Institute of History and Art.

206. Lady's dressing table, mahogany and satinwood, Baltimore, c. 1800. Painted flowers above looking glass, with five diamond-shaped painted panels at center. Oval painted-glass panels at sides, below acorn-and-oak-leaf glass friezes. W. 54″. Maryland Historical Society.

207. Lady's secretary-desk, mahogany, satinwood, holly, and ivory, Baltimore, c. 1800. Five black-and-gilt glass panels on outside with allegorical figures. Temperance and Justice on the doors. W. 30½″. The Metropolitan Museum of Art.

During the last two decades of the eighteenth century, many skilled Irish and English craftsmen migrated to rapidly growing Baltimore. Their productions were of the highest order, including a select group of inlaid mahogany cased pieces with inset painted glass panels (shown here and on page 130) and fine fancy furniture (pages 132–141). The designs of the three examples on these pages were derived from Sheraton's *Drawing Book*. He termed 206 a "Lady's Combined Dressing Table and a Dressing Chest," and the same Sheraton design appears on the trade card or label of William Camp, an early nineteenth-century Baltimore cabinet-maker.[66] Stylish English painted neoclassical furniture sometimes made use of paintings on inset copper panels, a practice not followed in this country. However, these Baltimore examples added allegorical, mythological, and biblical painted-glass panels to forms which were already very ornate. Commerce and Industry are shown on the dark-blue ovals of 206, while Temperance and Justice are featured on 207, with Moses on the top center panel. Charles Montgomery pointed out, in his *American Furniture: The Federal Period,* that the center oval of 208, with a female seated on a klismos-type Grecian chair, could be the earliest American representation of this form of chair.

208. Lady's cabinet and writing table, mahogany and satinwood, Baltimore, c. 1800. Five black-and-gilt oval glass panels with allegorical figures on door fronts of upper section. W. 30⅞″. Winterthur Museum.

210. Lady's secretary-desk, mahogany,
Boston–Salem area, c. 1800. W. 38″.
Museum of Fine Arts, Boston.

In the Boston–Salem area gilded, silvered, and painted glass panels were used on rare occasions in door panels of high-style cased pieces. The panels were used only on glass doors and were not set into wooden areas as they were in Baltimore. In the three examples shown on these two pages, one can see the affinities of the lighter panels to those used in the upper sections of looking glasses. The doors painted with black-and-gold ovals on 210 are similarly decorated to those on 211, which have looking-glass ovals. The two scenic panels on 210 of a cottage scene and an eagle are charmingly dissimilar, while those of flowers and their classical arrangers on 211 add a bright unity to this fine desk.[67]

209. Lady's secretary-desk, mahogany
and ivory, Boston–Salem area, c. 1800.
W. 36″. Photograph courtesy Ginsburg
& Levy, Inc.

211. Gentleman's secretary, mahogany and satinwood,
probably Essex County, Massachusetts, c. 1800. W. 75¼".
Winterthur Museum.

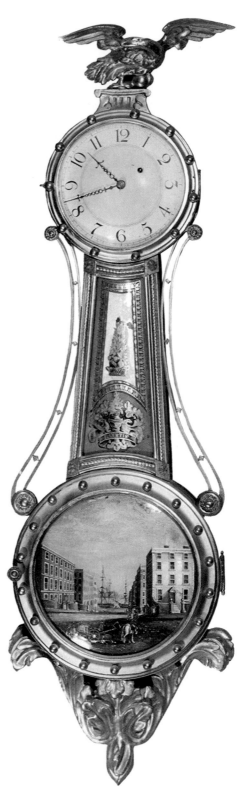

212. Wall clock, "Willard's Patent," Boston area, 1819. H. 40". The Seamen's Bank for Savings.

213. Wall clock, made by Lemuel Curtis, Concord, Massachusetts, 1816–1821. H. 45". Old Sturbridge Village.

One of America's best-known craftsmen is Simon Willard. His contributions to clockmaking were so varied and gifted that, to this very day, fellow craftsmen have emulated his works. In fact, some recent imitations have been the insincerest form of flattery. In 1802 he received a patent for an "improved timepiece," which he always called his "patent timepiece," and we today refer to as a "banjo clock." John Doggett made and gilded many of the delicate elements of the cases. Decorative painters included Aaron Willard, Jr. (Simon's nephew), and Spencer Nolen, who were in partnership in Boston from 1805 to 1809. On the back of the white-and-gilded glass tablets of 214 (at the right) appears "Willard & Nolen, Boston" in red paint. It is thought that the fine white-and-gilded banjo clocks were made as presentation pieces for weddings or other deservingly important occasions. The man in the moon appears in the upper tablet and an eagle in the lower one. Simon Willard's wall clocks usually contain simple geometric decorations in their glasses. However, Willard, not the best businessman, permitted his apprentices (and even others) to make wall clocks using his patent mechanism, and these were often signed "Willard's Patent" on the glass. Elnathan Taber, an apprentice and good friend of Willard, might well have been the maker of 212, which is dated 1819. It has an acorn finial and typical rope moldings. The upper tablet is decorated with the figure of Hope. The lower one is inscribed "HULL" and colorfully recalls Captain Isaac Hull's significant victory of his *Constitution* over the *Guerrière* off Nova Scotia in 1812. While it is not known who painted this clock, other ornamental painters of the Roxbury school included the well-known John Ritto Penniman, his protégé Charles Bullard, Samuel Curtis, and Stillman Lothrop. Their work included dial painting as well as the glass tablets, and they formed an important part of the armada of Roxbury craftsmen. A clockmaker who apprenticed there was the brother of one of the painters. Lemuel Curtis went on his own in 1811 and moved to Concord, Massachusetts. He patented some improvements on the Willard timepiece and made a more ornate version of the banjo clock called the "girandole clock," obviously after the convex mirrors it resembles (213). It has exquisite gilding and an unidentified view (perhaps lower State Street in Boston) done in polychrome on the lower convex glass.[68]

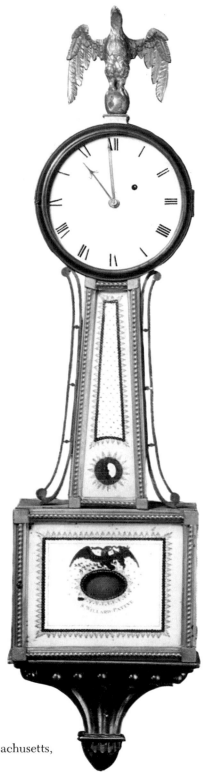

214. Wall clock, made by Simon Willard, Roxbury, Massachusetts, 1805–1809. H. 42″. Winterthur Museum.

215. Sideboard, mahogany, ebony, satinwood, silver, and glass panels, Baltimore, c. 1795–1800. Silver inlay and drawer pulls. Painted oval glass panels and plaques. W. 65½″. The Metropolitan Museum of Art.

The most dazzling piece of American Federal furniture known is the sideboard above ordered in Baltimore by David Van Ness for his home, Maizefield, in Dutchess County, New York. Fine inlays of wood are used, the griffins and swags at the bottom center copied from an "Ornament for Frieze or Tablet" in Sheraton's *Drawing Book*. The extensive use of silver inlays on the front and drawers of the sideboard and attached knife boxes is most unusual in American furniture. Glass panels between the front legs have floral urns and are gilt and black on a rose ground. Small glass plaques above the columns have masks, lyres, swags, and plumes in gold. As early as 1790, Walker and Chandless, Baltimore painters "from Dublin and London," advertised "Painting on Glass and Transparent Painting." [69]

216. Chimney glass, gilded pine and painted glass, probably New York, c. 1800–1805.
Glass panels gilded and painted in shades of blue and pink. W. 74¾". The Metropolitan
Museum of Art.

216a. Detail showing landscape in bottom-center portion of chimney-glass frame.

Verre églomisé is the French term for gilding and silvering glass on the back.
While this practice has gone on for centuries, it has taken its name from an
eighteenth-century Parisian collector and framer, Jean Baptiste Glomy. Above
is a chimney glass that combines gilding and reverse painting on glass panels
which are decorated in gold leaf with blue and pink paint. The scenes are fascinating. At the top center a pauper huddles by a fire; he is surrounded by floral
sprays. The sides feature grapes and leaves (left) and roses and pinks (right),
with four round vignettes. These show two girls at a swing, a tomb by a weep-
ing willow (left), a man fishing, and a farmhouse (right). The bottom scene includes boats and a harbor, a farm scene near a village, and a gentleman shoot-
ing. These genre scenes are charming, and it is tempting to interpret the
decoration as a from-rags-abroad-to-riches-in-the-new-country biography.

Fancy Furniture

217. Settee, painted black, with polychrome-and-gilt decoration, attributed to John and Hugh Finlay, Baltimore, 1805. L. 51″. The Baltimore Museum of Art.

217a. Detail of top-right oval on 217.

Hepplewhite and Sheraton popularized stylish painted furniture in their designs and comments and were most instrumental in its move from porch to parlor. In *The Cabinet Dictionary* (1803) Sheraton devoted an entire section to the techniques and the designs of painted furniture, as well as later japanning. He felt that "varnish colors" were much better and more effective than "common oil painting," which was less expensive and easily done. By 1797 fancy chairs were advertised in New York by William Challen (see page 102). In the early nineteenth century the rage for fancy furniture swept the country, and this popularity went on through the first half of the century. Of all the cities and towns producing fancy furniture, Baltimore excelled in the variety of forms and quality of decoration. In 1800 nearly fifty makers and painters of fancy chairs worked there.[70] Among the best known were John and Hugh Finlay, brothers from Ireland, who were in partnership in Baltimore from 1803 to 1833. When Benjamin Latrobe undertook the refurnishing of the White House for James Madison in 1809, he ordered chairs and sofas from the Finlays (see pages 150–151). They were paid $1,111 for them by Latrobe, and in true bureaucratic tradition he was not reimbursed for them until 1812.[71]

While the Finlay furniture made for the White House was destroyed in the fire of 1814, an existing set of two settees, ten armchairs, and a pier table made for John B. Morris was, according to family tradition, made by the Finlays in 1805. A settee and armchair shown here demonstrate the Finlays' abilities. Delicate leafy borders and columns in gold are foils for painted trophies on the seat rails and central splats. In 1803 "views adjacent to this city" were advertised by the Finlays; and on the top rail of the settee (217) are three Baltimore buildings, two of which remain today. From left to right are Homewood, the bank building of Baltimore, and Mount Clare (217a), built about 1760 by Charles Carroll and owned by his nephew, James Maccubbin Carroll, in 1805. On the top rail of the armchair (218) is Mount Deposit, built for David Harris. The decoration is extremely well done and recalls an 1805 advertisement of the Finlays listing "CANE SEAT CHAIRS, SOFAS, RECESS and WINDOW SEATS of every description and all colors, gilt ornamented and varnished in a stile not equalled on the continent —with real Views, Fancy Landscapes, Flowers, Trophies of Music, War, Husbandry, Love, &c. &c."[72] The "real Views" make the set one of documentary delight.

218. H. 33½".
The Baltimore Museum of Art.

133

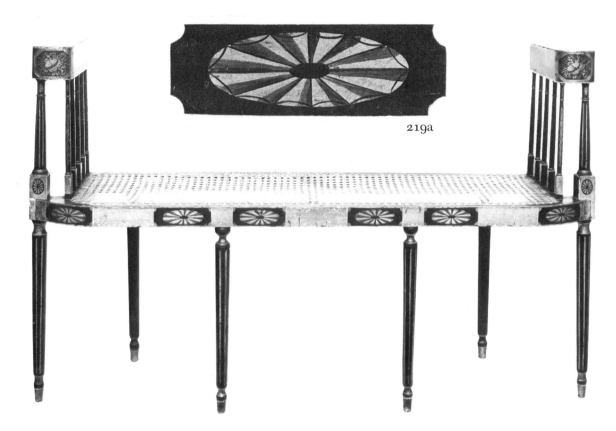

219a

219, 219a. Window seat, maple and tulip, Baltimore, 1800–1810. Caned seat. Part of a set with 220 and 221. L. 50″. Winterthur Museum.

The forms of Baltimore fancy furniture were highly varied. The 1805 Finlay advertisement quoted on the previous page lists these:

> A number of sets of new pattern Rush and Windsor Chairs and Settees; Card, Tea, Peir, Writing and Dressing Tables, with Mahogany, Satin-Wood, Painted, Japanned and real Marble Top Sideboards; Ladies' Work Wash-Stand and Candle-Stands; Horse Pole, Candle and Fire Screens; Bedsteads, Bed and Window Cornices, the centers enriched with Gold and Painted Fruit, Scroll and Flower Borders of entire new patterns, the mouldings in Japan, Oil and Burnish Gold, with Beads, Twists, Nelson Balls, &c. Likewise Brackets, Girondoles and Trypods; Ladies' Needle Work, Pictures and Looking Glasses Frames; old Frames Regilt; real Views taken on the spot to any dimension, in oil or watercolors; Coach, Flag and Masonic Painting; and particular attention paid to Gold Sign Lettering on Glass, Pannel or Metal. JOHN & HUGH FINLAY.[73]

The Finlays and other American fancy painters frequently mention japanned finishes. In this country these refer to transparent varnish colors—usually black and gold—and not to the use of transparent colors over whiting or size as often done on English fancy chairs.

220a

The three pieces shown on these pages are from a large set of fancy furniture which has been attributed to Robert Fisher of Baltimore, based on a signed piece of the set unfortunately destroyed by fire a few years ago.[74] Painted black with gold decoration, the set has striped legs, imitating carving or inlay, and well-delineated paterae (219a). Dentil-edged gold panels flank the central decoration on both the side chair and the pier table. The stretcher of 220 is little short of amazing, and the polychrome scene (220a) is of two houses built by William Buchanan for his daughters about 1800. The side chair (221) has a trophy of musical instruments on its top rail.

221. Side chair, maple, etc., Baltimore, 1800–1810. Part of a set with 219 and 220. H. 33¼″. Winterthur Museum.

220, 220a. Pier table, tulip and pine, Baltimore, 1800–1810. Part of a set with 219 and 221. W. 45¼″. The Baltimore Museum of Art.

THO⁵ RENSHAW Nº 37 S. Gay Sᵗ Baltᵉ   John Barnhart Ornamenter.

222a. Detail of 222 showing signature.

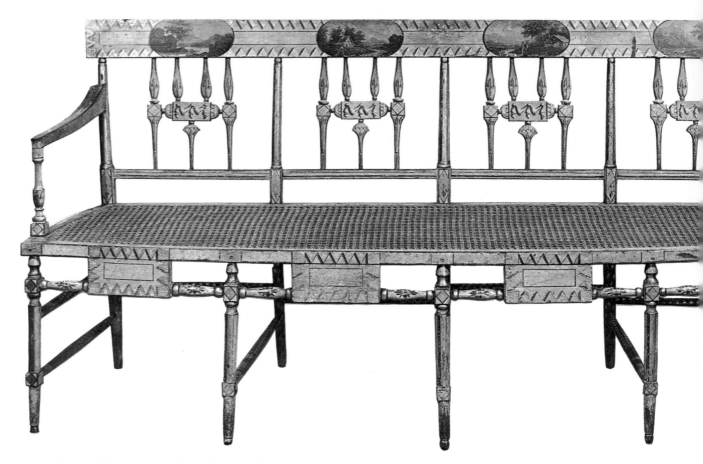

222. Settee, Baltimore, c. 1814–1815. Made by Thomas Renshaw and painted by John Barnhardt. Ivory and gold, with polychrome landscapes. L. 75½". The Baltimore Museum of Art.

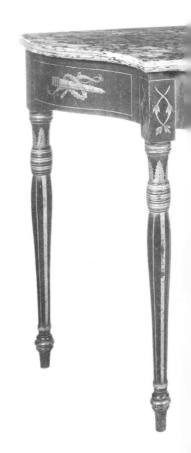

The only signed piece of Baltimore fancy furniture now known is the quadruple-back settee above. It is signed on the lower rails of the center sections of the back (see 222a). Thomas Renshaw is listed in Baltimore directories in 1814 and 1815, and John Barnhardt appears in them in 1822 and 1823. Elements of the settee are heavier than in earlier fancy furniture, but the "feel" of this piece, with landscape scenes on the back, the gilt dentil borders on flat surfaces, and the vertical stripings on the legs, is typically Baltimore. The armchair (224) at far right provides a fascinating study in attribution. While its color is different from the Renshaw–Barnhardt settee (a deep-red ground rather than ivory), the decoration is extremely similar. The construction of the chair, with its rather ungainly squared-off sections on the legs at the junctures of the stretchers, is almost identical to the settee. Thus, with so many major similarities, the armchair can be attributed to Renshaw and Barnhardt with certainty rather than hope. The colored landscape views on both pieces are unidentified. Figure 225 is another later Baltimore chair, made between 1810 and 1815. It is both highly stylish and rather fussy; and its decoration, in white and gold on a red ground, is most unusual for the three chinoiserie scenes on the top rail, center splat, and on the tablet below the seat rail. The pier table (223) was made in the preceding decade and is Baltimore at its best. Gilt stripings and leaves accent the legs. Trophies of music and love (223a) are shaded in brown on the gold leaf, all on a black ground. A marble top sets off the decoration nobly. The inventory of Charles Ridgely (1760–1829) of Hampton shows how popular fancy furniture was in fine houses of the area. Over fifty painted chairs were noted in yellow, green, "light colored," red-and-green, and gold-and-green. Painted settees, lamp stands, pier tables, and card tables were also listed.[75]

225a. Detail showing chinoiserie decoration on tablet under seat of 225.

224. W. 21″. Winterthur Museum.

223a

223, 223a. Pier table, cherry, etc., Baltimore, 1800–1810. W. 53½″. Winterthur Museum.

225. W. 20½″. Winterthur Museum.

226a

226

We have already seen three magnificent Baltimore cased pieces made of mahogany with inset painted-glass panels on pages 124 and 125. Here a pier table (226) and a corner table (227) feature gilded glass panels at the center on a blue background. The scene, directly from Sheraton's *The Accompaniment* to *The Cabinet-Maker and Upholsterer's Drawing Book* (1802), is of Diana's visit to Endymion (226a). The leafage at the top of the legs of the pier table is gilded, and all other decoration on both pieces is inlaid. Charles Montgomery has suggested that these tables, part of a very small group having Baltimore histories, might have been made by the Philadelphia cabinetmaker Joseph B. Barry, who advertised "Marble pier and corner tables" in Baltimore in 1803.[76] The single-cross-backed side chair at the right (228) is painted light red and features a gardening trophy on its top rail and paterae on its front and back stretchers.

227. Corner table, mahogany, inlaid, marble; Philadelphia or Baltimore, 1802–1810. W. 27⅝″. Winterthur Museum.

226. (Opposite). Pier table, mahogany, inlaid, marble; Philadelphia or Baltimore, 1802–1810. W. 36¾″. Winterthur Museum. 226a. Detail from *The Accompaniment* to Sheraton's *Drawing Book* (1802). Photograph courtesy Library, Cooper–Hewitt Museum of Decorative Arts and Design, Smithsonian Institution.

228. Side chair, maple, etc., Baltimore, 1800–1810. Painted red and gold. H. 33½″. Winterthur Museum.

229. Oil painting of the house and shop of David Alling (1777–
1855), Newark, New Jersey, chairmaker. The sign on the shop
identifies Alling as a "Fancy Chair Maker." Fancy chairs stand
outside both buildings. Several others are in the shop window,
while one lurks inside the open door of the Alling house. Painted
1810–1835. 21″ x 30″. The Newark Museum.

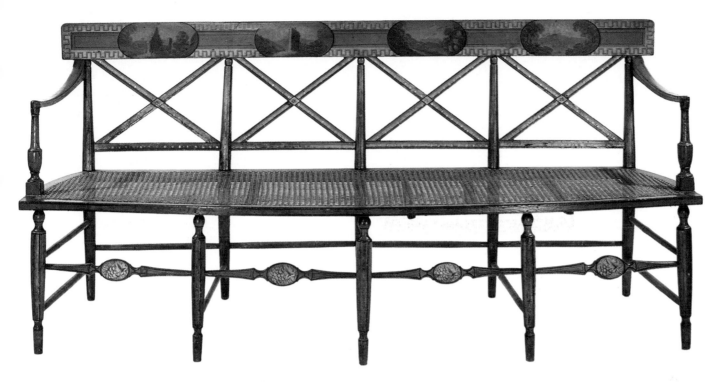

230. Settee, maple, etc., Baltimore, 1805–1815.
Painted sepia, brown, yellow, and black. L. 70¼".
The Henry Ford Museum.

The settee above is another Baltimore example ex-
hibiting some unusual details. The Greek key
borders of the top rail differ from the dentil edgings frequently seen, and the ball turnings at the
top of the vertical members of the back (at the
juncture of the top rail) vary from the normal
treatment. However, the broad vertical striping on
the legs, the grapes and leafage on the stretchers,
and the four polychrome romantic landscapes are
typical of Baltimore fancy work. It was probably
made by one of the many unknown competitors of
the Finlays, Renshaw and Barnhardt. The graceful
marble-top pier table (right) is unusual in that
much of its ground is done in bronze powder. The
painting of the Alling house and shop (opposite) is
a very rare view of a fancy craftsman's establish-
ment.

231. Pier table, pine, marble top, probably Baltimore,
1800–1815. Decoration in bronze and green, with
gilt covered urns and trophies of beribboned horns on
the skirt; leaves and flowers on the legs. W. 44¼"
The Henry Ford Museum.

232, 232a. Side chair, one of a set of six, maple, etc. Connecticut or New York, 1815–1825. Black and gilt, with polychrome scene. H. 34½″. Photograph courtesy Mr. and Mrs. Jerome Blum. Collection of Stewart E. Gregory. 233. Side chair, one of a set of ten, maple, etc., New York City, 1815–1820. Orange-red ground, with black and gold; polychrome scenes. H. 33½″. Photograph courtesy Ginsburg & Levy, Inc.

232

233

While fancy chairs were made everywhere after 1800, more were made in New York, our largest city, than anywhere else. Many chairmakers advertised their wares, frequently with small linecuts in the newspapers showing an actual chair. Since more than one maker could use the same cut, one must tread on lily pads of doubt when attempting to be too definite about who made what. In 1817 Wheaton and Davis, of Fulton Street, offered "an elegant assortment of Curl'd Maple, Plain Painted and Ornamented, Landscape, Conversation and Rocking Chairs, Settees, Sofas, Loungees, Music Stools, &c. all of the newest fashion." [77] Whether they made the handsome fancy chair opposite (234) is not known. It is most stylish, with splayed and reeded front legs, a sweeping, rounded seat, fine curled-maple graining, and a fine riverscape that seems an adumbration of the Hudson River School of landscape painting. The steamboat is interesting, since this new type of motive power had been only recently introduced to the river, by Robert Fulton's *Clermont* in 1807. The chairs on this page also are "landscape chairs." Figure 233 features two imaginary landscapes, with a carved back decorated in gold leaf. Its legs are reeded. Figure 232 above has a great deal of snap to it. Simpler than the other two, it nevertheless has an unusual back, with interlaced circles and balls. The hesitant splay of the front legs is noteworthy, but not so much so as the charming scene on the back (232a), which seems far removed from the advertisements of the big city.

234, 234a. Side chair, one of a set of six, maple, etc., New York City, 1815–1820. Curled-maple graining, gilt and red-brown striping. Polychrome composite Hudson River Valley views differ on each chair. Owned in the Van Rensselaer Manor House in Albany, New York. Figure 234a is a detail of the back, showing a steamboat. H. 32¾". Winterthur Museum.

234

234a

235. Armchair, maple, etc.,
New York, 1805–1815. H. 33½″.
Winterthur Museum.

236. Couch, maple, etc., New York, 1805–1815.
L. 77″. The Brooklyn Museum.

237. Side chair, maple, etc., New York, 1805–1815. H. 33¾″. The Metropolitan Museum of Art.

Fancy furniture is sometimes called "Fancy Sheraton" in honor of the designer who did so much to popularize it. It was actually produced before and after his reign of influence. One of the best descriptions of contemporary terminology for fancy chairs is an 1812 advertisement of Asa Holden of Broad Street, New York:

. . . highly finished Fancy Chairs, such as double and single cross, fret, chain, gold, ball and spindle back, with cane and rush seats, etc., of the latest and most fashionable patterns. The cane seats are warranted to be American made, which are known to be much superior to any imported from India.[78]

The elegant set shown here includes two armchairs, six side chairs, and a Grecian couch (235–237). All are painted dazzling vermilion and have mounts of gilt bronze as well as gilt-painted decoration and yellow-varnished rush seats. The delicate ball-and-spindle backs and outward-flaring front legs of the chairs combine with the decoration to produce the ultimate in stylishness in New York fancy furniture.

145

238. Side chair, one of a pair, birch and maple, Massachusetts, 1805–1820. Blair House, Washington, D.C.

239. *Nathan Hawley and Family, Nov.ʳ 3ᵈ 1801*, watercolor by William Wilkie, Albany. 16″ x 20″. Albany Institute of History and Art.

The appeal of fancy chairs was universal. Nathan Hawley was Sheriff of Albany County and head of the jail. An inmate, William Wilkie, painted the picture above showing Hawley and his wife seated on yellow fancy chairs. The table is grained and the children small. In New England, fancy chairs were popular after 1800. They tend to be more delicate than chairs made in other areas, and side chairs predominate. Richard Austin, a Salem chairmaker, charged $2.50 each for "not Stript" bamboo chairs, $2.66 for striped chairs, and $3.33 for "Gold Leaf" chairs in 1805.[79] Both chairs shown here are from the Salem area. Figure 238 has a black-and-red ground, with the drapery folds and urn on the back in gold, green, and red. Figure 240 was bought by James Barr, Jr., of Salem in 1812. The decoration is in gold, green, and brown on a light-yellow ground and is deceivingly delicate. Both chairs have very thin strips of wood over the seat edges. The rush seats, by the way, were always originally painted or stained on fancy chairs.

240. Side chair, one of a set of six, birch, probably Salem, Massachusetts, 1812. H. 36″. Essex Institute.

241. Side chair, one of a set of nine, maple, Baltimore, 1815–1820. H. 34½". The Metropolitan Museum of Art.

242. A New York Greek Revival interior by Alexander Jackson Davis, 1845. 13¼" x 18¼". The New-York Historical Society.

243. Side chair, one of a pair, Philadelphia or Baltimore, 1815–1820. H. 35". Philadelphia Museum of Art.

Revivals in the nineteenth century were much like women's hemlines in our own time—constantly on the move. The French interpretation of Roman and Greek arts was felt in England and America. Designers Thomas Hope and George Smith—with the later works of Thomas Sheraton—show these exact archaeological influences. The results were shock waves of influence from the English Regency and the French Empire, with bits of ancient Italy, Greece, and Egypt liberally sprinkled in. Thus, furniture made in America from 1815 to 1840 can vary tremendously in form and decoration. A new wood, rosewood, came into vogue in fine furniture; and in painted decoration new pigments and a new technique, stenciling, were introduced. Tables and cased pieces assumed an architectural monumentality; while many chairs, based on the Greek klismos, shown on ancient vases, featured serene lines and outward-flaring saber legs. Figures 241 and 243 are based on this prototype. Figure 241 has turned front legs, and it is painted yellow ochre, with decoration in green, black, red, and ochre. Figure 243 is decorated in black, red, ochre, and gilt. Both feature Greek, Pompeian, and Egyptian motifs in the new "modern" or "Grecian" style. The Greek Revival had arrived for a long, popular stay,[80] and its spacious scale can be seen in the watercolor above by Alexander Jackson Davis, America's leading mid-century eclectic architect.

IV. AMERICAN EMPIRE

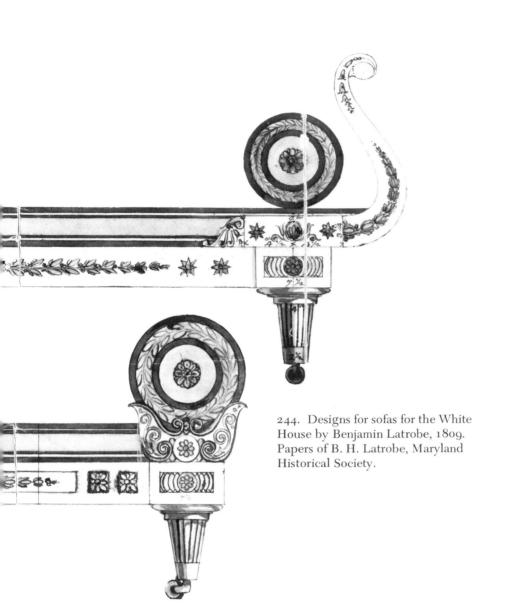

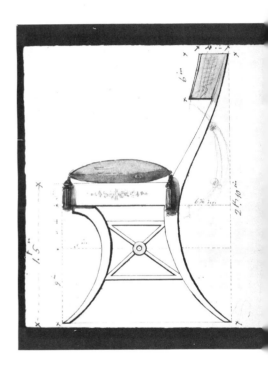

244. Designs for sofas for the White House by Benjamin Latrobe, 1809. Papers of B. H. Latrobe, Maryland Historical Society.

The architect Benjamin Henry Latrobe served as Surveyor of Public Buildings in Washington from 1804 to 1812. A great proponent of the Greek Revival, he expressed the hope, in an 1811 address to the Society of Artists in Philadelphia, that "the days of Greece may be revived in the woods of America, and Philadelphia become the Athens of the Western world." [81] During the Madison era Latrobe supervised the furnishing of the White House, working closely with Mrs. Madison. In 1809 he drew the designs on these two pages. The drawings of the sofas and chairs were sent to John and Hugh Finlay in Baltimore, with a note from Latrobe requesting, "I hope you will be able to bend your whole force to them immediately." [82] The chairs were based on the Greek klismos form as shown in Thomas Hope's *Household Furniture and Interior Decoration*, published in London in 1807; and the sofas were modeled after a Hope design for a "couch shaped like the ancient *Triclinia*." Not only were the forms new, but the decoration, with rosettes, husks, and anthemia, came from a heftier vocabulary than did earlier neoclassical devices. The large pier glass at the right, unfortunately broken in transit to the White House, was white, blue, and gilt, with marble panels surrounding the glass. Even the pieces that survived the journey during Latrobe's modish renovations could not survive the disastrous fire at the White House in 1814 (see page 133). The drawings are testimony to the popular, new "modern" style.

245. Designs for side chairs for the
White House by Benjamin Latrobe,
1809. The chairs were painted and
the cushions red velvet. Papers of
B. H. Latrobe, Maryland Historical
Society.

246. Design for "looking glass" for
the White House by Latrobe.
Library of Congress.

247. Side chair, maple, New York, 1815–1825.
Rosewood graining with gilt decoration.
H. 32⅛". Winterthur Museum.

248a. Detail showing freehand gilding on front rail of 248. Photograph courtesy Peter Hill.

248. Couch, maple, New York, 1815–1825. Rosewood graining with gilt decoration. L. 84". Museum of Fine Arts, Boston.

French influences were strong in New York cabinetmaking. Indirect inspiration came from designers such as Charles Percier and Pierre François Fontaine, whose ideas were incorporated into the works of such English designers as the later Thomas Sheraton, Thomas Hope, and George Smith, whose book *A Collection of Designs for Household Furniture and Interior Decoration* (1808) was the most comprehensive statement of the English Regency period. Direct influences from France came in the form of skilled cabinetmakers migrating to New York. Their abilities resulted in New York's becoming the style leader for the new country.

Grecian chairs were greatly modified in America. Carved ornamentation on backs and legs became bolder and heavier; and freehand gilt decoration, frequently of very high quality, was used in place of gilt ormolu mounts. Backs of chairs progressed from the simpler cross or double-cross to carved scrolls, harps, lyres, and eagles. The two examples here combine carving with excellent imitative rosewood graining and gilt painting. The side chair (247) has an eagle on its top rail with carved cornucopias, and paw feet. On the couch (248) are gilt masks and simulated mounts. Its carved feet and ankles are painted dark green.

The couch or stool below features rosewood graining, and its gilt decoration is looser than that on the preceding chair and couch. The gilt rosettes, leaves, and honeysuckles are most tastefully done and are complemented by elegant brass casters. D. R. Hay, an English decorative painter and author who did a great deal of graining in the 1820s, later wrote:

> The humble art of imitating woods and marbles is in some measure allied to the high art of portrait-painting, in being also an imitative art, and requiring a degree of natural genius in the grainer, as such artists are technically called, to enable him to avoid the faults so common in both arts, namely, that of producing a caricature of the object of which he attempts to produce a correct resemblance.[83]

The grainers of 247, 248, and 249 produced correct resemblances. On the opposite page is a side chair made for a dinner honoring the Marquis de Lafayette in Baltimore on October 7, 1824. Lafayette was, without doubt, the most wined and dined visitor this country has ever had, and his triumphal return in 1824 and 1825 attested to (and tested) his enduring strength. The chair has sturdy turned legs. The black-and-gilt decoration features a polychrome bust of Lafayette on the top rail.

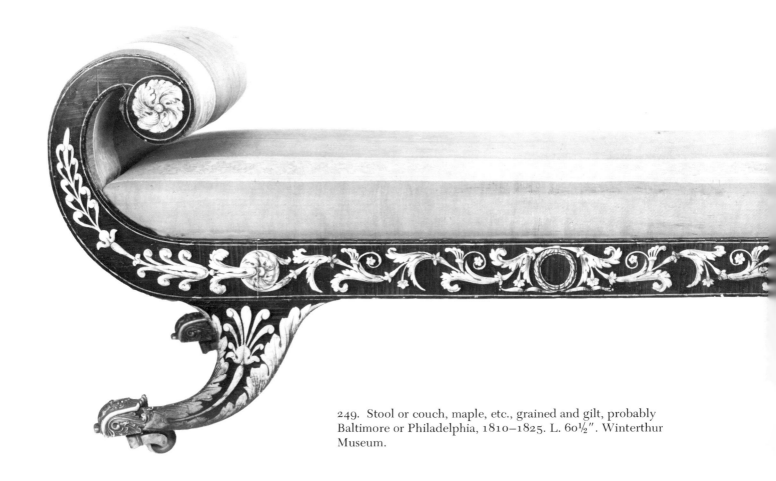

249. Stool or couch, maple, etc., grained and gilt, probably Baltimore or Philadelphia, 1810–1825. L. 60½″. Winterthur Museum.

250. Side chair, black and gilt, Baltimore, 1824.
H. 31″. 250a. Detail showing portrait of
Lafayette. The Baltimore Museum of Art.

250a

New York's most famous cabinetmakers in the earlier nineteenth century were Duncan Phyfe, Michael Allison, and Charles-Honoré Lannuier. Working in the Regency tradition, Phyfe and Allison preferred mahogany and other fine woods, with the emphasis on carving rather than gilding. Lannuier, working in a simplified French idiom, softened it with Anglo-American whispers and whiffs, creating, as in the card table below, the New York Empire style. Made for Philip Hone, a prominent New York businessman diarist, and mayor in 1826, the table features a gilded winged caryatid and leafy hocks above the carved and ebonized paw feet. With bird's-eye maple on the top and on the sides of the platform, rosewood, satinwood veneer inside the top, and brass inlays of stars, circles, and anthemia on the edge of the folding leaf, the table is one of the most highly textured and glowing of Lannuier's works.[84]

The pier glass (252) is gilded and has "double twist" columns at the sides. Urns with flame finials, two anthemia, and a central shell with a reclining sea horse are at the top. This elegant pier glass was purchased at an auction of the effects of Salem's most famous literary figure, Nathaniel Hawthorne.

The pier table (253) is grained in imitation of mahogany and features gilt decoration. The lyre base with its eagle gives the illusion of carving. It is signed "W. Pringle/Painter," a name not found among the Pringles of New York and Philadelphia directories.

251. Card table, rosewood, maple, satinwood, and gilt. Attributed to Charles-Honoré Lannuier, New York, c. 1813–1817. H. 31″. The Metropolitan Museum of Art.

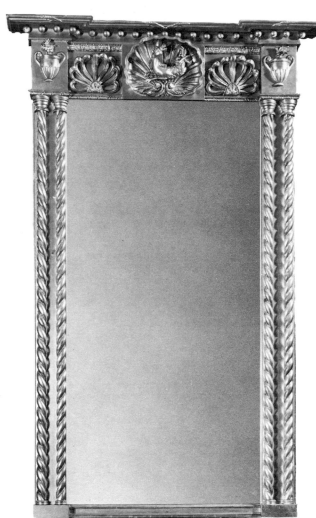

252. Pier glass, gilt, Boston–Salem area, c. 1820.
H. 75″. The National Society of the Colonial
Dames of America in the Commonwealth of
Massachusetts.

253. Pier table, one of a pair, poplar, grained and
gilt decoration by W. Pringle, Middle States,
1820–1835. W. 42″. Photograph courtesy Craig
and Tarlton, Inc.

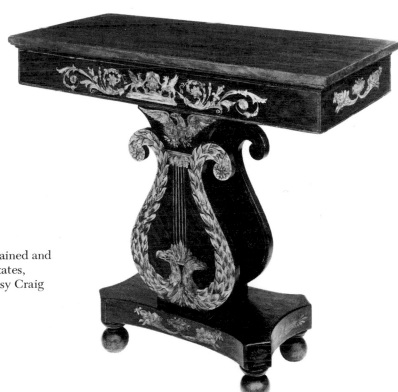

254. Pier table, tulip, probably Baltimore, 1825–1835. Grained, with bronze gilding. W. 44⅝″. Photograph courtesy Peter Hill.

255. Grecian couch, poplar and pine, possibly Baltimore or Philadelphia, 1815–1820. Gilded all over. L. 90″. The Bayou Bend Collection, The Museum of Fine Arts, Houston.

257. Card table, mahogany, etc., attributed to Charles-Honoré Lannuier, New York, 1815–1819. W. 36½″. The Henry Ford Museum.

256. Cellarette, mahogany, rosewood, etc. Attributed to Charles-Honoré Lannuier, New York, 1815–1819. W. 34″. Photograph courtesy Israel Sack, Inc. Yale University Art Gallery.

The rapid style changes of the nineteenth century were abetted by technological advances on many fronts. In the case of gilding, less costly bronze powders were substituted for gold leaf. Then the bronze powders could be imitated for even less by heating tin, mercury, ammonia, and sulfur.[85] Modern radiator paint was imminent! About 1815 stencils made their appearance, and this American innovation permitted more rapid decoration of running borders and other repetitive designs that were so costly in time when done freehand. Copies of ormolu mounts soon became copies of copies, and technology was on its way to control both style and quality.

Egyptian influences are seen in the examples shown here. The pier table (254) is grained in imitation of rosewood, the bronzed gold frieze painted in black, red, silver, and orange fruit designs. Its most unusual feature is its slate top, which is painted to imitate black-and-gold marble. The Grecian couch (255) is based directly on a design of Thomas Sheraton from *Designs for Household Furniture*, published in 1812 after his death. While his designs are in black and white, colored plates came into use in nineteenth-century design books, aiding the cabinetmaker, painter, and upholsterer greatly.

Both pieces on this page are attributed to Charles-Honoré Lannuier. The feet and sphinxlike figures of 256 are painted black, with gilt decoration, as is the entire startling base of 257, except for the platform top.

On the next page, 258 relates to a similar pair in the Museum of the City of New York and a mahogany chair in the manner of Phyfe.[86]

259. Made of whitewood and pine in New York about 1825, the base of this center table is painted black, with gilt decoration. H. 27½". Photograph courtesy Ginsburg & Levy, Inc. The Bayou Bend Collection, The Museum of Fine Arts, Houston.

258. This "beastly" painted maple armchair, partly gilded and stenciled, from New York, 1820–1825, is similar to a pair owned by Stephen Whitney. H. 38". Winterthur Museum.

259a. The top of 259 features a
composite Hudson River view in
polychrome. The delicate border
is gold on very dark green.
Diameter 36½".

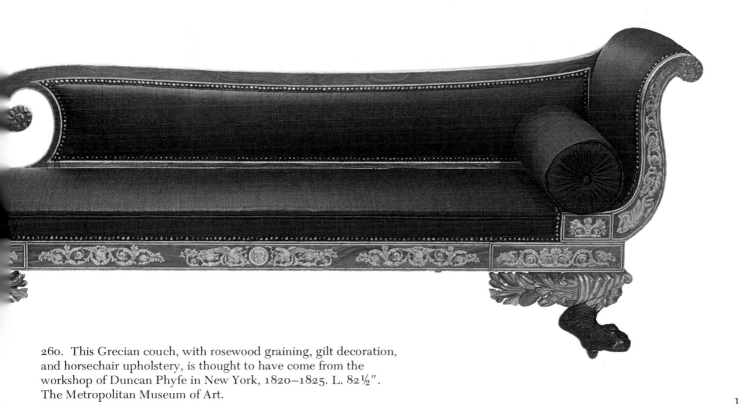

260. This Grecian couch, with rosewood graining, gilt decoration,
and horsechair upholstery, is thought to have come from the
workshop of Duncan Phyfe in New York, 1820–1825. L. 82½".
The Metropolitan Museum of Art.

"Improved" pigments and oils had been advertised since the eighteenth century. In fact, one New Yorker featured a quick-drying oil, which "if used on bedsteads will destroy any vermin."[87] Patent paints were mentioned in Philadelphia by 1800. The advent of two synthetic colors, chrome yellow in 1797 and artificial ultramarine in 1806, were foreign inventions that spurred on American manufacturers. Chrome yellow was produced in Baltimore right after 1800; and in 1808 "American Manufactured PRUSSIAN BLUE . . . equal to any imported" was made there.[88] Dr. James Mease, in *The Picture of Philadelphia* (1811), mentioned on page 75:

> Paints of twenty-two different colours, brilliant and durable, are in common use, from native materials; the supply of which is inexhaustible. The chromate of lead, that superb yellow colour, is scarcely equaled by any foreign paint.

Colors were constantly improving. However, in the high-style American Empire pieces of the first half of the nineteenth century, freehand and stenciled gilding was the single most-used color. The armchair at the left (261) combines acanthus and anthemion motifs in gilt painting and stenciling on rosewood graining. The small chest below is ebonized in part, with stenciled leafage and gilded stripings. The singing mahogany dressing bureau (263) uses gilt stenciling quite sparingly to punctuate the carving and fine veneers. These three examples, with the three shown on pages 164 and 165, show the range and glories of the American Empire style.[89] It truly could be called a "gilded age."

261. Armchair, one of a pair, whitewood, Baltimore, 1830–1840. Rosewood graining; gilt decoration. H. 34½″. The Baltimore Museum of Art.

262. Miniature chest of drawers, mahogany, probably New York City, 1825–1840. Gilt-stencil decoration. W. 11″. Collection of Allen Prescott.

263. Dressing bureau, mahogany veneers, New York, c. 1830. Gilt-stencil decoration. Partial label in frieze drawer reads "H & H / no. 154" (probably Haines and Holmes). W. 37″. Munson–Williams–Proctor Institute.

264. This secretary represents the ultimate in New York stenciled and painted furniture. Made about 1825, possibly by Joseph Meeks & Sons, it features various gilded motifs on ebonized mahogany. It combines wood, carving, gilding, brass, glass, and silk in a stunning fashion. W. 55¾″. The Metropolitan Museum of Art.

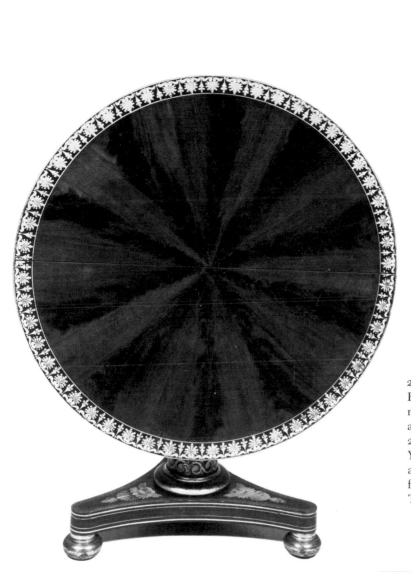

265. The center table at left, made in Philadelphia or Baltimore, 1825–1830, has a handsome section-veneered mahogany top, with gilt stenciled decoration on its edge and also on the ebonized poplar base. Diameter 29¼".
266. The mahogany sideboard below, made in New York, 1825–1835, features gilt decoration—freehand and stenciled—and ebonized columns and drawer fronts. W. 68". Both, The Bayou Bend Collection, The Museum of Fine Arts, Houston.

The rather serene card table below is reminiscent of the work of the Philadelphia cabinetmaker Anthony G. Quervelle. The gilt scrolls on the skirt resemble Plate XX, "Furniture Painting Arabesque Ornaments," in Nathaniel Whittock's *The Decorative Painters' and Glaziers' Guide,* published in London in 1828. One of the most important books on ornamental painting in the nineteenth century, it is a mine of information on all phases of graining, marbleizing, painting on glass, stenciling, and coloring. It details a history of design, and its plates (many are colored) provided innumerable sources and examples for professionals and amateurs in both England and America.

On the opposite page is an 1815 Albany advertisement (268) of the fancy chairmaker William Buttre, who had worked in New York City from 1805 to 1814. The unusual eagle and shield in the back of the chair shown in the cut are apparently loosely based on the Great Shield of the United States. Although the eagle's head and neck do not extend above the back, nor is there a sunburst on the front stretcher, chair 269 has many similarities to the one shown in the advertisement, including the shield on feathered eagle's legs, the five balls below the stretcher, and the squared-and-turned legs. Fancy chairs were made throughout the Empire period. They bring to mind Sheraton's definition of a rout chair: "Small painted chairs with rush bottoms, lent out by cabinet makers for hire, as a supply of seats at general entertainments or feasts; hence their name rout chair." [90] In the realm of genteel catering, lighter examples still exist.

267. Card table, one of a pair, mahogany and rosewood, gilt-stencil decoration, Philadelphia, 1820–1830. W. 35⅝". The Metropolitan Museum of Art.

268. Advertisement from *Albany Advertiser*,
February 16, 1815, reprinted in *Albany Register*,
May 19, 1815. Albany Institute of History and Art.

269. Side chair, ash, etc., probably made by William
Buttre, Albany, New York, c. 1815. Brown paint with
gilt decoration. H. 35″. Winterthur Museum.

270. *Cleopatra's Barge*, gouache, by George Ropes, Salem, Massachusetts, dated 1818. 17½″ x 22¼″. The Peabody Museum of Salem.

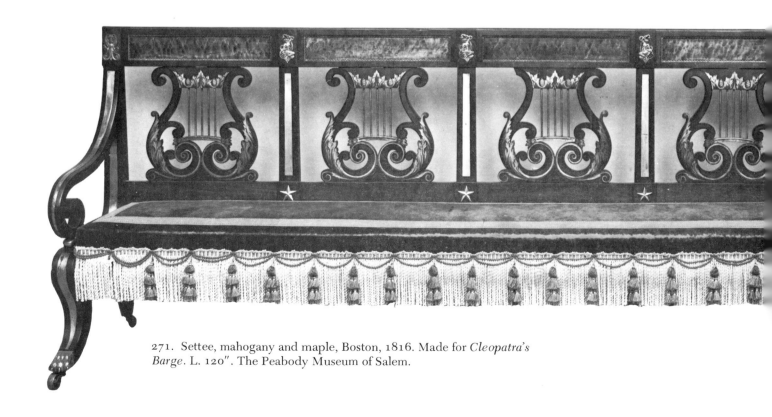

271. Settee, mahogany and maple, Boston, 1816. Made for *Cleopatra's Barge*. L. 120″. The Peabody Museum of Salem.

Launched in 1816 for amiable George Crowninshield of Salem, *Cleopatra's Barge* was as much a dandy as her owner. She measured eighty-three feet on the waterline and was the first major yacht built in America. Her elaborate stern decorations and herringbone-painted port side can be seen in the 1818 painting (270) by George Ropes, a Salem artist. The starboard side was painted with horizontal stripes, and this lively exterior was a perfect foil for the splashy furnishings below. Dr. William Bentley visited the yacht in 1816 and vastly admired the "elegant settee with velvet cushions, chairs with descriptive paintings, mirrors, buffets loaded with plate of every name, & the best glass & porcelain." The rich mahogany and maple of the Boston-made settee (271) combine ormolu mounts with gilt striping and leafage on the lyres. Five of the chairs with "descriptive paintings" on green backgrounds (272 and 273), thought to have been painted by Samuel Bartoll, have survived with many other mementos of this fabulous brigantine.[91]

272 and 273. Two fancy side chairs, maple and ash, painted green with different scenes, Salem area, Massachusetts, 1816. H. 33¼″ The Peabody Museum of Salem.

274, 274a. Night table, mahogany, and detail of top painted by Maria Crowninshield, Salem, Massachusetts, 1814. W. 27½". Privately owned.

The Empire style did not completely overwhelm conservative Massachusetts. Sheraton tables were made until the middle of the 1800s, the heftiness of their legs constantly on the increase. This mahogany night table (274) bears some similarities to the work of William Hook of Salem. The top was decorated by Maria Crowninshield (Hannah's sister, see page 101) as a wedding present to her husband and first cousin once removed, John Crowninshield. His initials are on the table, and the cupid seated on a forlorn dog points to these verses:

Tempted by love, by storm beset
Thy image I shall ne'er forget
                    Maria Crowninshield, 1814

Boston, however, could go all out, and Henry Sargent's glittering painting of a tea party (275) ably documents the urbane stylishness of the day.

275. (Opposite). *The Tea Party*, oil painting, by Henry Sargent, Boston, c. 1821–1825. 64¼" x 52¼". Museum of Fine Arts, Boston.

277. Shelf clock, maple, by Aaron Willard, Boston,
c. 1820. H. 34″. The Brooklyn Museum.

276, 276a, 276b. Shelf clock, mahogany, by Aaron
Willard, Boston, 1817. H. 36″. Museum of Fine Arts,
Boston.

Aaron Willard (1757–1844) was the youngest of the four famed clockmaking Willard brothers and an excellent craftsman. His son, Aaron, Jr., was the painter of the glass on the Simon Willard banjo clock shown on page 129, and he took over his father's business in 1823. The abilities of the elder Aaron can be easily seen in the shelf clocks shown here. Figure 276 was bought from Willard by Louisa Adams of Quincy, Massachusetts, in 1817 for $50. With convex moldings on its base and brass paw front feet, it is definitely in the Empire style, while still retaining an air of conservatism when compared to the more modish banjo and girandole wall clocks of the period (page 128). The glass painting is extremely well done. On the opposite page are details of both sections, the borders

of which are painted in black and gold. The background of his nameplate is bright red (276a). The border of the lower section shows the continuing predilection for shells in the Boston area. The scene, in colors, shows a mother with baby seated in a very stylish side chair of the klismos type, painted yellow.

The clock above (277) is slightly simpler. The wood is maple, and the finial and feet are more mundane than those on the other one. However, the glass painting is most colorful, with vermilion used with black as ground colors for the gilt decoration. Chronos himself sits with his scythe and hourglass, contemplating a clock face. In the hands of Aaron Willard, the Massachusetts shelf clock continued on in timeless dignity.

276a

276b

278. Shelf clock, mahogany, labeled by Solomon Stow, Southington, Connecticut, 1836–1840. H. 30″. American Clock & Watch Museum.

279. Wall clock, mahogany, etc., unsigned, Boston area, 1825–1840. Bronze stenciling on case. H. 40″. Winterthur Museum.

The Connecticut shelf clock, introduced by Eli Terry about 1816, was one of the most popular timepieces made here. Within ten years its delicate mahogany cases had given way to those in the Empire style. Figure 278 is an "Eli Terry's/Patent Clock," labeled by Solomon Stow of Southington. The case is ebonized, with bronze stencil decoration. The dial and glass tablet have been attributed to Mrs. Stephenson of Plainville. The view of the village green in Southington is based on page 105 of J. W. Barber's *Connecticut Historical Collections* (1836).[92]

Banjo clocks were made throughout the 1800s. This unsigned example (279) was made by one of the Boston–Roxbury group. The carved brackets at the sides and stenciled decoration on both the case and bottom bracket are features of the Empire style. In fact, the clock is quite close to a lyre clock in feeling. Scrolls are painted on the waist glass, while Aurora being drawn in her amphibious chariot occupies the lower rectangular tablet. Elnathan Taber, who had taken over Simon Willard's business after he retired in 1839, cleaned this clock in 1847.

281. Shelf clock, rosewood, signed by Forestville Manufacturing Co., Bristol, Connecticut, 1847–1850. H. 24″. The Henry Ford Museum.

280. Wall clock, mahogany, signed by Simon Willard & Son, Boston, c. 1850. H. 33½″. Old Sturbridge Village.

Taber might have made this banjo clock (280), which is signed "Simon Willard and Son." It is a simple banjo clock, with the two glass panels painted to resemble mahogany. John Ware Willard talks of the decline in the quality of glass painting about 1850. He cites the youngest son of Simon, Jr., Zabadiel Willard, the last of the family to make clocks, as stating "the work was so bad that the Timepieces made for his store had to have the glass fronts painted in imitation of mahogany, owing to the lack of good artists." [93] The results were not at all bad.

A shelf clock that seemed to grow out of the lyre clock is the so-called acorn clock (281). It was developed in the late 1840s by Jonathan Clark Brown at the Forestville Manufacturing Company in Bristol, Connecticut. This example has a painted dial, and the Greek Revival house painted on the glass tablet is identified as the "RESIDENCE OF J. C. BROWN, Esq. BRISTOL CT." Built in 1832, the house was purchased by Brown in 1847. Other views on acorn clocks include the Hartford State House, St. Paul's Church in New York, and flowery scrolls. [94]

V. NINETEENTH CENTURY

Academy Painting

282. *The Drawing Class*, watercolor, American, 1810–1840. 14⅜″ x 22⅛″. The Art Institute of Chicago.

After 1800, private academies grew and flourished throughout the country from Maine to Kentucky. At these "female schools" or seminaries,

> in addition to knitting and plain sewing, ornamental needlework was taught, and in some, instruction was given in drawing in India ink and painting in water colors.[95]

The emphasis on art training in such academies was on stitchery and painting on either paper or velvet; in New England, however, fond parents often obtained from cabinetmakers boxes or tables on which their daughters could demonstrate their newly acquired proficiencies.

283. Worktable, maple, New England, 1810–1825. W. 19″. The Metropolitan Museum of Art.

284a

284b

284, 284a, 284b. Chamber table, birch and pine, painted by
Wealthy P. S. Jones, Bath, Maine, and dated March 6, 1815.
W. 32″. Winterthur Museum.

285. Box, curled maple, Massachusetts, 1810–1825. W. 4″. Privately owned.

286. Worktable, maple and pine, eastern New England, 1810–1825. W. 15½″. Winterthur Museum.

At the Vermont Literary and Scientific Institution in Brandon, regular tuition cost $12.00 for two terms of forty-four weeks, room and board cost $1.50 a week, and drawing and painting were $1.00 extra per quarter. Drawing manuals, prints, and book illustrations provided sources and inspiration for the young ladies, whose abilities often varied greatly.

From Bath, Maine, have come several tables with painted decorations by young seminarians. The landscapes on the top and sides of the table at the left (284) derive undoubtedly from a school drawing book or engravings. The delicate floral borders, the posies on the drawer, the inscription, and the musical trophy were all drawn in India ink before muted watercolors were applied. Fringes with knots and tassels decorate the legs. The table itself is no triumph of cabinetmaking, but a great deal of charm is added by the decoration. Another table from Bath at Winterthur is verbose indeed, with many poems and even anagrams of classmates' names on the front!

The tiny box above came from Andover, Massachusetts, and features a landscape on the top; a rosy wreath on the front, and a musical trophy on the left side.

The table at the right is of bird's-eye maple, a favored wood for schoolgirl art. Vines twine about the square, tapered legs, and the fruit on the top foreshadows the theorem paintings of the 1820s and later.

287a

287, 287a, 287b. Small drop-leaf table, Connecticut, 1815–1835. The turnings, glass knob, and lack of ruled joint on the leaves make this table stylistically the latest shown in this group. W. 33". Shelburne Museum, Inc.

287b

288

288. Watercolor theorem painting on paper, New England, dated 1825. 17½″ x 22¼″. Privately owned.

289, 289a. Box, wood covered with paper, watercolor decoration, probably New England, c. 1820. W. 16¾″. Abby Aldrich Rockefeller Folk Art Collection.

290. Workbox, maple, inlaid, New England, 1820–1830. Polychrome painting on wood. W. 12″. The Henry Ford Museum.

289a

The table on the opposite page has a rather bumpkinesque quality about it. The elements of decoration on the top and leaves lack the delicacy and unity that is usually found on pieces of academy furniture. The borders are also coarser, as is the bemossed roping of the legs. However, the table is far more colorful than most of its mates. The scene on the top looks almost like an American setting, but, like the top of the box (289a) on this page, it was most certainly taken from an exercise book.

The freehand-painted plaited baskets of fruit and flowers on the leaves of the table (287a) represent a most popular painting-class exercise. Countless watercolors (288) of similar fruit baskets are known; and later, with the development of stencils, or "theorems" as they were known, less talented young ladies could practically be assured of instantaneous success in their endeavors. The theorems were perforated or cut out of paper. The transfer of color by this technique was accomplished easily, and velvet became very popular as the material used, since the fibers hid the separations of the stencils far better than the flatter, harder surface of paper.

The wood of the octagonal box (289) is covered with paper panels, their joints hidden by applied gilt strips of paper. On the panels are flowers and vines in reds and greens, and a well-executed river landscape in an oval graces the paper top. It is not far from this technique to that of decoupage, which was also taught in academies later in the century. This box, however, is excellently painted.[96]

The box at right (290) belonged to Alice Upson of Hartford County, Connecticut, and features a polychrome scene on the top and flowers, fruit, shells, and musical instruments on the front and sides—all painted directly on the wood. The sources of academy art were drawing books. Even those printed in this country featured scenes from England and the Continent. A castle in England or an Italian view were more in the vocabulary of schoolgirl artists than local views. Scenes from mythology, the Bible, and novels—especially Scott's works—were also used.

289

290

291a

291

After Mary Ann Colman of Newburyport took over her father's private school for "Misses" in 1810, she was described as a

good teacher of water color painting; the fruit and flower pieces executed at her school were natural and well done. She also taught painting on wood; several work-boxes and work-stands, painted under her instruction, are still to be seen in the residences of some of our older citizens.[97]

Evidently the different technique needed in painting on wood was not taught at all female academies.

In this final trio of what can literally be termed "academic art," the table at the left (291) runs the gamut of decorative sources. Vines spiral the legs, and garlands of grapes and strawberries enframe the top. Groups of shells in seaweed bathe in the rectangles above the legs. The scene on the top is of Moses and the vision in the burning bush. On the apron, scenes of foreign buildings fill the panels, with a rather improbable view of Florence, Italy, on the drawer front. The *décorateuse* of the table could paint her borders well, but her India ink draftsmanship left much to be desired!

American scenes rarely appear on seminary furniture. On the back of the box below (292), however, is a painting of Front Street in Thomaston, Maine, showing the buildings and fences of the town. The sewing box is veneered and is inscribed on the

291, 291a. Octagonal table, curled maple, New England, 1815–1825. W. 23″. Photograph courtesy of Israel Sack, Inc.
292. Sewing box, mahogany with maple veneer, decorated by Jane Otis Prior, Maine, and dated March, 1822. W. 12″. Privately owned.

292

bottom, "Miss Sarah McCobb's, painted by Miss Jane Otis Prior, March, 1822. Remember your friend Jane when far distant from each other—when you look at this. J. O. P." A shell border runs around the top, and other scenes include Henlon Park, Northumberland, the village of Egington, England, and the Boston State House. Its two American scenes make the box unique. It could have been decorated at Miss Tinkham's school in Wiscasset, Maine, where painting was taught at that time,.

With delicate carved and reeded legs, the worktable at the right (293) is a truly fine example of American Sheraton-style cabinetmaking. It was made in the Boston area and was decorated by Sarah (Eaton) Balch of Dedham, a pupil at Miss Rowson's Academy. The front and the two sides are painted to simulate bird's-eye maple, with garlands of roses, and the top has an oval scene outlined in gold showing a mill with wheel, two figures, a house, and a lake with distant mountains. Another table with similar decoration exists, and it descended in another branch of the Eaton family of Dedham.[98]

Mrs. Susanna Rowson, the famous Anglo-American actress, dramatist, author, and teacher, ran her academy in Medford from c. 1798 to 1803, in Newton from 1803 to 1807, and in Boston from 1807 to 1822. Needlework pictures and paintings done there survive.

293a

293

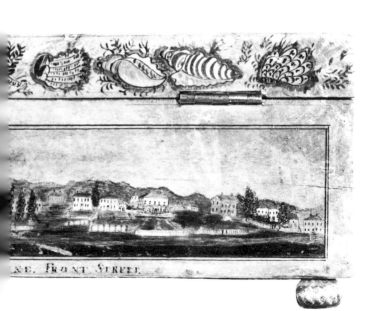

293, 293a. Worktable, maple and pine, decorated by Sarah Eaton Balch, Boston area, early nineteenth century. W. 17″. Privately owned.

Hitchcocks

294. Side chair, birch, etc., signed by Hitchcock, Alford & Co., Hitchcocksville, Connecticut, 1829–1843. H. 35″. Winterthur Museum.

295. Watercolor portrait of John Adam Munsell, New England, c. 1830. 3¼″ x 2⅝″. Museum of Fine Arts, Boston.

At the left, Mr. Munsell, with his shears, sits in a round-top Hitchcock-type side chair. This type evolved in the 1820s from a fortunate combination of bronze stenciling with elements borrowed from both Windsors and fancy chairs and is named after its most ardent adherent and popularizer, Lambert Hitchcock. Whether he invented this style of chair is not known, but he did believe in publicity and marked more of his products than any other maker. Hitchcock-type chairs and settees had their greatest popularity in the second quarter of the nineteenth century. Well made and decorated, they sold for $1.50 each in 1829, less than half the cost of a fancy chair. With varying shapes and designs, and with seats of rush, cane, ard plank, these inexpensive, stylish chairs had a wide appeal.

296. View of Hitchcocksville in the mid-1830s. From John W. Barber's *Connecticut Historical Collections*. Photograph courtesy The Magazine *Antiques*.

294a. Stencil mark on back of 294.

Lambert Hitchcock (1795–1852) moved to Barkhamsted, Connecticut, in 1818 and started making knock-down chairs, which were shipped to the South and Midwest for assembly. In 1821 the community was re-christened Hitchcocksville (now Riverton); and in 1826, having apparently decided the whole was worth more than its parts, Hitchcock built a large, three-story brick factory, seen at the left in the view above. Between 1826 and 1829 his chairs bore the mark "L. HITCHCOCK. HITCHCOCKS-VILLE. CONN. WARRANTED." After major financial reverses in 1829, the company was reorganized with Arba Alford, Jr., becoming a partner. Chairs made during this period (1829–1843) were marked as above (294a). In 1843 Hitchcock moved to Unionville, where he continued working until his death in 1852.[99]

Stencils made of paper were used on furniture. In the case of the unusual couch or daybed above, black-over-red rosewood paint was first applied. Then a coat of binder—such as varnish and turpentine—was put on; and when this had nearly dried, a stencil was laid flat on the surface to be decorated, and the metallic powders were brushed on with small velvet or leather pads. Several stencils were used to achieve a single design, each adding its bit to the fineness of detail. Bronze powder, which could be of several colors, was normally used due to its low cost, but any powdered metal, such as brass, zinc, aluminum, silver, or gold, could be used as well. Stripings were then added and the piece varnished. Every step could be varied greatly; and freehand work could be combined with stenciling, as could paints of different colors. The early work to about 1830 could be quite inventive and exciting in its variety, but later stenciling, often done with a single stencil and little shading, was usually hopelessly dull. The New York State settee converts into a bed when its extra front legs are pulled out and a mattress inserted in the widened frame. It is marked "C. Johnson. Patent" on the back under an arm. On February 24, 1827, Chester Johnson of Albany was awarded a patent for "Improvement in the manufacture of sofas, &c." [100]

297. Convertible settee, marked "C. Johnson. Patent," Albany, c. 1827. L. 78½".
Munson–Williams–Proctor Institute.

297a. Detail of back of 297.

299. Eagle-back side chair, 1825–1830. H. 34″. Old Sturbridge Village.

298. Turtle-back side chair, c. 1829. Privately owned.

On these two pages are variants of Hitchcock-type chairs. The only chair actually signed by Hitchcock is 303, which dates from his earliest period. Painted black, with bronze-gilded stenciling and a gray rush seat, it closely resembles those shown in the Moore family portrait (301). As we have seen, Hitchock was not the only maker of these chairs. Connecticut was their main spawning ground, with William Moore, Jr., of Barkhamsted, John L. Hull of Killingworth, Seymour Watrous of Hartford, and Holmes and Roberts of Robertsville among makers of existing signed examples. Others were made in Massachusetts, Rhode Island, New York, and Ohio. Figure 300, for instance, was made by Allen Holcomb (1782–1860) of New Lisbon, New York. One of a set of six, it is later than the signed Hitchcock, with less crisply turned legs and a plank seat. It is stenciled on the back and striped in yellow and green, the ground being rosewood-grained. A bowl of fruit is featured in the stenciling on the back. Fruit, flowers, and leaves appear with endless variety and varying quality in the stenciled decoration on the backs of Hitchcock-type chairs, with an occasional lyre, building, or a cornucopia. The "turtle-back" (298) was quite popular, while the handsome pierced eagle-back was a type less frequently made (299). Its decoration and striping are on rosewood graining, and the front legs flare rakishly as in the best fancy chairs. Figure 302 is a most unusual variant, with a painted polychrome scene on the back in place of the usual stenciling.

300. Round-top side chair, made by Allen Holcomb, New Lisbon, New York, 1830–1845. H. 35½″. New York State Historical Association.

301. Joseph Moore, a hatter and itinerant dentist of Ware, Massachusetts, had his family portrait painted by Erastus Salisbury Field about 1845. Moore married Almira Gallond in 1828, and perhaps that was the year they bought their Hitchcock chairs. 82¾" x 93¼". Museum of Fine Arts, Boston.

302. Side chair, probably Connecticut, 1825–1835. H. 33". Lyman Allyn Museum.

303. Side chair, signed "L. HITCHCOCK. HITCHCOCKS-VILLE. CONN. WARRANTED." 1825–1829. H. 34". The Henry Ford Museum.

304. Parlor of the Stencil House, Shelburne Museum. Soft green background, with stenciled decoration in red, green, and brown.

The use of stencils extended beyond furniture decoration. They were also used extensively on tinware and in wall decoration. The room above is from a house built near Sherburne, New York, and it was stenciled probably in the 1820s. The great age of American wall painting was in the early part of the nineteenth century, and it was not long until it was found that stencils could duplicate the borders and repetitive patterns of wallpapers with more ease and less cost. These developments coincided with the use of stencils on furniture, and the second and third decades of the century became the heyday of stenciled decoration. Stenciling is not difficult to do, but not easy to do well. In the room above, the artist used his restrictive medium very well, varying his designs and borders constantly. Some of the patterns are similar to those used by the best of the itinerant stencilers, Moses Eaton.[101]

In furniture, shaded stenciling done with powders of varying colors can be quite striking. From the 1830s on, however, the care given to the earlier work vanished, and single tones in mass-produced designs seemed to be made by the mile rather than for the object they were to adorn.

Many furniture forms were stenciled. On the opposite page are three stenciled frames. The two looking glasses use stenciled rosettes at the corners to copy the brass appliqués on high-styled examples. This practice continued the American innovation several decades earlier of imitating gilt ormolu mounts by stenciling. The columns, corners, and central tablet of 305 are ebonized; the remainder of the frame is mahogany veneer. Figure 307 has a glass tablet above the looking glass. The grained and stenciled frame of 306 encloses a beguiling portrait of two members of the Chase family of Deerfield, New Hampshire.

306. Watercolor portrait, attributed to
J. Evans, New Hampshire, 1825–1840.
Original stenciled frame. 9½″ x 13½″.
Privately owned.

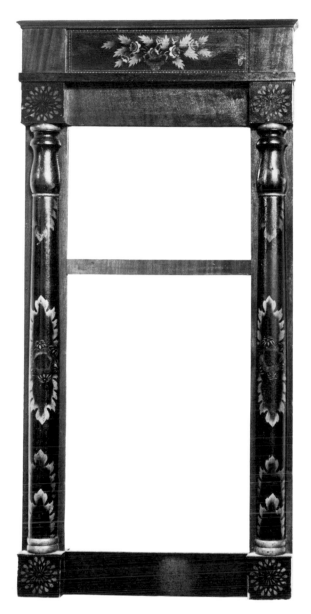

305. Looking glass, pine, New England, 1820–
1830. Stenciled sections are ebonized; remainder is mahogany. H. 36½″. Privately owned.

307. Looking glass, pine, New England,
1825–1840. Black paint, with gilt stenciling.
H. 22″. Old Sturbridge Village.

308. Side chair, maple, American, 1815–1825. Freehand decoration on smoke-grained ground. H. 33″. Collection of Mr. and Mrs. John Gordon.

Even though he was a poor businessman, Lambert Hitchcock was an excellent salesman. He traveled as far as Chicago on business trips and served as a state Senator. One of his best sales devices was the use of the word "warranted" in the markings of his chairs. This early form of a guarantee must have given an immense comfort to the vast number of middle-class owners whom Hitchcock reached so effectively. He sold his products wholesale to jobbers and dealers, and he even set up his own store in Hartford, where he offered both his and other makers' furniture for sale. In 1834 he advertised a "NEW CHAIR STORE" which sold

> Chairs from the Factory of Hitchcock & Alford (Hitchcocksville,) comprising a general assortment of Cane, Flag, and Wood Seats, of the best materials and workmanship, and warranted. Will furnish, at short notice, Chairs boxed in good shipping order.
> Has also on hand, an elegant assortment of *Mahogany* and *Curl-Maple* CHAIRS, made after the latest fashions, and a superior article.
> He will keep low priced Chairs from other Manufactories, which he will sell as low as they can be purchased in this market.
> ALSO, Curl Maple and Plain CANE SEATS.
> HITCHCOCK & CO., continue to keep at their Establishment in Hitchcocksville, a general assortment of CHAIRS AND CABINET FURNITURE.
>
> LAMBERT HITCHCOCK
>
> Hartford, August 25, 1834.[102]

Lambert Hitchcock had done and said it all far better than any of his contemporaries.

A fascinating problem is posed by the two side chairs shown in color on these pages. Figure 308 is a fancy chair that preceded the Hitchcock type. The freehand decoration is done in gold, red, and black. Its main feature, however, is smoke graining on yellow that in this instance suggests curled maple. Where it and 309 were made is unknown. Note how similar the bases of the two chairs are. Figure 308 has a New York history, while 309 was found in Pennsylvania. They relate to a side chair with rosewood graining at Winterthur which is considered to be Philadelphia or New Jersey.[103] However, all three relate to another chair, with an unbroken Maine history from 1817 on. Any problem makes valid points; and, in this case, we must realize how much exporting of fancy chairs went on, and how little we know of many chairmakers of the nineteenth century.

Figure 309 relates to the Hitchcock type through the stenciled decoration and especially through the shape of its top rail. The turnings and convex tablet at the center are found frequently on Hitchcocks and served as a central pinnacle for the stenciled decoration of the chairs.

Painted, decorated, and gilt bed and window cornices were available in this country by the 1790s, when the resurgence of stylish painted furniture occurred. By the late 1820s many were stenciled. There is a group of very fine New York State examples, with stenciled landscape scenes, that were done in the 1830s. The one below is a pine window cornice, probably made for venetian blinds in New England about 1830. This pleasing shape was also made in New York.[104]

309. Side chair, maple, American, 1820–1835.
Stenciled gold and green on black ground.
H. 32½″. The Henry Ford Museum.

310. L. 38¼″. The Henry Ford Museum.

311. Dressing table, pine and maple, New England, 1820–1840. Rosewood graining, with olive banding and gilt-bronze stenciling. Long bottom drawer is a false one. W. 34″. Collection of Dr. and Mrs. William Greenspon.

312. Dressing table, pine, etc., New England, 1820–1840. Brown rosewood graining, with red-and-yellow banding; red panels. Gilt-bronze stenciling of vine, fruit, and leaf decoration. W. 36″. Collection of Mr. and Mrs. Peter H. Tillou.

313. Inside of chest lid with sample stencils in bronze, gilt, and silver. The Stephens factory was in Cooperstown, New York. Dated 1832. W. 41½″. Photograph courtesy New York State Historical Association. Collection of Francis M. Reynolds.

314. Chest, pine, probably New York State or Pennsylvania, 1825–1840. Painted red, with gilt-stencil decoration. W. 32″. The Henry Ford Museum.

The dressing tables opposite combine paint and stenciled decoration. Figure 311 is dignified and rather elegant, while 312 rejoices in its decorative abandon (see color plate page 1). The rosettes at the edges of the backboard of 311 are brass; on 312 they are stenciled. The inside lid of a plain, black chest (313) reveals a pleasant surprise in the display of the stencils of the N. R. Stephens Chair Factory. Rosettes, leaves, Masonic devices, baskets and urns, and an eagle are included in the extensive decorative vocabulary of this manufacturer. They are typical of the variety of stencils owned by proficient makers. The chest (314) bears a balanced assortment of stencils that lack the delicacy of the Stephens examples. In even later work the clarity and shading of the stenciling are lost almost beyond definition (see pages 270–271).

315. Stencil for chair back made by William Eaton (1819–1904), New Hampshire and Massachusetts. Part of a large collection at The Society for the Preservation of New England Antiquities.

Pillars and Scrolls

316. W. 42″. Collection of Jack F. Fenstermacher.

The exuberant carving of high-style Empire furniture gave way to simpler lines and plainer surfaces in the late 1830s. This influence of the French Restoration was felt in painted furniture, but many makers preferred to hark back to earlier Sheraton and Empire forms for their inspiration. Greek Revival architecture was favored in villages and towns up to the eve of the Civil War, and it set the style for local craftsmen to emulate in furnishings. The various styles of the big cities, coming in machine-gun-like bursts from shortly after 1800 on, were as bewildering as they were intriguing to most people. In rural areas some were accepted while others were rejected. The result of all this coming together of influences was encouraging to the country craftsman. He could do what he (and his clients) wanted. Thus, the twenties, thirties, and early forties became the golden age of American painted furniture.

The serving table above combines a Sheraton form with rosewood graining, marbleizing on the top, and bellflowers and baskets painted in gilt. Found in New York State and made between 1825 and 1830, it is high in spirit and deep in scrolls.

318. Watercolor portrait of James and Sarah Tuttle by Joseph H. Davis, Strafford, New Hampshire, 1836. 9½″ x 14½″. The New-York Historical Society.

317. Side chair, maple and pine, Baltimore, 1820–1835. Roscwood graining, with gilt decoration. H. 33″. Collection of Mr. and Mrs. Charles V. Hagler.

Rosewood graining could be achieved by the use of different colors. Black over red was used on the serving table (316), while a brownish red was used with the black on the side chair shown in two views on this page. Its decoration is in painted gilt, and the swooping scrolls of both its front and rear legs certainly are a sweeping variation of the Greek klismos form. It was made in Baltimore in the 1820s and is representative of a type made up and down the coast at that time. They were popular and inexpensive, and it took an experienced painter less than five minutes to grain one of them.[105]

If the period 1820–1845 was the age of liberation for the ornamental painter, it was for the folk artist as well. Joseph H. Davis, or "Left Handed" Davis, itinerated through southern New Hampshire and Maine between 1832 and 1838, painting explosively decorative portraits.[106]

317a. Side view of 317.

319

319, 319a, 319b. Set of fourteen graining combs, steel, made by Henry H. Taylor, Sheffield, England, mid-nineteenth century. Privately owned.

319a

Graining was accomplished by various means. Usually the dark color was brushed over a ground of the lighter color in sweeping, freehand brushstrokes, as on the bold secretary at the right. Note how the painter has achieved considerable effect and much more interest by making his decoration asymmetrical. He has created a fanciful conceit that adds life and movement to a staid Greek Revival form. Graining on furniture usually was done in oils, although distemper could be used. One author advised that "one gallon whiskey" be used as the vehicle, adding, "With a graining brush, grain it according to fancy." [107] In addition to brushes, rollers were used for graining, as were combs made of gutta-percha and cork. Steel combs, made in Sheffield at the Acorn Works and the Times Works by Henry H. Taylor, have been found in this country. They sped up the process but did not allow the glorious freedom of brushwork.

320. Secretary, pine, New Hampshire, 1825–1840. Red-and-black
rosewood graining. W. 49″.
Photograph courtesy Richard
Withington.

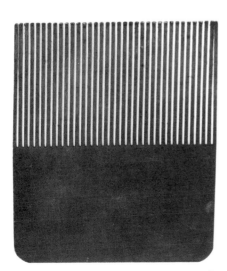

319b

321. Box, pine, Maine, 1830–1840
W. 10½″. Privately owned.

322. Drop-leaf table, maple, probably Maine, 1830–1840.
W. 41″. Privately owned.

323. Worktable, pine, Maine, 1825–1835. W. 23″. Privately owned.

In 1820 Maine freed itself from Massachusetts and became the twenty-third state of the Union. Manufactures were encouraged, and in the next generation definite contributions were made to American decorative arts through painted furniture, painted tin, and britannia, all made in Maine. On these two pages and page 202 are examples of Maine rosewood painting. The decoration of the sewing table above (323) is in black over deep red, with stripings not in bronze powder but in mustard paint. The legs are red. The graining is well done, with simulated crossbanded veneers on the edge of the top. On the opposite page are two examples that bear delightfully loose, almost abstract rosewood graining. The table (322) is in black over an orangish red and almost looks as if it had just stepped out of a watercolor by Joseph H. Davis (see page 197). The box, painted reddish brown with black striping, has a very modern feeling and shows how effective the simplest freehand brushwork can be. Maine had started to lead the way in northern New England painted decoration, and more will be seen from this rural state.

325. Side chair, maple, signed by Walter
Corey, Portland, Maine, c. 1841–1850.
Rosewood graining; bronze striping.
H. 33¼″. Privately owned.

324. Commode, pine, Maine, 1825–1840.
Rosewood graining; gilt striping. W. 28″. Privately
owned.

In the *Kennebunk Gazette* in July 1832, a cut showed a fancy chair of a generation earlier, and the advertisement of Lauriston Ward of Saco offered "Fancy Flag Bottom CHAIRS; Imitation do. Double Back Yellow and Rose WOOD do." [108] At the left, excellent imitative rosewood graining adorns the commode, which is signed "Y. Nowell Kennebunk" in pencil and "Y. Nowell Bangor" in paint. Unfortunately, records fail to reveal whether Mr. Nowell was its maker or its owner. The small box on the commode also bears rosewood graining, and both have blue interiors. The fiddle-back side chair was made at the most prolific chair manufactory in Maine, owned by Walter Corey of Portland, who was listed in Portland directories from 1841 to 1867. Other chairs, including klismos types and plain farm chairs, were signed by him. On this page are two late Empire "pillar-and-scroll" examples, both grained more soberly in imitation of mahogany.

326. Card table, pine, northern New England, 1835–1845. Mahogany graining in orange-red and ochre. W. 34″. Privately owned.

327. Chest of drawers, pine, northern New England, 1835–1845. Brownish-red mahogany graining. W. 42″. Privately owned.

328. Low-post bed, pine and maple, probably New Hampshire, 1800–1830. Red-and-black graining. W. 53″. Old Sturbridge Village.

329a

329

329. Night table, pine and maple, New England, 1830–1840. W. 18″. 329a. Detail of decoration under drawer. 330. Footstool, pine, Connecticut, 1830–1840. W. 14⅞″. Both privately owned.

330

All sorts of variations can occur in the simplest black-over-red graining, and the results can be imitative of rosewood or mahogany, or they can be flights of fancy beyond the realm of imitation. The imaginative, bold decoration of the bed (328) would have made no one think he was actually looking at the grain of real wood and is a carry-over of the suggestive graining of the eighteenth century. The small night table, however, features differing methods of combining red and black graining. The top is crisscrossed, the sides stippled and striped, the drawer is stenciled over the graining, the rail below the drawer is stippled, and the legs are sponged! Mustard-yellow striping is used, and the design below the drawer (329a) is a delightful exercise in geometrics. The footstool is painted a bright red and black with yellow striping. The washstand (331) is marvelous! The graining is adequate, but the eagles' heads and pseudo-armorial decoration certainly dress up the piece immensely. Washstands strong in armorial bearings and nationalism are not often encountered!

331. Washstand, pine, found in Pittsburgh, Pennsylvania, 1830–1845. Rosewood graining, gilt decoration. W. 18⅝". Collection of Herbert W. Hemphill, Jr.

332a. Detail from bellows below.

Paint for Paint's Sake

332. Bellows, traditionally made for Johanna Henrietta Harsen of New York by a convict on Welfare Island, c. 1820. Polychrome and gilt. L. 21″. Museum of the City of New York.

333. Armchair, pine, etc., Connecticut, 1825–1840. Yellow, with polychrome stenciled-and-painted decoration. H. 30½″. Collection of Russell Carrell.

334a

334, 334a. Box, pine, New England, 1830–1840. Pinkish red, with decoration in black and cream. W. 18½". Collection of Jean and Howard Lipman.

Decoration of furniture in the nineteenth century went far beyond the more somber rosewood graining. All stops were pulled out, and figures, animals, and birds joined with fanciful and imitative graining in a kaleidoscopic riot of color and decoration. On the opposite page, the bellows owned by Mrs. Cornelius Harsen of New York was traditionally made by one of the convicts on Welfare Island. Green predominates, with blue, red, and gold (see color plate page 2). Its "AMERICAN ARTIST" (332a) bears little resemblance to our workaday ornamental painters! A writer, reminiscing about her grandfather's house in the 1820s, wrote, "The west room was the family 'keeping room,' also lighted up at night by a roaring backlog. The brush and bellows in this room were pretentious with green and gold, and the shovel and poker were headed with brass knobs." [109]

The armchair (333) is a late Windsor survival and is painted yellow, with freehand and stenciled decoration in gold, silver, green, and black. The box on this page features a charming, elongated dog and a swirling tiger.

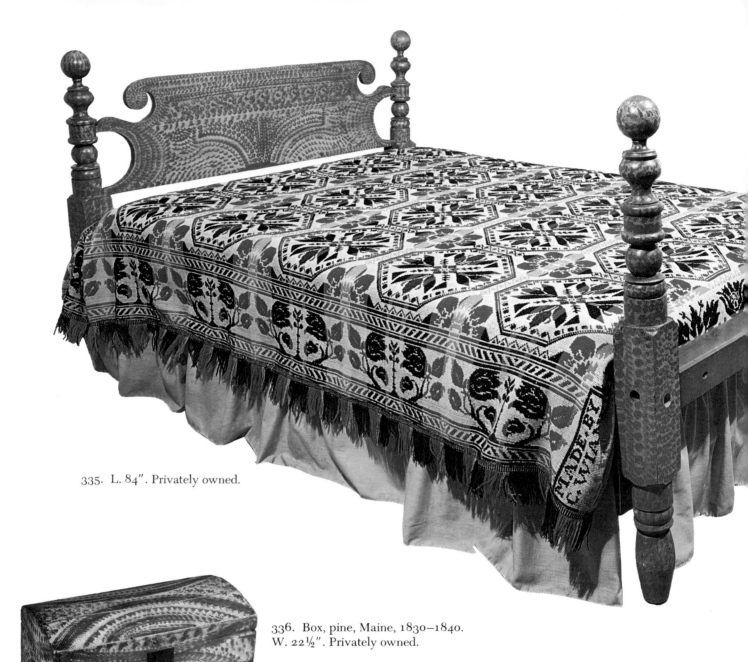

335. L. 84". Privately owned.

336. Box, pine, Maine, 1830–1840.
W. 22½". Privately owned.

337. Chest, pine, New England,
1830–1840. W. 39¼". Collection of
Stewart E. Gregory.

Various techniques of decorating were used to achieve the effects on the colorful quintet on these pages. The bed, from eastern Connecticut and made between 1830 and 1845, has sponged decoration in red and yellow. The box (336) is more hesitantly done in the same manner, probably with a less absorbent sponge. Any lack of technique is vividly made up for in bright coloring. The chest (337) is boldly decorated in sweeping swirls of brown with touches of green on the beige ground. Occasional sponged areas are used to contain the fantastic graining. On the next page, the candlestand is an earlier form, the top of which is very well marbleized in gray, yellow, red-brown, and black. The blanket chest (339), with its wild but at the same time carefully ordered decoration in shades of ochre and brown, was probably painted with crinkled paper to achieve its segmented swirls. The skirt is neatly accented by a thin stripe of ochre along its bottom edge.

339. Chest with drawers, pine, New England, 1830–1840. W. 40″. Privately owned.

338. Candlestand, maple, New England, 1800–1830. W. 19¾″. Collection of Jean and Howard Lipman.

Nathaniel Whittock prophesied in 1828 what would come to be in America, when he ended his section on furniture graining in *The Decorative Painters' and Glaziers' Guide* by saying:

> Furniture painting, which is now only done with cheapness and effect in London or other large towns, could be executed with elegance in every village, and would become a source of profitable and pleasing employment.[110]

While one can ruminate on the order of profit and pleasure, the fact remains that in America furniture painting became a product of towns and villages alike. Fancy painting, "in the New York style," was advertised by itinerants in more than one small town.[111] Another advertisement, in Raleigh, North Carolina, in 1835, not only gave the worthy heritage of Joseph Meadway but contained one of the best definitions of graining to be found anywhere:

> Coach Painting, &c. &c. Joseph Meadway, from New York and formerly of England, respectfully informs the Citizens of Raleigh, and its vicinity, that he is prepared to execute any kind of Coach, House, Sign and Ornamental Painting; also Graining, that is, Painting in imitation of any kind of Wood or Marble that has beauty in its appearance. . . .[112]

209

340. Chest, pine, Hudson River Valley,
1820–1835. W. 42½". Privately owned.

341. Chest, pine, Maine, 1825–1840.
W. 30″. Collection of Gary R. Davenport.
341a. Detail from side of 341

341a

Swags and drapery folds were an important part of the neoclassical decorative vocabulary. Their survival into the 1800s can be seen in the examples shown here. Figure 340 is painted an ochre ground, with brown graining and green-and-black swags. The tassels and drapery folds of 341 and 341a are loosely sketched in black on a grayish blue-green ground. The box (342) is initialed "W. K." on the top and is painted red-orange, with blue banding and black-and-white "stringing." The tucked-in drapery is painted in mustard yellow. Another box, with identical decoration and initialed "M. C.," is also privately owned.

342. Box, pine, Vermont, 1825–1840.
W. 11¼″. Privately owned.

343

344

345

This galaxy of painted boxes and chests demonstrates the range and rage in painted decoration of the 1800s. Flowers can be delicate (344 and 350), a lion can be regal (355), and an eagle and two other birds beguiling (352). Patterns may be unconsciously abstract (349) or flamboyantly geometric (351). The decoration can quaver (354), shimmer (347), or be incontrovertibly defined by the box itself (353). A chest features a play on paterae (343), while a box (348) seems almost elegantly modern in feeling. Their colors—not words—sing their song.

343. Chest, New York State, 1825–1850. W. 32″. The Henry Ford Museum. 344. Box, New England, 1810–1820. W. 15″. Collection of Mr. and Mrs. Samuel L. Meulendyke. 345. Box, Middle States, 1830–1840. W. 13″. The Henry Ford Museum. 346. Box, New England, 1825–1840. W. 14″. Collection of Jean and Howard Lipman. 347. Chest, New England, 1820–1840. W. 43½″. Collection of Jean and Howard Lipman. 348. Box, New England(?), 1830–1850. W. 14″. Collection of Herbert W. Hemphill, Jr. 349. Chest, New York State, 1830–1840. W. 35″. Privately owned. 350. Box, New Hampshire, 1820–1840. W. 18″. Privately owned. 351. Box, New England, 1820–1840. W. 23¾″. Collection of Jean and Howard Lipman. 352. Box, New England, 1820–1840. W. 14¾″. Collection of Jean and Howard Lipman. 353. Box, New England, c. 1830. W. 14⅛″. The Henry Ford Museum. 354. Chest, New England, 1830–1840. W. 45½″. Collection of Mr. and Mrs. Samuel L. Meulendyke. 355. Box, Massachusetts, 1840–1850. W. 9″. Collection of Mr. and Mrs. Christopher Huntington.

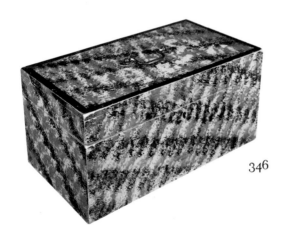

346

347

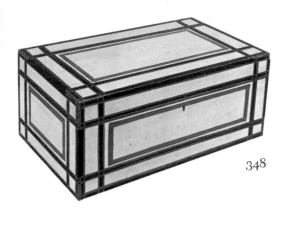

348

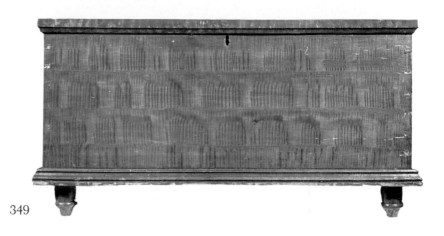

349

350

351

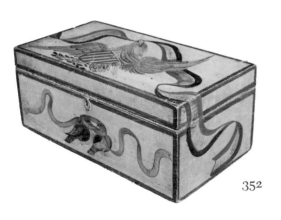

352

353

354

355

356. W. 43".

357. W. 9¾".

358. W. 7½".

359. W. 8⅝".

From Maine to Ohio, boxes and chests provided one of the best vehicles for decoration. Figure 356 is a New England sea chest of the 1830s, with black moldings and polychrome scenes on a cream ground (Collection of Jean and Howard Lipman). Figure 357 is a pine box from New England, probably made in the 1830s. The decoration in red, green, and black features five cherry trees on the top (Collection of Mr. and Mrs. Samuel L. Meulendyke). Figure 358 is from Maine and shows a bird drawn in calligraphic script chasing a fly. The box is pinkish-red, with black-and-white decoration and is signed "C. Rice 1892" (Privately owned). Figure 359 is an excellent

example of curled-maple imitative graining. It was made in Massachusetts between 1815 and 1825 and bears the name of its owner, Henry W. Nichols, of Sturbridge, on wallpaper lining the inside (Old Sturbridge Village). Figure 360 is a Pennsylvania chest of the 1830s, with ordered sponged work in yellows and browns (The Henry Ford Museum). Figure 361 is a charming small domed box of poplar from Seville, Ohio, 1820–1840. The decoration is in red, white, and two shades of green on a cream ground (Privately owned). Painted by amateurs and professionals alike, all these pieces show the varied "pleasures" of painted decoration.

360. W. 49¾".

361. W. 8⅝".

214

362a. Side view of 362.

362. This handsome chest features very bold combed decoration in reddish brown and black. Note the variety of patterns obtained by this simple technique. It was made in New York State between 1825 and 1830. W. 39″. Collection of Russell Carrell.

363. Chest with drawers, pine, Massachusetts, 1825–1835.
W. 42″. Collection of Jean and Howard Lipman.

The three chests on these pages show how different methods of painting can result in vividly pleasing decoration. Figure 363 combines regular painting with sponging and crinkled-paper work. Red and black combine with red, cream, and black in the carefully planned decoration. It closely resembles another chest, privately owned, which was found in North Brookfield, Massachusetts. Figure 364 is one of the gems of imitative graining. Brownish red is used on yellow to imitate mahogany, and dentiled inlay is carefully outlined in black on the edges of the top and drawers. Made by E. Morse of Livermore, Maine, in 1814, the chest is one of the earliest and most important documented examples of nineteenth-century decorated furniture. If the painting of 363 is fanciful and 364 is imitative, that of 365 must truly be termed fantastic. When the red was put on the yellow, a solvent was added that made the final combination of colors run together ever so slightly, producing a mildly mottled effect. This technique was allied to "vinegar painting" or "putty painting," a means used to achieve dripping, seaweed-like designs on chair seats and other surfaces occasionally.[113] The added dottings above the drawer impart a delightfully contagious quality to the success of the decoration.

364. Chest of drawers, pine, signed in pencil "Made by
E. Morse/Livermore [Maine] June 7th 1814." W. 36⅝".
The Henry Ford Museum.

365. Chest with drawer, pine,
New England, 1825–1840. W.
40″. Collection of Jean and
Howard Lipman.

366

367

366. Chest, pine, New England, 1825–1840. Green, brown, and yellow decoration. W. 29″. Smithsonian Institution.

367. Box, pine, Maine, 1830–1840. Brown-on-yellow decoration. W. 12⅜″. Privately owned.

368. Table, pine, Essex County, Massachusetts, 1820–1830. W. 18½″. Smithsonian Institution.

369. Tall clock, works by Silas Hoadley, Plymouth, Connecticut, 1825–1841. Pine case, smoke-grained on ochre. H. 85″. Collection of Gary R. Davenport.

368

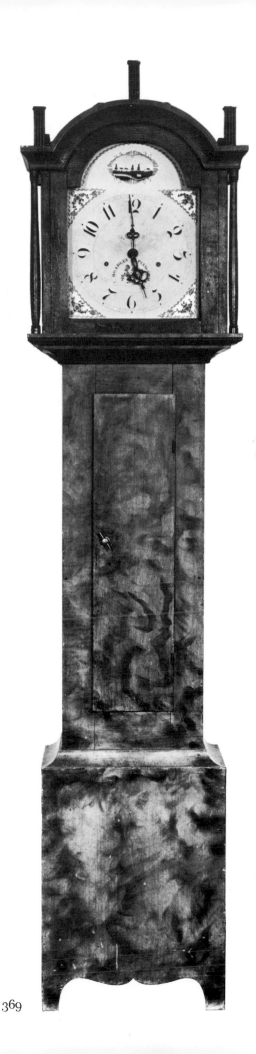

369

"Vinegar painting" was accomplished by "walking" the second coat of paint over the ground color with a piece of putty or soft substance, such as leather. Vinegar was used in the overcoat, and as it dried, the linseed oil in the putty caused a separation in the darker glaze producing unusual seaweed-like patterns as in the chest, box, and table shown on these pages. The table has a two-tone combination, with reddish brown and yellow on the legs and sides, while green and yellow are on the top and drawer fronts. The case of the Silas Hoadley tall clock at the right is smoke-grained on an ochre-painted background.

370

370. The enrichment of this pine blanket chest-on-chest of drawers consists of grained, burled, and webbed fancies in black over a rust ground. Also see detail 370a opposite. The unique form was made in Maine in the 1830s and originally had wooden drawer knobs. Its great glory, however, is its astonishingly different decoration, which almost seems a preview of modern Abstract Expressionism. W. 39⅞". Privately owned.

371 and 372. (Opposite). Chest and chest of drawers, pine, both signed by Thomas Matteson, South Shaftsbury, Vermont, and dated 1824. Brown decoration on mustard ground with green banding on both pieces. Chest, W. 40½", The Henry Ford Museum. Chest of drawers, W. 40½". Collection of Mr. and Mrs. Langley Smart.

373. (Opposite). Chest of drawers, maple, probably made by Matteson about the same time as 371 and 372. W. 37¼". Collection of Mr. and Mrs. William F. Carr.

371

372

If one picture is worth a thousand words, the blanket chest-on-chest of drawers on the preceding page succinctly sums up all that can be said of American painted furniture in the nineteenth century! On this page is an exercise in attribution. The two chests above and right (371 and 372) are signed and dated 1824 by Thomas Matteson of South Shaftsbury, Vermont. Using a quiet palette of brown on mustard with bandings of dark green, Matteson achieved an effective and distinctive decoration on the two chests. The sides of the chest of drawers repeat almost exactly the pattern on the front of the small chest. When the decoration on these chests is compared to that on the chest of drawers below, there are so many similarities that an attribution of 373 to Matteson seems warranted. The shapings of the front and side skirts and the lipped drawers on both chests of drawers are the same. The decoration on all three has very close affinities, except that the colors of 373 are somewhat stronger than on 371 and 372, nor does it have the green bandings. It is fascinating to compare three examples of one man's work, and it appears that the attributed example was painted with more maturity and deftness than the other two. South Shaftsbury is in the southwestern corner of Vermont, located just north of Bennington.

373

370a. Detail from top-right drawer of 370.

374. Chest of drawers, pine, northern
New England, 1810–1830. W. 37½".
Collection of Jean and Howard Lipman.

Dating painted pieces can be a problem. If the example strikes
toward the heights of a style, one is tempted to assign it an earlier date than the piece that wallows rather helplessly in a stylistic imbroglio. While this practice is usually proper, one must
be on guard at all times when considering productions made in
rural areas. As in the eighteenth century, not only did a time lag
exist in the transmission of the latest mode to the country, but,
even more importantly, a conscious rejection of these newer
"whims" was firmly implanted in the minds of most rural people.
Thus, while one is forced to date these four chests differently,
they all could have been made about the same time.

375. Chest of drawers, pine, probably
Rhode Island, 1815–1830. W. 39½".
Collection of Mr. and Mrs. Edward
L. Steckler.

376. Chest of drawers, pine, probably
southern New Jersey or Pennsylvania,
1815–1835. W. 38⅞". Privately owned.

The six-drawer chest (374) recalls the tall maple chests of northern New England of the late 1700s. It is stunningly painted to resemble mahogany and satinwood in golden brown and reddish brown. The side ovals in invected rectangles have received a monumental treatment by the decorator. Figure 375 is in the Sheraton style and is grained in red and black to imitate mahogany. The two chests at the right are in the Hepplewhite style and show an imaginative play on woods. Figure 376 emulates rosewood in yellow and shades of brown, while 377 more sketchily suggests rosewood and curled (or waved) maple in black, red, and two shades of yellow (on the drawer fronts). As a group, these chests of drawers exemplify the most popular types of nineteenth-century graining.

377. Chest of drawers, pine, Maine,
1820–1840. W. 40". Collection of Mr.
and Mrs. Peter H. Tillou.

378

378. Washstand, whitewood and pine, signed by Isaac Wright & Co., Hartford, Connecticut, 1828–1838. W. 18¼″. The Connecticut Historical Society.

379 and 380. Matching washstand and dressing table, pine, the former signed by William A. Mason, Fryeburg, Maine, and dated August 24, 1829. White background, with polychrome fruit, flowers, and scenes. Washstand, W. 18¹/₁₆″; dressing table, W. 34¾″. The Henry Ford Museum.

Documented examples of painted furniture—that is, pieces signed and/or dated by their makers—are unusually difficult to find. The Connecticut and Maine examples on these pages assume great importance, since their makers are known. The Connecticut washstand (378) has a yellow ground with decoration in black and bronze powder. It is representative of many washstands of the 1820s in its quick, economical decoration of grapes, leaves, and scrolly tendrils. Colored bandings are omitted from the rear legs. "ISAAC WRIGHT & CO./ CABINET / CHAIR / & UPHOLSTERY / WARE- HOUSE/HARTFORD/CON." is stenciled on the underside of the drawer. Wright worked in Hartford from 1828 until his death in 1838.

The dressing table (379) and matching wash- stand (380) made by William A. Mason of Frye- burg, Maine, in 1829 were probably originally part of an even larger set of bedroom furniture. They are painted white with thin green trim. The deco- ration is done in vivid colors, with pink roses on green leaves on the backboard (380a), and a bril- liant clutch of fruit on the drawer front of the dress- ing table (380b). Red strawberries on green leaves, orange-and-red apples and pears, and brilliant purple grapes are all succulently depicted. The washstand is also covered with scenic delights, and the decoration of both pieces has much in common with the seminary art of the period. Both amateurs and professionals had access to prints and drawing books for their common inspiration.

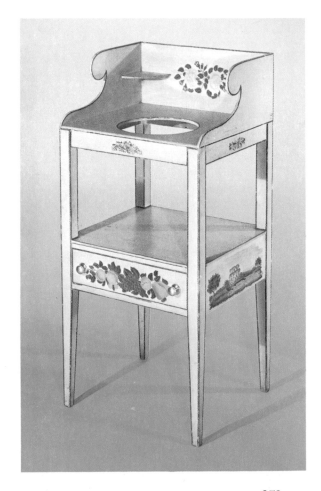

379

380a. Detail of backboard.

380

380b. Detail of drawer.

381. Card table, pine, etc., probably New Hampshire, 1810–1825. Mahogany graining in red and black; mahogany veneered skirt with figured birch tablet. W. 36″. Collection of Barbara Johnson.

Imitative graining and real woods are sneakily combined in the card table above (381). Actual veneers are used in the skirt, while the top, leaf, and legs are painted to simulate mahogany. The actual method of mahogany graining was explained by Rufus Porter in 1825 in his manual *A Select Collection of Valuable and Curious Arts, and Interesting Experiments*. The ground coat was made of white lead and ochre, with a mixture of boiled linseed oil colored by Venetian red and burnt terra-de-sienna making the red coloring when applied with a flat brush.

> For this purpose a common sash-brush may be made flat, by having a small piece of wire, or wood, bound on each side, near the handle. Some of the darker shades may be drawn with burnt umber and black, ground together, which may be applied with a camel hair pencil. If any part is to be made very light, the staining may be wiped off carefully with a ball of cotton. Light stripes, or lines may be produced by drawing a piece of cork or soft wood over the work, thus taking off, or removing the dark colors, that the original ground may appear.[114]

If one were asked, "When is a card table not a card table?," the only answer should be "Figure 382." This captivating table is a thoroughly charming, deceitful conceit. Its apparently folding top is actually of one piece of wood, with two rounded arches forming what appear to be two boards. Its paint is unusual also. Red paint imitates cherry or mahogany on the top and legs, but humble pine is copied in lighter paint on the skirt.

382. Pseudo card table, pine, New England, 1810–1825. W. 35⅞″. Privately owned.

383. Combinations of decoration can be intriguing. On the pier table above, plain ochre painting on the base is enriched with black stripings on the legs. The drawer front (originally without pulls of any sort) is set off by a painted bamboo band in black, cream, and transparent brown. The top is marbleized neatly in grays, white, and a deep blue. These disparate decorations unite harmoniously to produce an exciting piece of country furniture. Although the table is made completely of white pine, which would indicate a northern New England origin, it was found several years ago in Ohio. Whether it was made there or transported there by nineteenth-century settlers from New England is not known. The table is 30¼″ in height and is privately owned.

384

385

The objects on these pages show a definite sea turn. The pipe box was carved and painted by a sailor, presumably on the ship shown in the oval watercolor set into the box above the drawer and covered with glass. The box is light blue, the vines and flowers brown, and the legend "For Eliz." is white on a black banner. An air of exoticism was added by the upper pagoda cresting. The sea chest (385) is painted green, with yellow rope decoration. Two black sea monsters are on the front, and on the top an Indian at the left and an African native at the right by a palm tree flank a full-rigged vessel in the center. Figure 386 is a later sea chest, lacking the moldings and finesse of the preceding example. Red, blue, black, white, and yellow are naïvely used on a dark-green ground to depict a vessel and a lighthouse on the front and various geometric forms on the top. The original beckets are well braided. Figure 387 is the top of a box found in Portland, Maine, traditionally used to carry a compass. Painted black with putty-colored borders and red and dark pinkish-red quarter circles, its compass rose is in red, black, and putty colors. On the opposite page are three views of the inside of a plain green sea chest, owned by a whaler's cooper, Manoel E. de Mendonça. The till (388) is decorated with an eagle, a shield, and flags on a field of flowers, while the inside of the lid (389 and 389a) has a colorful view of the harbor of New Bedford. It has been suggested that de Mendonça had his name painted by a sign painter and later did the view himself.[115]

384. Pipe box, probably Nantucket, Massachusetts, 1800–1835. Blue ground. H. 21¾". Winterthur Museum. 385. Sea chest, pine, probably Massachusetts, 1800–1835. Green ground. W. 44¾". The Henry Ford Museum. 386. Sea chest, pine, New England, 1835–1850. W. 42". Old Dartmouth Historical Society Whaling Museum.

387

387. Top of compass box, pine, Maine, 1840–1880. Black ground. W. 15". Privately owned.

388

389, 389a. Inside of lid with detail and top of till (388, above) of a sea chest, painted dark green on the outside, made in Massachusetts about 1865 for Manoel E. de Mendonça, a Portuguese-American who was the cooper on a whaling ship. Scene on inside of lid shows New Bedford harbor. W. 45". Old Dartmouth Historical Society Whaling Museum.

386

389a

389

The simplest decoration can add a great deal of warmth to the plainest piece of furniture. On the table below, found in western Massachusetts, are blotches of black brushed over its bluish-gray background. Swirling brushstrokes can easily be seen on the blanket chest on the following page. Simple strokes of black on a white ground make up the undulating pattern of this chest (391). The cradle (392) was made by Wyman H. Stebbins, a carpenter of Deerfield, Massachusetts, for his daughter Frances about 1833. It has simple black sponged decoration over an orangish-red ground.

The economy of painted work can be seen in a Boston bill to Miss Lois White from H. P. Page in 1848, wherein he charged her fifty cents for "marking" a trunk and one dollar for "Painting & Graining Chest." [116]

390. Table, pine and maple, Massachusetts, 1830–1840. W. 37½". Collection of Mr. and Mrs. Edward L. Steckler.

391. Blanket chest, pine, New England, 1820–1840.
W. 39″. Old Sturbridge Village.

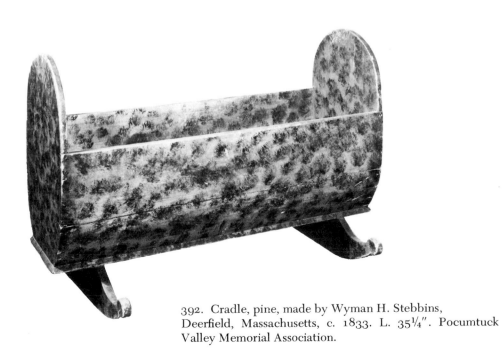

392. Cradle, pine, made by Wyman H. Stebbins,
Deerfield, Massachusetts, c. 1833. L. 35¼″. Pocumtuck
Valley Memorial Association.

393. Chest with drawers, pine, northern New England, 1820–1835. W. 40¾". Collection of Jean and Howard Lipman.

394. Candlestand, birch, probably northern New England, 1810–1830. W. 14¾". Collection of Jean and Howard Lipman.

395. Chest of drawers, pine, Maine, 1825–1840. Brownish-red-and-black graining, green banding, yellow stripes. W. 41". Collection of Mr. and Mrs. Christopher Huntington.

Maine ornamental painters had a mania, it seems, for using endless combinations of black-and-red graining, frequently set off with thin yellow stripes and broader green bandings. The chests of drawers at the bottom of these pages (395 and 398) are decorated in this manner; and chairs, tables, commodes, a bed, a secretary, and a rocking armchair (see figure 427, page 247) have been found, all with this same type of decoration. Fountain-like patterns of black paint on 395 almost outdo crotch mahogany itself, while the graining on 398 is more somber and reflective of the sober character of the chest itself. The two candlestands (394 and 396) are similar to those seen in primitive paintings of northern New England and are painted in red and ochre. They combine the delicacy of form with the fancy of painted decoration most expressively in the rural manner.

When done well, imaginative graining can be one of the strongest statements of the rural vernacular. Figures 393 and 397 were boldly decorated by the same person in sweeps of red and green on a yellow ground. They are both blanket chests, having two false drawers at the top. Figure 393 never had knobs or brasses of any kind, while 397 has glass pulls. Their paint is superb. It goes far beyond the framework of reality supplied by the compartmented areas representing veneers and inlays, and both chests delightfully writhe with motion that would be difficult to achieve through the use of real woods. Truly, nature herself was excelled by the ornamental painter in whose work could be found rural sublimity. On a more mundane level it should be noted that 397 was purchased in Vermont, and both chests relate to the work of Thomas Matteson shown on page 221.

397. Chest with drawers, pine, northern New England, 1820–1835. W. 40¾". Privately owned.

396. Candlestand, birch, probably northern New England, 1810–1830. W. 14¾". Winterthur Museum.

398. Chest of drawers, pine, Maine, 1830–1840. Brownish-red-and-black graining, green banding, yellow stripes. W. 43¾". Collection of Mr. and Mrs. Charles V. Hagler.

233

399. Cupboard, pine, Vermont, 1825–1835. Brown on tannish-gray background. W. 56¾". Collection of Mr. and Mrs. Charles F. Montgomery.

Zooming paisleyesque graining enriches the wide expanse of the base of the cupboard above. The decoration is slightly tighter on the chest opposite (400), but on both pieces the patterns soar across their fronts. The triangulated decoration of the table (401) carries out in mild staccato the angularity of its chamfered legs, made of mahogany. Its top is curled maple, the drawer front plain maple, and pine is the secondary wood. On the legs are faceted cuffs where the transition from octagonal to round members occurs. While the figured maple top has been painted over here, Rufus Porter gave directions for its imitation: "The birds' eyes and curls are formed by removing the staining from the ground with a piece of stiff leather, the edges of which are cut in notches so that several points will touch the work at the same time." [117]

400. Chest, pine, probably northern New England, 1825–1835.
Orange-red, with black decoration. W. 39″. Privately owned.

401. Table with drawer, maple, etc., New England, 1820–1845
Brown, yellow, and red. W. 38⁵⁄₁₆″. The Henry Ford Museum.

402. Cornice board, pine, American, c. 1830. Freehand polychrome landscape decoration. W. 54″. Privately owned.

Furniture was but a part of the work of the ornamental painter. Henry E. Spencer, formerly of Philadelphia, advertised in 1828 in North Carolina:

> He will execute Ornamental Work, such as Fire-Boards, Fire Screens, and Pictures, painted in landscape, naval victories, &c. for ornamenting Rooms. He will do all kinds of small jobs, such as painting Windsor Chairs, Gigs, &c. on as moderate terms as can be done in this country.[118]

As early as 1723 John Custis of Williamsburg, Virginia, ordered fireboards for his house:

> It is to put in ye summer before my chimneys to hide ye fire place. Let them bee some good flowers in potts of various kinds and whatever fancy else you think fitt.[119]

He gave the size of his fireplaces and ended by saying, "I had much rather have none than have daubing." Fireboards were made in America until Victorian times, and they could be painted on wood or canvas or covered by cutout wallpaper designs made for this purpose in France. Figure 403 appears to be a translation of one of these wallpaper designs into paint. Figure 405 is most unusual, with a handsome "pott" of flowers, fireboard-like decoration on the front of a typical New England six-board blanket chest. Figure 404, with scrolly and ecclesiastical overtones, is probably the work of a carpenter-carver. The view through the windows behind the catafalque shows trees in the sunset. We have already seen a stenciled corniceboard on pages 192–193. Few exist done in freehand painting, and 402 is a part of one of these. The scene shows a house and inn, and the top was originally scalloped and topped with acorn finials.

403. This pine fireboard was made about 1840 and is painted black, with decoration in dark cream and brown. W. 40¾″. Collection of Mr. and Mrs. Harvey Kahn.

404. Fireboard, pine, Connecticut, 1840–1850. Carved, and painted in polychrome. W. 46½". Collection of Jean and Howard Lipman.

405. Chest, pine, New England, 1820–1840. Painting on front in blue-green, brown, and pink on off-white ground. Sides and top grained. W. 41". Historic Deerfield, Inc.

406. Tall clock, pine, Pennsylvania, dated 1832 and signed by J. D. Green, probably its decorator. Reddish-brown-on-yellow graining, with gold stenciling. H. 85″. Photograph courtesy The Hudson Shop. Collection of Mr. and Mrs. Peter H. Tillou.
407. Tall clock, pine, made by Riley Whiting, Winchester, Connecticut, 1813–1835. Painted black, with graining in shades of light and dark brown. H. 88″. The Henry Ford Museum.

407

The two tall clocks on this page combine imitative and fanciful graining and stringing on their cases. This elongated form was particularly well suited for inventive decoration, and it is sad that so few painted clocks have survived unscathed.[120] The works of figure 407 were made by Riley Whiting, one of the more prolific clockmakers of the nineteenth century, while 406 is signed on its base by J. D. Green, presumably its decorator.

On the opposite page are three later pieces, made about the middle of the century. The candlestand (408, 408a) is painted in three colors, and the segmented geometrics of its octagonal top are distinctive. The box (409, 409a) is fitted inside with a looking glass and wallpapered compartments, and it features an extremely well-painted Hudson River view on its lid. The small grained and stenciled chest (410) has its original glass knobs, molded with threads and screwed directly onto the drawer fronts.

406

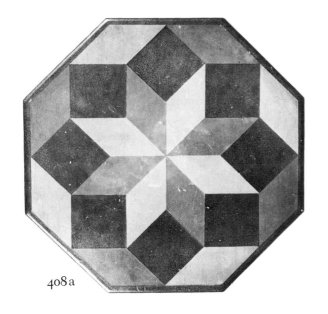

408a

408. Candlestand and detail of top (408a), American, 1840–1860. Green, black, and vermilion. H. 30″. Privately owned.
409. Box and detail of top (409a) showing the Narrows on the Hudson River near West Point; pine, American, 1845–1865. Cream ground; polychrome decoration. W. 11⅛″. The Henry Ford Museum.
410. Miniature chest of drawers, pine, probably New England, 1835–1860. Mottled graining in various shades of brown, with gilt-stencil decoration. W. 15″. Privately owned.

409a

409

408

410

Later Windsors

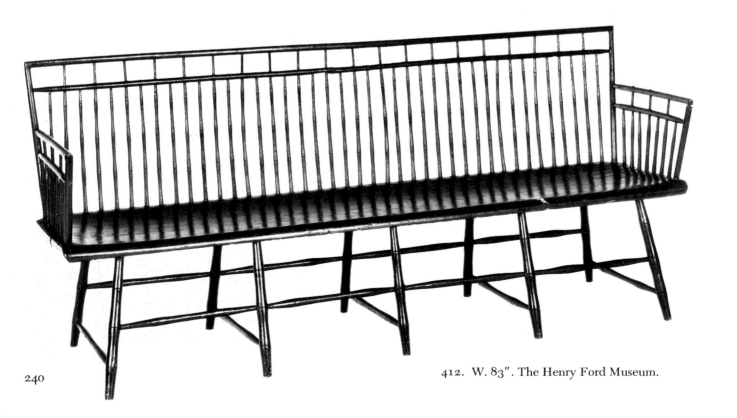

412. W. 83″. The Henry Ford Museum.

411. W. 77″. The Metropolitan Museum of Art.

Nineteenth-century Windsors were more colorful than their predecessors, but without so great a variety of forms. As the century started, old forms persisted, and fan-backs and bow-backs, with the new bamboo-turned legs, were popular. In 1801 a Connecticut maker gave this classic receipt for green paint for Windsors:

> To paint green on windsor chairs take your verdigrease and grinde it with the linseed oil and a small matter of white lead as to give a Boddy grinde this as thick as you can with the oil and when ground put it in your Paint pot and Stur in as much common Chair varnish as to thin it Down proper for your Brush.[121]

In 1800 in Philadelphia, Lawrence Allewine advertised his perfected, patented paints for all branches of decoration. The old and the new coexisted during the early part of the century. The settee above (411) dizzily combines continuous arms, bow-backs, and slightly arthritic bamboo turned legs—all established practices—with a series of flat, undulating splats and stretchers that would have been unknown in the 1700s. It is painted oyster white with black decoration. The rod-back Windsor, with a medley of bamboo turnings, appeared shortly after 1800, and the black settee (412) opposite is a New England example of this type. The dark-green settee below is a serene, balanced low-back version of the 1820s.

413. W. 79″. Collection of Jean and Howard Lipman.

414

The design and decoration of fancy chairs influenced Windsors in the nineteenth century. Rod-back Windsors (see figures 412, page 240, and 428, page 248) were popular at the turn of the century, and variations of these became quaintly known as "birdcage" or "chicken-coop" Windsors. After the War of 1812, a new type became fashionable, the arrow-back, which is seen on these pages. By this time country craftsmen were producing Windsors in great abundance. City influence was still strong, but the large firms such as Thomas and William Ash of New York, who had provided quantities of Windsors for both domestic and foreign markets after the Revolution, had been supplanted by a greater number of smaller firms and individuals, many working in rural areas. As techniques of mass production grew and interchangeable parts came into use more and more, quality was sacrificed for quantity. The rugged baluster turnings, generous scooped seats, and towering, forest-like backs of early Windsors were gone. Simpler types, with broader top rails and splats, came on the scene. Fortunately, so did decorative painting, which had replaced the plain paint of the early Windsors. The new decoration found a most suitable ally in these plainer forms.[122]

415. Watercolor portrait of G. Phillips, attributed to Asahel Powers of Springfield, Vermont, 1820s. Found in Concord, Massachusetts. 6″ x 4¾″. Figures 414 and 416, arrow-back Windsor side chair and rocking armchair, New England, 1820s. Side chair, H. 35½″; armchair, H. 44″. All privately owned.

416

417. Watercolor of the Talcott family by Deborah Goldsmith, upper New York State, 1832. 14″ x 18″. Abby Aldrich Rockefeller Folk Art Collection.
418, 418a. Arrow-back Windsor side chair, maple and pine, probably Rhode Island, 1820–1830. H. 35½″. New York State Historical Association.

418a

418

Figure 414 opposite is painted a buff ground, with shells, grapes, and stripings in red, brown, and black. It and 417 have round shoulders flanking the tablet in the center of the top rail, while the rocker (416) has a flat rail. It also has more vertical arrows and is painted yellow, with oak leaves and acorns for decoration. The old-looking young Phillips lad perches in a wiggly side chair with a sinuous back stile. Deborah Goldsmith's fine document of the Talcott family features all sorts of intriguing details from the grained clothes press to the suspicious beast behind the footstool at Mr. Talcott's feet. Sitting on white Windsors with green vines are Mary (seventy) in the rocker, Betsey (thirty) and Emily (three months) on one side chair, and Samuel (thirty-eight) and Charles (three) on another. The arrow-back chair on this page features an elongated lioness on the top, with grapes in the back. Another from the same set has a lemur on the top. The chair is black, with striping in yellow, the grapes are gold and yellow with red flourishes, and the jungle scene is polychrome. The legs of the chair "tuck in" like those on earlier Rhode Island Windsors. A lady reminiscing on her youth in Connecticut in the 1830s wrote:

> There were six wooden chairs painted red with bunches of grapes and grape leaves on the top slat of the back. There was a rocking chair to match with a cushion covered with some of the calico like bed curtains. There was a small green rocking chair without arms, very uncomfortable to sit in as it threw anyone forward.[123]

419. Rocking arrow-back Windsor settee, maple and pine, American, c. 1830. W. 44½″. The Henry Ford Museum.

Windsor furniture for children included high chairs, regular chairs, cradles, settees, and miniature dolls' furniture. The arrow-back rocking settee (419) is black, with gold-and-yellow stenciled and painted decoration. This type, with its detachable retainer for babies, was a popular form and was made in many areas. The incised turnings on the legs and back supports are striped in yellow. Invariably, these incised stripes are a part of bamboo turnings, providing a needed contrast for plainer legs.

The miniature side chair and settee (421 and 422) are part of a set including another side chair and a rocker. They were probably home-made for a young lady's dollhouse and have a good scale—always the making or breaking point for miniature pieces. Another similar set, made by a Salem sea dog, is at the Essex Institute.

The cradle (420) is not the most successful rod-back variant—scale holds true for larger pieces, too—but it has a chunky charm which its occupant(s) must have found satisfying.

421 and 422. Miniature arrow-back side chair and settee, pine, 1825–1835. Painted red-brown, with mustard-yellow decoration. Chair, H. 6⅞″; settee, H. 7⅛″. The New-York Historical Society.

420. Windsor cradle, maple and pine painted green, New England, 1810–1840. L. 40¾″. The Henry Ford Museum.

So-called Salem rockers developed in the teens, their Windsor heritage apparent in their bamboo turnings, scooped seats, and top rails with shouldered tablets. Figure 423 is a graceful example, with an exotic scene on the back. The Boston rocker developed in the 1820s. Its spool turnings, rolled seat and tablet, scrolled shoulders, and lower back are characteristic of this type. Figure 424 features very accomplished stenciling on rosewood paint, with a brindle seat. These rockers became extremely popular and were made beyond the Boston area. "1 Boston Rocking chair" was listed in the inventory of Gerard Beekman of New York in 1833. Sarah Anna Emery, describing life about 1830, wrote, "Life at Harvard was much more primitive than at present. The dormitories were uncarpeted and furnished with common bedsteads, pine washstands, tables and chairs. What were termed Boston rocking chairs were luxuries recently introduced by some of the students into their rooms." Armless rockers and rockerless armchairs were also made.[124]

423. Rocker, Salem type, maple, pine, mahogany arms; stamped by Benjamin Newman, Gloucester, Massachusetts, c. 1815–1825. H. 46″. Essex Institute.
424. Boston rocker, maple, pine, mahogany arms; stamped by J. Raymond, Essex County, Massachusetts, 1825–1835. H. 37¼″. Privately owned.

425

426

The three chairs on this page show how much original decoration added to the success of Windsors. Figures 425 and 427 are painted with rosewood grounds, and 426 is painted like curled maple. The colors of the decoration vary, and all have fine, neat stripings. Figure 425 is of the thumb-back type, and 426 has a stepped top rail and base turnings reminiscent of fancy chairs. Similar tops, with the stiles running into (but not beyond) the top rail, are known as step-down Windsors. Like so many nineteenth-century examples from arrow-backs to Boston rockers, the top rails frequently were variations on a central rectangular tablet flanked by rounded ends. Flat top rails were also used, as in 425. A reward of fifty dollars was offered in 1804 in New York for six Windsors, with "green backs and black seats, ornamented with yellow," which were stolen from Christian and Paxton, auctioneers. They said, "The frequent depradations committed in this way, has determined us to prosecute the first detected to the utmost extent of the law." [125]

425. Thumb-back Windsor side chair, maple and pine, New York State, 1815–1835. H. 33½". Privately owned.
426. Arrow-back Windsor side chair, maple and pine, New England, 1815–1835. H. 36". Collection of Jean and Howard Lipman.
427. Arrow-back Windsor rocking armchair, maple and pine, Maine, 1825–1835. H. 41". Privately owned.

427

428

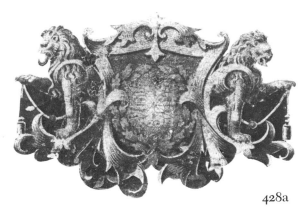

428a

428, 428a. Rod-back Windsor side chair, maple and ash, labeled by George Fry, Philadelphia, c. 1820. Painted black-green, with red striping, polychrome-and-gilt mantling. H. 34″. The Newark Museum.

Figure 428 is a highly elegant nineteenth-century Windsor, with well-defined bamboo turnings and a pleasingly shaped seat. The stripings are delicately done, as is the armorial cartouche (428a), typical of heraldic design about 1820. The chair is one of a set of six, three of which bear Fry's label.

Figure 429 is practically an end-of-the-road example. Turnings and the top rail lack definition, and the round scooping of the seat neither relieves its thickness nor fits the contours of the sitter very well. It heralds the arrival of the simple farm chairs of the middle of the century. It was made in a small town by a chairmaker who labeled other later Windsors. Another maker, Joel Pratt, Jr., also worked in Sterling and made Windsors. Their work reflects the role of craftsmen in rural areas in the 1800s and brings to mind the advertisement of William R. Hughes of Salisbury, North Carolina, in 1831: "He keeps on hand a large supply of well made windsor chairs both Gilted and Painted which he will sell low for Cash or Country produce."[126]

429. Flat-top Windsor side chair, maple and pine, labeled by G. Brown, Sterling, Massachusetts, 1830s. Painted green, with black-and-yellow decoration. H. 33¼″. Privately owned.

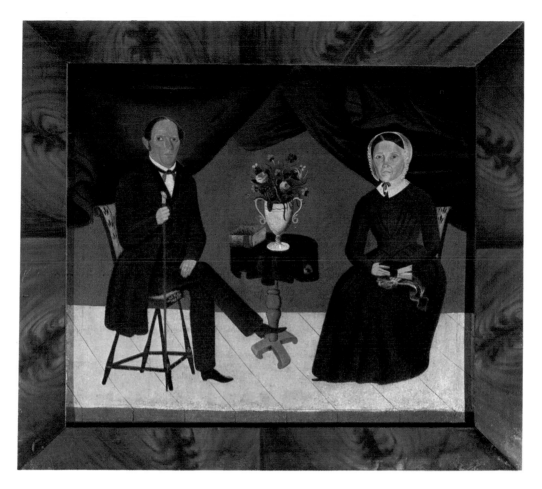

430. This portrait of Mr. and Mrs. William Vaughn was painted by Sheldon Peck of Lombard, Illinois, in 1845. The Windsors have black and yellow decoration, and the wooden frame is grained to simulate mahogany. 30″ x 33¾″. Privately owned.

431. Decorated furniture from the deep South is rare. This settee, with a cypress seat, is painted mustard with dark-green scrolls on the top rail. It was traditionally made for Oakland, a plantation in the country near Natchez, Mississippi. W. 79½″. Collection of Mrs. Douglas MacNeil.

432. Armoire or cupboard, poplar with brown graining, Louisville, Ohio, 1820–1840. W. 60″. The Henry Ford Museum.

433. Cupboard, Southern pine, signed by Nathan Overton, Randolph County, North Carolina, working 1821–1850. Green, with brown-grained panels, white bevels, marbleized molding and cornice, brown base molding. W. 40½″. The Colonial Williamsburg Foundation.

PATTERNS

435a

434

435

434 and 435, 435a. Chest and *trastero*, both pine, northern New Mexico, c. 1830. Cupboard has marbleized red field with olive moldings; panels are light blue and black; shell is blue-green and pumpkin, with black lines and green dots. Floral interior panels (435a). Chest, W. 27⅝"; cupboard, W. 29⅛". Museum of New Mexico.

While England was the main source of cultural influences in America, settlers from other lands also left their marks. French taste had exerted itself in the rococo and in the Empire style, and furniture in the French manner was made from Canada down the Mississippi Valley. However, most American versions of French furniture used dark woods and veneers. A stunning exception (432) is an armoire, or cupboard, made in the French settlement of Louisville, Ohio, which flourished from about 1820 to 1840. The form is decidedly French, but the wood, the hardware, and the brown graining are far removed from Normandy.

The corner cupboard (433), in the more familiar English tradition, is unusual, since it is a documented Southern piece made about the same time.

In the Southwest, Sante Fe became the capital of a widespread Spanish colony in 1610. By the end of the eighteenth century the decline of the Spanish Empire had started; and New Mexico, twice removed from the motherland, took on a remoteness that was to continue through American occupation until the building of the railroad in 1880.

The arts survived, however. *Santos* and *retablos*, religious pictures, were painted there, and simple carved or painted furniture was produced. Occasionally, itinerant artisans came up from old Mexico with oil paints in the early 1800s (434). Most of the decoration done by local craftsmen, however, was in tempera (435). The chest has a pinkish-tan ground, with polychrome decoration, while the cupboard (or *trastero*) is marbleized.[127]

251

436. Sewing table, painted red, New
Lebanon, New York, 1810–1840. W. 24⅝".
The Metropolitan Museum of Art.

437. Washstand, cherry graining,
probably New Lebanon, New
York, 1810–1840. W. 20″.
Collection of Charles H. and
Mary Grace Carpenter.

In 1774, with the arrival of Mother Ann Lee and her followers in New York, the Shakers had come to America. The tenets of the United Society of Believers in Christ's Second Appearing, the formal name of the group, were ascetic. The Believers had little interest in worldly issues, relying instead upon the eternal value of the human spirit. They separated from the world into their own communities, and women separated from men so their goals could be more easily reached without distraction. From their first community at Watervliet, New York, established in 1776, the movement spread first to New England, and after 1800 to Ohio and Kentucky. By the mid-1800s there were some 6,000 Shakers in eighteen communities; and the movement, made up of native Americans, was one of the few indigenous ones to achieve success here. Purity was the key; and their furniture, like their own lives, was inspired from above. Truly it can be termed soul furniture.[128]

Shaker Furniture

Shaker furniture has a functional purity of line and form that results in a timelessness that transcends the dictates of style. While frills of any sort were forbidden, color was allowed; and some Shaker pieces were either painted or stained with a thin wash. The "Family" at New Lebanon, New York, became the headquarters of the Believers, and the sewing table (436) and washstand (437) at the left were made there. The table is red, and the washstand, made of cherry, is quite unusual in having a subtle, wavy graining over the wood. Few grained Shaker examples are known. The slat-back side chair is typical; many of these were sold to the "outside world" throughout the nineteenth century. They were stained many colors, in this case a handsome mustard. The blue table (439) is most unusual in that remnants of a deeper blue-green trailing vine decoration—a most un-Shakerly practice—remain on the back skirt and, to a lesser degree, on the front of the drawer.

438. Side chair, stained mustard, Hancock, Massachusetts, c. 1830. H. 37¼". The Shaker Museum.

439. Table, painted blue, Canterbury, New Hampshire, early nineteenth century. W. 34½". Privately owned.

440. Wardrobe, or *schrank,* pine, marbleized and painted,
Lancaster County, Pennsylvania, c. 1790. Blue-green ground;
polychrome decoration. W. 88″. The Henry Ford Museum.

Pennsylvania German Furniture

Shortly after the founding of Pennsylvania the first German immigrants arrived. In the eighteenth century they came in thousands, eventually settling in southeastern Pennsylvania. They made their land incredibly rich through their sober industry. Perhaps as a compensation for their plain, devoted ways, their spirits sang forth brashly harmonious songs of design and color. Their furniture combined Continental inspiration with more than a whiff of the English on occasion. This, plus their own inventiveness, resulted in an exciting and lively folk art that was truly American. It could be as stylized as it was symbolic, but it was always vibrant.

The three examples on this page are plain painted; the dark green being a favorite color for "English" Philadelphia beds. The wardrobe, opposite, startlingly combines plain colors with floral decoration and marbleizing.

441. Armchair, maple, painted mottled red, Pennsylvania, last half of the eighteenth century. H. 43″. The Metropolitan Museum of Art.

442. Table, pine, painted brown, Pennsylvania, c. 1750. H. 24⅞″. Philadelphia Museum of Art.

443. Daybed or couch, maple painted dark green, Pennsylvania, 1710–1750. L. 65″. Collection of Mr. and Mrs. David Pottinger.

444

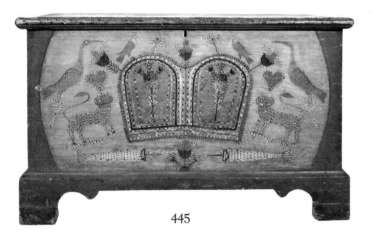

445

446

Most of the German settlers had come to America from the Palatinate, an area which included much of the Rhine Valley and adjacent lands reaching from Switzerland downriver to Holland. By 1770 they made up nearly one third of the population of Pennsylvania. Many lived in Germantown, but most continued their agrarian ways and moved out to the countryside in Lancaster and Berks counties, which were later split to include Lebanon, Dauphin, Northumberland, and Schuylkill counties.

They were mostly Lutherans and members of the German Reformed Church, although Moravians and the pietistic sects such as Amish, Mennonites, and Schwenkfelders also settled here.

They persisted in their traditions, led mainly by their religion. Christopher Sower printed a German edition of the Bible in 1743, antedating by more than a generation the first production of an English Bible in this country. The art of medieval illumination was practiced and taught at the Ephrata Cloisters as early as 1746; and from this developed the art of *fraktur*, including *Vorschriften* (copybook exercises and religious lessons), *Taufscheine* (birth and baptism certificates), New Year's greetings, house blessings, bookplates, and games. This art form aided both in the preservation of Old World traditions and in the dissemination of a Christian iconography.

Symbols were rife. The unicorn was the symbol of purity, and the peacock signified resurrection. Fish, living in water, were linked with baptism, while griffins and pelicans represented Christ. All sorts of flowers, animals, and birds had their special connotations. However, it must be borne in mind that decorative symbols can rapidly lose their meanings and become stylized. Thus, the true meaning of the tulip was sometimes little more than a love for the new plant; and six-pointed stars had long since become conventional motifs, before masquerading as hex signs on later barns.

444. Chest, Pennsylvania, dated 1774. W. 60″. A very early decorated example. Privately owned. 445. Chest, pine, Center County, Pennsylvania, c. 1800. W. 38″. Decoration and colors unusual. Collection of Mr. and Mrs. John Gordon. 446. Chest, pine, Jonestown, Pennsylvania (Dauphin County), signed by Christian Seltzer, its painter, and dated 1784. W. 52⅛″. An early example of the Seltzer–Rank "Jonestown school." The Henry Ford Museum. 447. Chest with drawers, yellow pine and poplar, Berks County, Pennsylvania, c. 1780. W. 52½″. An outstanding chest. The Metropolitan Museum of Art.

447

Describing a Pennsylvania German interior in 1783, Dr. Johann David Schoepf noticed "a great four cornered stove, a table in the corner with benches fastened to the wall, everything daubed with red, and above a shelf." [129] As can be seen on the opposite page, the daubings could be of many colors and could be glorious indeed. The date 1774 is early for a decorated chest (444), and its trestle feet and plain floral forms contrast with the later and more highly embellished examples. Figure 447 exhibits the best in technique and vocabulary of its painter, while 445 makes use of its devices and colors in a lighter, almost classical manner.

Decoration could be done by professionals or by amateurs, by stay-at-homes or by itinerants. Figure 446 is signed by its painter, Christian Seltzer, the first (and best) of a group that included his son and three members of the Rank family, all working at Jonestown, in Dauphin County. A professional itinerant, Heinrich Otto, painted many *frakturs*. He did a birth certificate for Rahel Friedrichin of Lancaster County and most likely transmitted many of the same designs onto a handsome walnut chest already owned by her parents (451).

Lancaster County cabinetmakers favored recessed panels (440 and 448), adding architectural frames within which the decoration could be contained. Figure 448 also features a cascade of peacock feathers on its ends. Bold red-and-yellow geometrics make up the decoration on 449, while Adam and Eve are the central decoration on 450. The ground color is a medium blue, with four black hearts outlined in red along the sides. The base is painted dark blue and red, and the flowers, birds, and figures are in polychrome.

Frequently, the decorative designs were lightly scribed onto the bare wood before the freehand decoration was applied. Many of these colorful chests were used as dower chests by their owners.

448. Chest, yellow pine, Lancaster County, Pennsylvania, c. 1780. Red ground, with black moldings; designs in red, black, green, brown, and tan. W. 52½″. The Metropolitan Museum of Art. 449. Chest, pine and tulip, Pennsylvania, early nineteenth century. Red and yellow. W. 44⅜″. Winterthur Museum. 450. Chest, pine, probably Berks County, late eighteenth century. W. 50″. Winterthur Museum. 451. Dower chest, walnut, Lancaster County, Pennsylvania; decoration dated August 15, 1791. Attributed to Heinrich Otto. Chest may be earlier. W. 54″. Collection of Mr. and Mrs. David Pottinger.

448

449

450

451

452. Desk-and-bookcase, pine, eastern Pennsylvania, c. 1800. Cabinetwork quite sophisticated. W. 40¾". Wintherthur Museum.

453. Cupboard, Mahantango Valley, Pennsylvania, early nineteenth century. Colors, red-orange (showing dark) and ochre (showing lighter in picture). W. 60". Philadelphia Museum of Art.

A turn-of-the-century author characterized Pennsylvania Germans as "distinguished for their temperance, industry, and economy."[130] Their labors flourished abroad as they had at home. They imported books and small objects such as oval brides' boxes and in this way perpetuated a great many of their traditions from the old country. Yet they had to become self-sufficient, and they did, being constantly tweaked by English influences from stylish Philadelphia. It is this segregation and integration of cultures that make Pennsylvania German productions so fascinating. Figure 452 is really a "gone English" piece, its form inspired by a Philadelphia Chippendale desk-and-bookcase. The decoration and the carved ornaments at the top preserve the heritage of its maker. The basic color is green, with dark blue-green base, reddish-brown ornaments, and white trim.

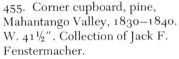

454. Dresser, poplar and walnut, Lancaster area, early nineteenth century. W. 80″. Collection of Mr. and Mrs. David Pottinger.

455. Corner cupboard, pine, Mahantango Valley, 1830–1840. W. 41½″. Collection of Jack F. Fenstermacher.

456. Cupboard, pine, Mahantango Valley, dated 1830. Ochre ground, with red graining; dark blue-green moldings; ivory upper doors; decorations in blue, yellow, salmon, and red. W. 60⅜″. Philadelphia Museum of Art.

A close study, based on the forms, decorative devices, and construction, reveals that many Pennsylvania German pieces were made later than they might appear at first glance. The four cupboards on these pages are all nineteenth-century productions. Figure 453 effectively combines carved demilunes, pinwheels, and late gadrooning with a two-toned color scheme. Figure 454, above, is painted a greenish yellow, with dark-green moldings and natural walnut doors with red trim. The eagle at the top is gilt, and the floral sprays and birds are dark green and red. Graining in Pennsylvania usually has a spirited snap to it, and ochre and burnt sienna combine heftily on the Sheraton corner cupboard (455). A cupboard (456) dated 1830, and made by the Consortia guild, handsomely revives and combines the form and decoration of earlier times.

457. Bed, Pennsylvania German, 1820–1830. H. 85″. Philadelphia Museum of Art, Titus C. Geesey Collection.

The graining on these four pieces is anything but imitative! This is fancy graining at its best and boldest, with sweepingly broad sponged surfaces hinting at fanciful hearts, tulips, and stars in the strongest Pennsylvania German manner. The bed is painted in a loud red-orange, with brown sponging achieving a flattened heart on the headboard. The graining on 458 is made up of red, brown, and ochre. A six-pointed star is on the top, tulips grace the ends, and two knotlike eyes stare forth from the abstracted forms on the front. Figure 459 is similarly, though less surely, decorated in brownish red and ochre, with the two moldings along the base painted in dark green. The table is decorated in brown and black, with a swirling four-pointed star on the top and a chattery sort of decoration on the edge, the skirt, and the drawer. The black also twines down the delicate legs. Like 462, the drawer has an opalescent glass knob.

458. Chest with drawers, pine, Pennsylvania, c. 1830.
W. 38″. Collection of Jean and Howard Lipman.

459. Chest with drawers, pine, Pennsylvania, c. 1830.
W. 46″. Privately owned.

460. Table, pine, Pennsylvania, c. 1830. W. 28¼″.
Collection of Jean and Howard Lipman.

461. Side chair, maple and poplar, Pennsylvania, 1820–1840. Walnut graining; stenciled decoration. H. 32¾″. The Metropolitan Museum of Art.

462. Desk, pine, Pennsylvania, c. 1825. Mahogany graining; dull beige ground on drawer; gilt and polychrome decoration. Commemorates Jackson's victory at New Orleans in 1815. W. 30″. Philadelphia Museum of Art.

The Pennsylvania Germans contributed much to their new land. Music was respected and featured by the Moravians more than by any others in the Colonies. German "mechanicks" developed the Conestoga wagon and the "Kentucky" rifle, both contributing variously but forcibly to the winning and opening up of their new country.

In the nineteenth century Pennsylvania German cabinetmakers took on the newer national styles, their furniture retaining only a bit of an accent. The chair above has an overall husky feeling in both form and decoration. Its top rail has a "kick" to it, and the legs end in "blunt arrow" feet reminiscent of earlier chairs (see figure 441, page 255). With all these different features, however, it is still obviously a later fancy chair. The desk (462) has a Germanic heft and involved turnings on the feet, but its decoration seems more in the tradition of the coach painter. On the chest (463) can be seen a shower of six-pointed stars and thumbprint designs, on delectably bowlegged feet.

463. Chest of drawers, pine, Pennsylvania, c. 1830. Dark blue-green ground; red-and-buff decoration. W. 37¾″. The Henry Ford Museum.

464. Chest of drawers, pine and poplar, Mahantango Valley,
Pennsylvania, probably 1820s. Panels show Germanic influence.
W. 43¾″. Philadelphia Museum of Art.

465. Desk, inscribed "Jacob Maser, 1834."
W. 39″. Winterthur Museum.

466. Chest, dated 1834.
W. 48⅜″. Winterthur Museum.

In these later pieces from the Mahantango Valley (see also figures 453, 455, and 456, pages 258–259), the strong devices of earlier Pennsylvania German decoration have become highly stylized and lessened in scale. They are used almost like inlay on Federal furniture, more as a whisper than a bang. However, with their bright colors, these case pieces have a charm and character of their own.

The desk (465) and chest (466) above are both dated 1834, the desk also being inscribed "Jacob Maser." [131] Both have quartered corners on the drawers, delightful eight-petal posies in red and yellow along the stiles, and birds galore in red, yellow, and black. The quarter fans are repeated on the sides, with large stars centered on the panels. Two horses prance on the lid of the desk, which has a strong green background. The chest is dark blue-green.

The devices on the late, printed *fraktur* at the right represent an obvious source for these lingering, yet lovely, examples.

467. *Taufschein,* printed by Moser and Peters, Carlisle, Pennsylvania, dated 1826. Philadelphia Museum of Art.

468

469

470

Smaller objects with Pennsylvania German decoration usually have great flair. The early nineteenth-century portable desk (468), found in Lancaster County, is made of pine and painted with a reddish-brown ground. Paterae, quarter fans, dots, and diagonals seem to poke fun at inlaid city work, while stars on the ends and a heart in the center are more traditional. It is 16¾″ wide and in the collection of Mr. and Mrs. Samuel L. Meulendyke.

On the wide pine looking-glass frame (469), painted a reddish brown, there are birds surrounded by oak leaves and acorns, in green, yellow, light red, and ochre. It was made about 1830, is 13⅝″ high, and is in the collection of Mr. and Mrs. Mitchel Taradash.

The candlestand (470), found in Sunbury, Pennsylvania, is a midcentury piece, also of pine. Its top is marbleized in green, blue, and yellow. The colossal turned shaft and swoopy legs are painted more in the style of a coach painter, the decoration in black and brown accented by yellow striping. It is 30″ high and owned by The Henry Ford Museum.

The doors on the opposite page show how decorative devices could spill over into architecture. Tulips and hearts abound on 472, while 471 features a bowl of tulips above a horseman. Two birds are in painted panels on the reverse side. The New Jersey origin of 471 is interesting, since Germanic settlements were made there, and several pieces of New Jersey German *fraktur* work are known—most with English writing.

472. Door from house in Berks County, Pennsylvania, late eighteenth century. Dull red stiles; white hearts on black; pink tulips on black. H. 69". Philadelphia Museum of Art, Titus C. Geesey Collection.

471. Door from house in Franklin Park, New Jersey, later eighteenth century. Reddish-brown ground, with swirls in black. Decoration in blue and red on beige. H. 72". University Art Gallery, Rutgers—The State University of New Jersey.

473

474

475

476

477

Not many decorated clocks have been found. This one is truly a charmer, with a spotted snake painted on the inside of the door! The ground color is red, with the decoration in black, yellow, and white. The urn of roses and bird on the door are very well done, but the problems of designing the two cups on the cornice and the washtub affair with truncated flowers on the base must have been all but overwhelming for the painter. A similar clock stood in a candy store in Shartlesville, Pennsylvania, years ago; and, according to tradition, the owner of the store used to warn children, "Don't touch the clock, because there's a rattler inside!" Such ferocities are as charming as they are rare in American painted furniture of all periods.[132]

The colorful clutch of painted boxes above shows a wide range of decoration, with hearts, leaves, grapes, strawberries, tulips, and a house featured. Figure 475 is in the shape of a book, and 477, with its sliding top, was used as a candle box. The salt box (476) is a form particularly suited for decoration and was highly favored by Pennsylvania Germans. How colorful they were!

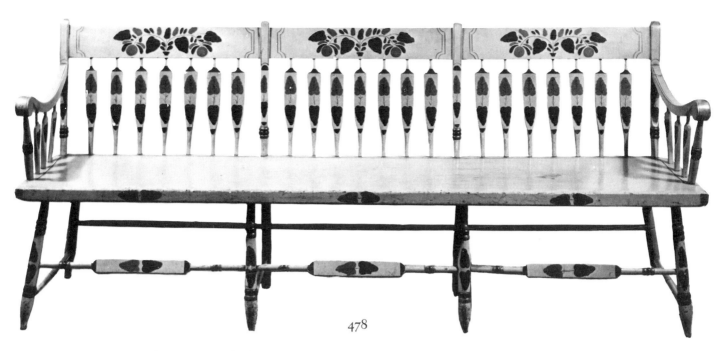

478

473. (Opposite). Tall clock, probably Schuylkill County, Pennsylvania, early nineteenth century. H. 91″. Philadelphia Museum of Art, Titus C. Geesey Collection. 474. Box, pine, Pennsylvania, 1830s. W. 5½″. Collection of Jean and Howard Lipman. 475. Box, pine, Pennsylvania, 1830s. W. 5¼″. Collection of Mr. and Mrs. Samuel L. Meulendyke. 476. Salt box, pine, Pennsylvania, 1820s. H. 7¼″. Collection of Mr. and Mrs. Samuel L. Meulendyke. 477. Candle box, pine, Pennsylvania, c. 1810. W. 12″. The Metropolitan Museum of Art.

478. The commodious arrow-back settee above was found in a farmhouse in Annville, Lebanon County, Pennsylvania, before 1845. It is painted yellow, with red-and-black decoration. It was made in the 1820s, is 84″ wide, and is in the collection of the William Penn Memorial Museum.
479. The unusual settee below has a stronger foreign accent. It was made in Pennsylvania about 1840 and is 80″ wide. The seat and arms are gray, and the rest is mustard with gold-and-black edgings to the splats. The landscape scene along the top rail is in varied greens. Collection of Mr. and Mrs. Robert C. Hartlein.

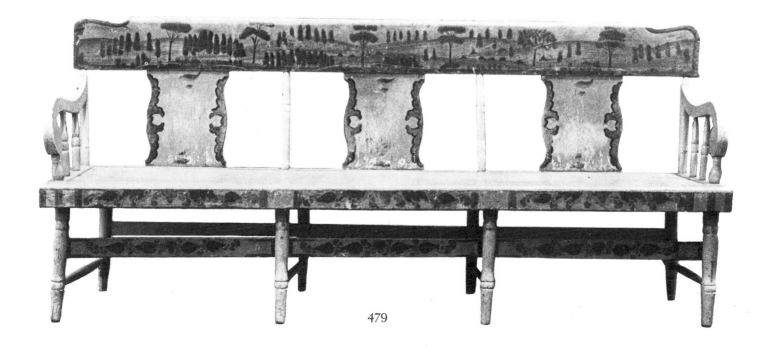

479

480. Tall clock, pine, Johnstown, Pennsylvania, mid-nineteenth century. H. 100½″. The Henry Ford Museum.

481. Chest, pine, Johnstown, Pennsylvania, dated 1854, and signed "MANUFACTURED BY CHRISTIAN BLAUCH W. 43¼″. The Henry Ford Museum.

482. Chest of drawers, poplar, Johnstown, Pennsylvania, dated 1850, and signed "MANUFACTURED BY JOHN SALA." W. 38⅛". The Henry Ford Museum.

483. Cupboard, poplar, Johnstown, Pennsylvania, dated 1851. W. 63¼". The Henry Ford Museum.

At Johnstown, in the southwestern part of Pennsylvania, some highly interesting furniture was made about the middle of the nineteenth century. These four examples display stenciled decoration, and the fact that three of them are dated shows how earlier forms lingered in rural areas. The clock is painted red, with black panels and trim, with stenciling in gold. The Christian Blauch chest (482) has red graining and black trim on the base and top molding. The elegant John Sala chest of drawers (481) has red graining, with black legs, top, and side panels. The stenciling and drawer beadings are yellow, while the maker's name, under the top double drawers, is in gold. The cupboard is painted much like the clock, with red ground, and black accents on the moldings, panels, and drawers. The black quarter columns on the sides are striped in blue-green.

484 (left) and 485 (right). Covered saffron cups, Lehnware, Clay, Lancaster County, c. 1860–1886. Figure 484 has a pinkish-cream ground with polychrome decoration in red, green, and dark blue, and a strawberry motif. Pomegranate motif is on 485, which is vivid red, with black and green. Both have pussy-willow banding on the top rim of the cup. H. 4½″ and 5″ respectively. Collection of Mr. and Mrs. Samuel L. Meulendyke.

486. Lehnware pail, probably mulberry, Clay, Lancaster County, c. 1860–1886. Red, with decoration in red, white, yellow, and green. Design on metal staves repeated on cover. H. 9¼″. Winterthur Museum.

487. Knife-and-spice box, poplar, Pennsylvania, c. 1830. Dark blue-green ground, with red drawer; tulips in black, red, and yellow. Light-blue bandings on edges. W. 13¼″. Philadelphia Museum of Art, Titus C. Geesey Collection.

489. Dough trough, poplar, Jonestown, Dauphin County, Pennsylvania, 1780–1800. Probably decorated by Christian or John Seltzer. Red ground, white panels; black vases with red-and-yellow tulips and green leaves. W. 28½". The Metropolitan Museum of Art.

488. Small chair, pine and maple, Pennsylvania, 1830–1840. Dark-green ground, with yellow leaves and stripings, red flower, and black outlining. H. 14". Collection of Mr. and Mrs. Mitchel Taradash.

490. Small dough tray, cherry, Pennsylvania, c. 1830. Polka-dotted hearts, circles, and stars on outside in yellow, dark green, and pale vermilion. Birds on top, horses inside lid. W. 17". Philadelphia Museum of Art, Titus C. Geesey Collection.

The objects on these two pages constitute a panoramic review of Pennsylvania German decoration. The earliest example here is the late eighteenth-century dough trough (489), made at Jonestown in Dauphin County (see figure 446, page 256). From the 1830 period come the delightful knife-and-spice box with its whalelike conjoined tulips (487), the spirited small chair (488), and the little bespeckled dough tray (490).

One of the latest practitioners of old-time decoration was Joseph Lehn (1798–1892) of Clay, in Lancaster County. After retiring from farming about 1860, Lehn started grinding his own colors and decorating small objects in vivid hues until 1886. Since other painters worked with him, "Lehnware" has become the proper term to describe the covered cups (484 and 485), pails (486), chests, boxes, tubs, toys, banks, and other wares covered with gaudy, waxlike paint.[133]

491. H. 26″.
The Litchfield Historical Society.

492. H. 28″.
Privately owned.

VII. VICTORIAN

In the last half of the nineteenth century the vortical changes of stylistic revivals and survivals progressed from the Gothic and rococo of the 1840s to Renaissance and Louis XVI revivals by 1870. Prior to the calming influence of the Mission style at the end of the century, influences of the Oriental, the Moorish, the Egyptian, the Old World, and the Colonial Revival were also felt. The Victorians had created a sweeping review of world furniture styles, and each "new" phase produced more demands on the rapidly developing technology. Different materials were also used. Marbleized table and bureau tops of slate and stone were made in New York and Vermont in the 1850s,[134] and cast-iron garden furniture, usually painted in dark green, was produced at the same time. The Victorian period was more an age of wood than of paint on furniture, although painted decoration was still used effectively at times.

While papier-mâché furniture had been made in England, it was not until 1850 that it was made in America, at the Litchfield Manufacturing Company in Connecticut, for a four-year period. Sheets of paper were glued together to form a type of millboard that could be cut and scrolled and finally finished with a japan varnish, painted, gilded, and inlaid with mother-of-pearl. The clock at the left was made there about 1852, and the shapely candlestand, with a papier-mâché top and white-pine base, could have been made in Litchfield also, although it was owned in Westbrook, Maine. The great P. T. Barnum was a director of the company, and his various enthusiastic undertakings may have been a factor in the demise of the organization in 1854.[135]

The box at the top of this page (493) is covered with painted oilcloth. The ground is black, and parrots, leaves, and flowers are dotted in red, yellow, and green. The technique of this precursor of linoleum was described fully in *The Painter, Gilder, and Varnisher's Companion,* the most popular painters' guide of the era.[136] The box is labeled by William P. Moody of Saco, Maine, who was a trunk manufacturer and harness maker before limiting himself only to harness work from 1855 to the 1880s. The book box (494) is most unusual, with an open book on betasseled drapery, all in painted pine! Inscribed "P. F. COIST," the feature of the decoration is a book opened to the poem "The Book of Liberty," on yellow pages.[137] The table (495), found in Maine and made about midcentury, is of walnut. Its Greek key border and leaves are red, yellow, green, and tan. A head of a classical warrior is pasted on the center scroll.

493. W. 12½".
Privately owned.

494. W. 19½".
Collection of Stewart E. Gregory.

495. W. 32".
Privately owned.

275

496. Bureau, poplar and marble, signed by Hart, Ware Company, Philadelphia, c. 1850. Black, with gold scrolls and polychrome flowers. W. 42½″. Philadelphia Museum of Art.

497. Side chair, probably New York, 1845–1855. Black, with gold-and-red decoration. H. 33½″. Museum of the City of New York.

Painted furniture's great moment in the Victorian period occurred in countless sets of cottage furniture. They were made everywhere and consisted of decorated chests, beds, commodes, dressing tables, night stands, towel stands, and chairs. Andrew Jackson Downing, a leading arbiter of mid-nineteenth-century taste, in describing the work of Edward Hennessey of Boston, wrote:

His reputation is an extended one, and he supplies orders from various parts of the Union and the West Indies. This furniture is remarkable for its combination of lightness and strength, and its essentially cottage-like character. It is very highly finished, and is usually painted drab, white, gray, a delicate lilac, or a fine blue —the surface polished and hard, like enamel. Some of the better sets have groups of flowers or other designs painted upon them with artistic skill. When it is remembered that the whole set for a cottage bed-room may be had for the price of a single wardrobe of mahogany, it will be seen how comparatively cheap it is.[138]

Figure 496 is a rather elegant cottage bureau, with a marble top and serpentine drawer fronts. Figure 499 is at Sunnyside (Washington Irving's home in Tarrytown, New York) and has applied split spindles in the Elizabethan manner. While large companies made cottage furniture, amateurs decorated these pieces also. Harriet Beecher Stowe painted three examples which are in existence today.[139]

498. Plate (fig. 268) from A. J. Downing's *The Architecture of Country Houses* (1850) showing a set of painted cottage furniture made by Edward Hennessey of Boston. With four chairs, a set cost from $70 to $100.

499. Bureau, pine, etc., possibly made by Edward Hennessey, Boston, c. 1850. Light green, with polychrome decoration. W. 38½". Sleepy Hollow Restorations.

At the first exhibition of the Salem Charitable Mechanics Association in 1849, John Jewett, a cabinetmaker, was awarded a diploma for five pieces of furniture, one of which was a refrigerator grained in imitation of black walnut. So graining, which had captured the imagination of decorative painters for a century and a half, had finally filtered down to everyday, utilitarian objects and occasional rural interpretations. In 1855 these deprecating remarks were made about graining:

> This has become so common that we may almost call it a rage. Like other senseless fashions, it will have its day, and pass away. It would be some satisfaction to us could we be instrumental in shortening its reign a single hour.[140]

Graining did continue in the last half of the century, but never with the quality and effervescence of earlier work.

For the New York City home of Robert Kelley, the architect Richard Upjohn selected the chairs shown here (500 and 501) as part of a parlor set including a piano, a center table, a sofa, and other similar armchairs and side chairs.[141] They are in the rococo revival style, with a strong French Louis XV influence. The side chair, with flowing curves and a supple, spring seat, became a favorite type and continued to be made through the fifties and sixties in mahogany and rosewood.

As the Chippendale style of the eighteenth century combined the rococo, Gothic, and Chinese, so did expressions of the nineteenth century combine more than one element. On the opposite page, the center table (502)—"the emblem of the family circle," as Downing described the form—combines japanned decoration with Gothic elements on an Empire form.[142] The japanning is very well done. Many of the individual scenes resemble those of earlier japanning, but the motifs are far more crowded here.

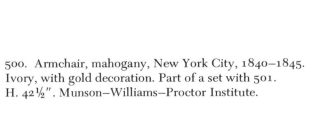

501. Side chair, mahogany, New York City, 1840–1845. Ivory, with gold decoration. Part of a set with 500. H. 33″. Munson–Williams–Proctor Institute.

500. Armchair, mahogany, New York City, 1840–1845. Ivory, with gold decoration. Part of a set with 501. H. 42½″. Munson–Williams–Proctor Institute.

502a

502. Center table, oak and mahogany, probably
New York, 1830–1840. H. 30″. Late black
japanning, with gold decoration. 502a. Top
of 502, diameter 44″. Fountain Elms, Munson–
Williams–Proctor Institute.

503. Cupboard, walnut and pine, Zoar, Ohio, c. 1850. Floral festoons, bowl of fruit, and birds, all on door, in polychrome. W. 48⅜". The Henry Ford Museum.

One of the most successful experimental communal colonies of nineteenth-century America was that founded by German Pietists at Zoar, Ohio. Led by Jacob Bimiler, they established themselves at Zoar in 1817 and continued after his death until final dissolution in 1898. They produced furniture, pottery, ironwork, and paintings, selling them to the public. Their early works were Germanic in character; but as they hired more local craftsmen, their productions became more typically Midwestern. The table (504) is a mirror of its time, while in the decoration on the cupboard door (503), the birds, flowers, and fruits are a faint echo of the Continent.[143]

On the opposite page, the sled is unusual in its woods, mahogany and curled maple, and the two scenes of a steamship and Indians are well done. Governor Frederick Robie of Gorham held Maine's highest office from 1883 to 1887.

The swinging cradle was traditionally made by Martin Linfield of Braintree, Vermont, for his daughter Sarah in 1875. It is decorated with oak graining. As we have seen, the popularity of graining had waned by this time, and pieces in oak graining spell the end of the cycle. An occasional set of late cottage furniture bears this decoration, and it is a mild shock to see pine grained to resemble golden oak!

The cupboard (507) is one of a pair made by a Mississippi City carpenter, G. H. Vierling, for Jefferson Davis' Beauvoir. Vierling was "head carpenter" for the Davis family, doing work at Briarfield and at the Hurricane, the plantation of Davis' eldest brother, Joseph. The cupboards are stained a celadon green. Southern furniture is often stained rather than painted.[144] Based on surviving examples, apparently little of it was decorated in the deep South (see figure 431, page 249).

504. Drop-leaf table, Zoar, Ohio, 1840–1850. Top grained in grays and brown; base stained brown. L. 40⅞". The Henry Ford Museum.

505. Sled, mahogany and curled maple, Maine, 1880s. Decorated in gilt on mahogany, with polychrome scenes. L. 45″. Privately owned.

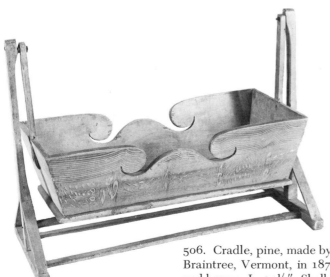

506. Cradle, pine, made by Martin Linfield of Braintree, Vermont, in 1875. Oak graining in yellow and brown. L. 34¼″. Shelburne Museum, Inc.

507. Cupboard, one of a pair, cypress, made in 1879 for Jefferson Davis by G. H. Vierling, Mississippi City, Mississippi. Stained green. W. 45½″. Beauvoir, Jefferson Davis Shrine.

508. The Metropolitan Museum of Art.

Variety was the keynote of the later nineteenth century—sometimes in overwhelming waves. Even cabinetmaking itself was on the move. With improved transportation, factories of the Midwest became the sources of furniture for the people, and the pre-eminence of a New York gave way to a Grand Rapids in the shift from handcraft to mass production. Many cabinetmakers changed professions. William Marcy Tweed, the son of a New York City chairmaker, made painted and gilt chairs as early as 1844 and owned a chair factory until 1858, when his leanings shifted to politics and he started on his way to become Boss Tweed. Not every craftsman was so meteorically fortunate, but the changes of the factory system brought about changes in the workers themselves.

One rather grim part of the painter's work that should be mentioned was the peril encountered in the grinding and handling of white lead and other poisonous materials. In *The Painter, Gilder, and Varnisher's Companion,* "painter's colic" and other maladies are discussed, with advice given to painters on how to avoid and minimize these problems. The author felt that the chewing of tobacco was a guard against poisonous fumes when done in moderation, "for the excessive chewing of tobacco will not only occasion a feeling of stupid languor, which unfits a man for exertion, but may in time bring on a disease almost as much to be dreaded as the evils which it is intended to guard against." [145]

509. Center table, rosewood and marble, probably New York City, 1865–1870. Finials, large boss, and feet are ebonized; gilt incised lines; polychrome porcelain plaque. W. 46¾". The Metropolitan Museum of Art.
510. Stool, labeled by Alexander Roux, New York City, about 1865. Decoration in umber, red, black, and gilt. W. 29¾". The Metropolitan Museum of Art.

The sitting room (508) from the Jedediah Wilcox house, built between 1868 and 1870 in Meriden, Connecticut, captures the opulence of the seventies. The huge over-mantel mirror and matching valances are made of rose-wood, partially ebonized and gilded, with mother-of-pearl cameos. A companion suite of Renaissance revival chairs and a sofa with the same decoration were original furnishings. The center table, also shown above, makes use of similar ebonized and gilt accents and has a col-ored porcelain plaque of a sphinx in the center of the skirt. The building of the Suez Canal in the late fifties was but one factor in the Egyptian craze of the sixties and seventies. It combined with Renaissance revival idi-oms in the center table. Ernest Hagen, a cabinetmaker working in New York at the time, criticized this "most awfull gaudy style" with gilt-brass sphinx heads, gilt en-graved lines, and painted-porcelain medallions. In a 1908 reminiscence of his contemporaries he said, "Other wise, their work was good; but the style horrible." [146] At the right is a stool in what Hagen called "Neo Grec," made by Alexander Roux about 1865. He was one of the best New York makers and his work spanned the middle of the century from Gothic to classical Renaissance. This departure into painted decoration and the "style an-tique" is a sprightly gem.

This large, unfinished "FANCY PAINTING" sign has a brown border and gray center oval, with scrolls, flowers, and cherubs in gold and polychrome. As is the case of so many painted pieces, its author is unknown. The left side of the sign is rather well completed, while the center and right side are not. A small cherub (over the word "PAINTING" at the lower right) blows a trumpet, perhaps unconsciously signaling the end of the era of the decorative painter in this country. From the painter-stainers of the seventeenth century to the fancy and ornamental painters of the 1800s, these men added a colorful and economical warmth to our furniture—a warmth that represents a lasting contribution to American decorative arts.

511. Painter's sign in the form of a palette and brushes, 1870–1885. Found in East Rochester, New Hampshire. H. 57″. Privately owned.

NOTES

NOTE: *While credit is not given for information provided by museums and owners in their catalogues, whether printed or on cards, the author would like to thank all those who have provided this most basic and crucial information.*

1. John Staniford is first recorded in Ipswich in 1678, when he married Margaret Harris. The arrangement of the drawers in the Staniford chest (which are not graduated and are all the same size) has varied over the years, giving different appearances to the chest. They are arranged here as originally shown in 1938 by Irving W. Lyon in articles in *Antiques* and *Old-Time New England* (see Bibliography). Another arrangement is shown in color in Marshall B. Davidson, *The American Heritage History of Colonial Antiques* ([New York]: American Heritage Publishing Co., Inc., 1967), pp. 18–19.

2. Quoted in Irving W. Lyon, *The Colonial Furniture of New England* (Boston and New York: Houghton, Mifflin and Company, 1891), pp. 53, 110. The standard reference on historical colors is Richard M. Candee, *Housepaints in Colonial America—Their Materials, Manufacture, and Application* (New York: Chromatic Publishing Company, 1967). See also John Stalker and George Parker, *A Treatise of Japanning and Varnishing 1688* (London: Alec Tiranti, 1960), pp. 6–8, 69–72; and L. M. A. Roy, "Paint Grinding and Decorating," *Antiques*, LIII (January 1948), 62–63. The earliest widely used manual of instruction for painters was John Bate, *The Excellent Arts and Sciences of Drawing, Colouring, Limning, Paynting, Graving, and Etching* in *The Mysteries of Nature and Art* (London: Andrew Crook, 1654), pp. 117–185. Certain decorative devices in the book, such as those on pages 167 and 189, have close affinities with furniture decoration of the period.

3. See G. R. Marvin, "'Painters Arms' Signs in the Society's Collections," *Proceedings*, The Bostonian Society, 1934, pp. 39–45. Also see Virgil Barker, *American Painting: History and Interpretation* (New York: The Macmillan Company, 1950), pp. 16–20; and *Antiques*, LIV (December 1948), 443.

4. See Houghton Bulkeley, "A Discovery on the Connecticut Chest," *Bulletin*, The Connecticut Historical Society, XXIII (January 1958), 17–19; and Patricia E. Kane, "The Joiners of Seventeenth Century Hartford County," *Bulletin*, The Connecticut Historical Society, XXXV (July 1970), 65–85.

5. Figure 17 is not recorded in Clair F. Luther, *The Hadley Chest* (Hartford, Connecticut: The Case, Lockwood & Brainard Company, 1935). It is similar in its distinctive decoration to those shown on pp. 90 (No. 42), 113 (No. 85), and 114 (not numbered) in Luther. See also Preston R. Bassett, "An Unrecorded Hadley Chest," *Antiques*, LXXV (May 1959), 450, 460–461. It would appear that the former "Coventry type" should now be called "Northampton type."

Figure 16 is similar to Luther, p. 129 (No. 108). Figure 18 is similar to the Hawks and Belding family chests, such as those shown in Luther, pp. 10 (No. 25) and 115 (No. 87).

6. The best discussion of Guilford–Saybrook chests is William L. Warren, "Were the Guilford Painted Chests Made in Saybrook?," *Bulletin*, The Connecticut Historical Society, XXIII (January 1958), 1–10. For use of printers' devices, see Luke Vincent Lockwood, *Colonial Furniture in America* (New York: Charles Scribner's Sons, 1951), I, 349; and Charles F. Montgomery, "Country Furniture: A Symposium," *Antiques*, XCIII (March 1968), 357–358. See also Gillam entry in Ethel Hall Bjerkoe, *The Cabinetmakers of America* (New York: Doubleday & Company, Inc., 1957), pp. 102–104.

7. An interesting photograph showing this chest before restoration is in Wallace Nutting, *Furniture of the Pilgrim Century* (Framingham, Massachusetts: Old America Company, 1921, 1924; reprinted New York: Dover Publications, Inc., 1965), fig. 68.

8. Quoted in Nina Fletcher Little, *American Decorative Wall Painting 1700–1850* (Sturbridge, Massachusetts: Old Sturbridge Village, 1952; reprinted New York: Dutton Paperbacks, 1972), p. 7.

9. Quoted in George Francis Dow, *Every Day Life in the Massachusetts Bay Colony* (Boston: The Society for the Preservation of New England Antiquities, 1935), p. 24.

10. Account book at Winterthur Museum. See Helen Comstock, "An Ipswich Account Book 1707–1762," *Antiques*, LXVI (September 1954), 188–192. White and colored chairs are also listed. The Gaineses also sold lampblack occasionally.

11. See *Antiques*, LXXII (August 1957), inside front cover.

12. This chest is described and discussed in William L. Warren, "More About Painted Chests," *Bulletin*, The Connecticut Historical Society, XXIII (April 1958), 53–54. The Deerfield chest is shown in *Antiques*, XXX (November 1936), 206.

13. "The Tantalizing Chests of Taunton," *Antiques*, XXIII (April 1933), 135–138.

14. See Jean Lipman, *Rufus Porter: Yankee Pioneer* (New York: Clarkson N. Potter, Inc., 1968), pp. 94–103. Porter's subsequent career as an important inventor is fully discussed here, as is his painting.

15. A chest with some similarities in the Garvan collection is illustrated in John T. Kirk, *Early American Furniture* (New York: Alfred A. Knopf, 1970), p. 84.

16. See [John T. Kirk], *Connecticut Furniture: Seventeenth and Eighteenth Centuries* (Hartford, Connecticut: Wadsworth Atheneum, 1967), p. 31. Many other painted chests are in this catalogue. See also Warren, "More About Painted Chests," 58. Reference below is to Dow, *Every Day Life in the Massachusetts Bay Colony*, between pp. 40 and 41.

A box with decoration similar to 53 is illustrated in *Antiques*, XLVI (July 1944), 26.

17. *The Diary of William Bentley, D.D.*, IV (Salem, Massachusetts: The Essex Institute, 1914), 392. For a color photograph of eighteenth-century cedar graining, see Little, *American Decorative Wall Painting*, opposite p. xvi.

18. See Esther Stevens Fraser Brazer, "Pioneer Furniture from Hampton, New Hampshire," *Antiques*, XVII (April 1930), 312–316; and *Antiques*, LXXXVI (July 1964), 85–86.

19. See Nina Fletcher Little, "The Conversation Piece in American Folk Art," *Antiques*, XCIV (November 1968), 744–749; and Mary Black, "The Gansevoort Limner," *Antiques*, XCVI (November 1969), 738–744. Two Dutch *kasten* brought to New York at an early date are shown in Maud Esther Dilliard, *An Album of New Netherland* (New York: Bramhall House, 1963), figs. 96, 97.

20. See Huyler Held, "Chests from Western Long Island," *Antiques*, XXXV (January 1939), 14–15

21. See Gertrude Z. Thomas, "Cane, a Tropical Transplant," *Antiques*, LXXIX (January 1961), 92–95.

Duyckinck quotation above from Rita Susswein Gottesman, *The Arts and Crafts in New York 1726–1776* (New York, The New[-]York Historical Society, 1938), p. 354. "Umber Cullin's Earth" (or Collin's Earth) came from peat bogs near Cologne. It resembled today's Van Dyke browns. Our umber today would have been called "brown ochre" in the 1700s.

22. See Davidson, *Colonial Antiques*, pp. 54, 55.

23. See Richard M. Candee, "The Rediscovery of Milk-based House Paints and the Myth of 'Brickdust and Buttermilk' Paints," *Old-Time New England*, LVIII (Winter 1968), 79–81.

24. See "Puzzles in Furniture," *Antiques*, XXX (September 1936), 207.

25. A handsome English japanned desk-and-bookcase owned by the Warner family of Portsmouth is shown in *Antiques*, LXXVII (January 1960), 78.

26. John Stalker and George Parker, *A Treatise of Japanning and Varnishing 1688* (London: Alec Tiranti, 1960), p. 16. Other quotations on this page from p. xvi. The original edition of Stalker and

Parker has only one "n" in the word "japanning" in the title.

27. Information supplied by Mrs. George E. Downing.

28. *The Boston Evening Post,* January 16 and February 6, 1749. See David Hansen, "Gawen Brown, Soldier and Clockmaker," *Old-Time New England,* XXX (July 1939), 1–9. Known Boston japanners include the following:

Davis, Robert, died 1739. A recently discovered high chest signed by Davis (the japanning in poor condition) is the only known signed example of American japanning.

Gore, John, born 1718. To Halifax, 1778.

Johnson, Benjamin (1740–1818). To Salem, 1763, and Newbury, Massachusetts, c. 1769.

Johnson, John (c. 1753–1789). Painter also.

Johns(t)on, Thomas (1708–1767). Working after 1732. Father of all Johnsons listed here.

Johnson, Thomas, Jr., born 1731.

Mason, David, working 1758.

Partridge, Nehemiah, working 1712 to c. 1714. To New Hampshire.

Pendleton, ——, working 1712.

Randall, William, working 1714–1760.

Rea, Daniel, II, working 1764 on.

Rea, Daniel, III, working 1789 on.

Roberts, Joshua, died 1719.

Waghorne, John, working 1739, 1740.

Whiting, Stephen, working 1758–1771.

William Price, print and map seller, advertised japanned furniture in 1726 "by one late from London," and Mrs. Hiller taught japanning to young ladies from 1748 to 1755. See also Esther Stevens Brazer, "The Early Boston Japanners," *Antiques,* XLIII (May 1943), 208–211.

29. Many later examples of Oriental lacquer work are at the Essex Institute and Peabody Museum, Salem. See also Helen Maggs Fede, *Washington Furniture at Mount Vernon* (Mount Vernon, Virginia: The Mount Vernon Ladies' Association of the Union, 1966), p. 45, for examples ordered by Washington in 1790 and 1795. For later japanning probably done in America, see *Antiques,* LXXXI (April 1962), 346. The changes in techniques of japanning are described in "Japanning," Dobson's *Encyclopædia* (Philadelphia, 1798), IX, 72–76.

30. See Frank Augustine Gardner, *Gardner Memorial* (Salem, Massachusetts: Privately printed, 1933), and Lawrence Shaw Mayo, *The Winthrop Family in America* (Boston: Massachusetts Historical Society, 1948).

31. See Esther Stevens Fraser, "A Pedigreed Lacquered Highboy," *Antiques,* XV (May 1929), 398–401; and an article on Loring, Eva Phillips Boyd, "Jamaica Plain by Way of London," *Old-Time New England,* XLIX (April–June 1959), 85–103.

32. See *Antiques,* XLIII (May 1943), 210. Several of these "combed" decorated looking glasses have been found. The quality of their painted decoration varies a great deal, suggesting that more than one person was responsible for their painting.

33. See Charles S. Parsons, "The Dunlaps of New Hampshire and Their Furniture," *Country Cabinetwork and Simple City Furniture* (Charlottesville, Virginia: The University Press of Virginia, for The Henry Francis du Pont Winterthur Museum, 1970), pp. 109–150; and Parsons, *The Dunlaps & Their Furniture* (Manchester, New Hampshire: The Currier Gallery of Art, 1970). The account book is fully transcribed in the latter, pp. 171–310.

34. Another similar tile-top table is shown in Joseph Downs, *American Furniture: Queen Anne and Chippendale Periods* (New York: The Macmillan Company, 1952), fig. 350.

35. For more on Pennsylvania painted furniture, see Nancy Goyne Evans, "Unsophisticated Furniture Made and Used in Philadelphia and Environs, 1750–1800," *Country Cabinetwork and Simple City Furniture,* pp. 151–203; and Margaret Berwind Schiffer, *Furniture and Its Makers of Chester County, Pennsylvania* (Philadelphia: University of Pennsylvania Press, 1966), pp. 269–277. Marshall advertisement quoted in *APT—Newsletter of the Association for Preservation Technology,* I (August 1969), 10. Ladner advertisement (below) from James H. Craig, *The Arts and Crafts in North Carolina 1699–1840* (Winston-Salem: The Museum of Early Southern Decorative Arts, Old Salem, Inc., 1965), p. 95.

36. George Washington, Mount Vernon Store Book, 1787, No. 798 (June 15). Library of Congress. The Punderson mortality picture is shown in color in Davidson, *Colonial Antiques,* p. 292.

37. For the history of the press and an exhaustive stylistic analysis, see Edwin Wolf 2nd and Robert C. Smith, "A Press for Penn's Pump," *Art Quarterly,* XXIV (Autumn 1961), 227–248.

38. A mahogany Philadelphia Chippendale high chest of drawers with black-painted outlinings is shown in Kirk, *Early American Furniture,* pp. 32, 33. The Blyth bill (above) is in the Edward Lang account book, Essex Institute.

39. See Nicholas B. Wainwright, *Colonial Grandeur in Philadelphia: The House and Furniture of General John Cadwalader* (Philadelphia: The Historical Society of Pennsylvania, 1964), pp. 46, 124, 125.

40. See Downs, *American Furniture,* figs. 281, 282.

41. See E. Milby Burton, *Thomas Elfe, Charleston Cabinet-Maker* (Charleston, South Carolina: The Charleston Museum, 1952), pl. 2, p. 26. A Chippendale Masonic armchair is at The Museum of Early Southern Decorative Arts. See *Antiques,* XCI (January 1967), 109. Also see Richard H. Randall, Jr., "Masonic Senior Warden's Chair," *Connoisseur,* CLXI (August 1966), 286–287.

42. See Harold E. Gillingham, "The Philadelphia Windsor Chair and Its Journeyings," *Pennsylvania Magazine of History and Biography,* LV (1931), 307. Quotation above from *Moreau de St. Méry's American Journey (1793–1798),* ed. and trans. by Kenneth Roberts and Anna M. Roberts (New York: Doubleday and Company, Inc., 1947), p. 264. The best survey of American Windsors is Nancy A. Goyne [Evans], "American Windsor Chairs: A Style Survey," *Antiques,* XCV (April 1969), 538–543.

43. See Nancy A. Goyne [Evans], "Francis Trumble of Philadelphia—Windsor Chair and Cabinetmaker," *Winterthur Portfolio One* (1964), pp. 221–241, especially fig. 5. The Newport Historical Society's chair (one of three) was made for Eliphal Sowle in 1743, according to family tradition. This would appear to be one generation earlier than the chair.

44. Letchworth bill reproduced in Alfred Coxe Prime, *The Arts & Crafts in Philadelphia, Maryland, and South Carolina, 1786–1800.* Series Two. (Topsfield, Massachusetts: The Wayside Press, for The Walpole Society, 1932), opp. p. 240. Apthorp inventory in the Joseph Downs Manuscript and Microfilm Library, Winterthur Museum. De Witt advertisement in Rita Susswein Gottesman, *The Arts and Crafts in New York 1777–1799* (New York: The New-York Historical Society, 1954), p. 115.

45. See Charles B. Wood III, "Mr. Cram's Fan Chair," *Antiques,* LXXXIX (February 1966), 262–264.

46. See Fede, *Washington Furniture at Mount Vernon,* p. 59; and *Antiques,* LXXXIV (December 1963), 725, 731. See also Joe Kindig III, "Upholstered Windsors," *Antiques,* LXII (July 1952), 52–53.

47. Joseph Barrell ms. letter book, 1 March 1795. Massachusetts Historical Society.

48. Quoted in Mabel Munson Swan, "John Ritto Penniman," *Antiques,* XXXIX (May 1941), 248. Seymour bill reproduced in Edwin J. Hipkiss, "A Seymour Bill Discovered," *Antiques,* LI (April 1947), 244.

49. Information supplied by former owner. Also see Joe Kindig III, "The Perspective Glass," *Antiques,* LXV (June 1954), 466–468. In 1793 Derby bought "an optical machine for viewing prints" and "6 doz. perspective prints" from John Prince, Salem clergyman and instrument dealer (Derby papers, Essex Institute, XXXI, 62). Two perspective glasses are listed in Derby's inventory: one in his mansion and one at his farm. Quotation below from Derby papers. Bill reprinted in Mabel Munson Swan, "Where Elias Hasket Derby Bought His Furniture," *Antiques,* XX (November 1931), 281.

50. Cabinetmaker unidentified. See *Bulletin,* The Connecticut Historical Society, IX (January 1943), 15.

51. Ms. account book, William Gray (1774–1814), Salem, Massachusetts, and Portsmouth, New Hampshire (for a few

years after 1800), Essex Institute.

Candlestand (fig. 165) is illustrated in color in Marshall B. Davidson, *The American Heritage History of American Antiques from the Revolution to the Civil War* ([New York]: American Heritage Publishing Co., Inc., 1968), p. 183.

52. *American Citizen*, June 6, 1804; quoted in Rita Susswein Gottesman, *The Arts and Crafts in New York 1800–1804* (New York: The New-York Historical Society, 1965), p. 273.

53. See "The Crowninshield–Bentley House," Essex Institute *Historical Collections*, XCVII (April 1961), 91. Corwin portrait illustrated in fig. 17 and described on pp. 152, 153. Box for Maria's wedding is illustrated in Dean A. Fales, Jr., *Essex County Furniture: Documented Treasures from Local Collections 1660–1860* (Salem, Massachusetts: Essex Institute, 1965), fig. 52.

54. *New-York Gazette and General Advertiser*, February 22, 1797; quoted in Gottesman, *The Arts and Crafts in New York 1777–1799*, p. 113. Whangee is a bamboo-like plant that grows in China and Japan. Similar mahogany chairs are illustrated in Charles F. Montgomery, *American Furniture: The Federal Period* (New York: The Viking Press, A Winterthur Book, 1966), figs. 61, 62.

55. See Montgomery, *American Furniture: The Federal Period*, fig. 184.

56. For a discussion of Boston and Salem dressing chests, see Richard H. Randall, Jr., "Works of Boston Cabinetmakers, 1795–1825: Part I," *Antiques*, LXXXI (February 1962), 186–189.

57. *Pennsylvania Packet*, April 30, 1787; quoted in Prime, *The Arts & Crafts in Philadelphia . . .* Series Two, p. 188. Armchair (fig. 182) is illustrated in color in Davidson, *American Antiques*, p. 23.

58. See Montgomery, *American Furniture: The Federal Period*, fig. 491; and Richard H. Randall, Jr., *American Furniture in The Museum of Fine Arts, Boston* (Boston: Museum of Fine Arts, 1965), fig. 183.

59. See Swan, "Where Elias Hasket Derby Bought His Furniture," *Antiques*, XX (November 1931), 282. Also see Mabel M. Swan, "The Man Who Made Simon Willard's Clock Cases," *Antiques*, XV (March 1929), 196–200; Montgomery, *American Furniture: The Federal Period*, pp. 60, 256; and Randall, *American Furniture*, pp. 150, 258–259. The entire bed is illustrated in Randall, figs. 214, 214a.

60. Swan, "Where Elias Hasket Derby Bought His Furniture," 282.

61. James Smith, *Maryland Journal* (Baltimore), November 16, 1792. For an excellent description of gilding, see Ralph Edwards, *The Shorter Dictionary of English Furniture* (London: Country Life Limited, 1964), pp. 320–321. Also see "Gilding" in Thomas Sheraton, *The Cabinet Dictionary* (New York: Praeger Publishers, 1970), II, 222–232. (Reprint of original 1803 edition.)

62. See Martha Gandy Fales, "Looking Glasses Used in America," *The Concise Encyclopedia of American Antiques*, ed. Helen Comstock (New York: Hawthorn Books, Inc., n.d.), I, 72–78. Girandole mirror (fig. 197) is shown in color in Davidson, *American Antiques*, p. 95.

63. In 1798 John Smith of Philadelphia advertised portraits of the Washingtons on "vitrified stained glass." See Prime, *The Arts & Crafts in Philadelphia . . .* Series Two, pp. 158–159.

Regarding figure 198, a print of the Robertson painting *New York from Hobuck Ferry House* was published in London in 1800 and probably served as the direct inspiration for the looking glass tablet.

64. Gottesman, *The Arts and Crafts in New York 1800–1804*, p. 164. Chimney glass (fig. 204) is shown in color in Davidson, *American Antiques*, p. 45.

65. See Norman S. Rice, *New York Furniture Before 1840* (Albany, New York: Albany Institute of History and Art, 1962), pp. 48, 49.

66. See *Baltimore Furniture: The Work of Baltimore and Annapolis Cabinetmakers from 1760 to 1810* (Baltimore: The Baltimore Museum of Art, 1947), p. 193. Other examples with painted-glass panels are shown on pp. 60, 61, 125, and 127. The large glass panels of figure 206 are restorations based on damaged extant originals. Montgomery citation (below), p. 233.

67. A lady's secretary very similar to figure 209 is shown in Vernon C. Stoneman, *A Supplement to John and Thomas Seymour: Cabinetmakers in Boston 1794–1816* (Boston: Special Publications, 1965), p. 29. Figure 211 is shown in color in Davidson, *American Antiques*, p. 63.

68. See Swan, "The Man Who Made Simon Willard's Clocks," *Antiques*, XV (March 1929), 196–200; and Montgomery, *American Furniture: The Federal Period*, pp. 191–194 and nos. 158–163.

69. See Prime, *The Arts & Crafts in Philadelphia . . .* Series Two, p. 160. From *Maryland Gazette*, December 28, 1790.

70. See R. L. Raley, "Irish Influences in Baltimore Decorative Arts, 1785–1815," *Antiques*, LXXIX (March 1961), 276–279. Also see Rodris Roth, "Interior Decoration of City Houses in Baltimore: The Federal Period," *Winterthur Portfolio 5* (1969), 59–86.

71. Letter from Latrobe to Madison, June 10, 1812, papers of James Madison, No. 48, Library of Congress: "Oct. 1809 To Messr. John & Hugh Finlay, chairs & sofas $1,111." See also R. L. Raley, "Interior Designs by Benjamin Henry Latrobe for the President's House," *Antiques*, LXXV (June 1959), 568–571.

72. Research done by John H. Hill on the Finlays' advertisements is in Montgomery, *American Furniture: The Federal Period*, pp. 446–448. For a listing of buildings (and owners) shown on the set, see *Baltimore Furniture . . . 1760 to 1810*, p. 156.

73. Advertisement in *Federal Gazette & Baltimore Daily Advertiser*, November 8, 1805. See preceding footnote.

74. Information supplied by The Baltimore Museum of Art. Pieces of this set include three side chairs, a settee, window seat, and card table at Winterthur; four side chairs and a pier table at The Baltimore Museum of Art; and other pieces privately owned.

75. Office of the Register of Wills of Baltimore County, Liber 38. Information kindly supplied by Robert L. Raley.

76. See Montgomery, *American Furniture: The Federal Period*, pp. 368–370.

77. Quotation in Montgomery, *American Furniture: The Federal Period*, p. 457.

78. Quotation in Emilie Rich Underhill, "Our Fancy Chairs Adopt Sheraton Details," in *The Ornamented Chair: Its Development in America (1700–1890)*, ed. Zilla Rider Lea (Rutland, Vermont: Charles E. Tuttle Company, for the Esther Stevens Brazer Guild of the Historical Society of Early American Decoration, Inc., 1960), p. 38.

79. Sanderson Papers, Essex Institute. See Mabel M. Swan, *Samuel McIntire, Carver, and the Sandersons, Early Salem Cabinet Makers* (Salem, Massachusetts: The Essex Institute, 1934), pp. 27, 28.

80. Figure 242 is shown in color in Davidson, *American Antiques*, pp. 114–115. For general introduction to this period, see Berry B. Tracy, "The Decorative Arts," in *Classical America 1815–1845* (Newark, New Jersey: The Newark Museum, 1963), pp. 10–33; and Tracy, Introduction, *19th-Century American Furniture and Other Decorative Arts* (New York: The Metropolitan Museum of Art, 1970), pp. x–xxxii.

81. From B. H. Latrobe, "Anniversary Oration Before the Society of Artists of the United States" (May 11), *Port-Folio*, V (June 1811), 10–17.

82. Raley, "Interior Designs by Benjamin Henry Latrobe for the President's House," p. 569. See footnote 71.

83. From *The Laws of Harmonious Colouring* (London, 1847), quoted in Marjorie Ward Selden, *The Interior Paint of the Campbell–Whittlesey House 1835–1836* (Rochester, New York: The Society for the Preservation of Landmarks in Western New York, 1949), pp. 22, 23.

84. See Berry B. Tracy, "For 'One of the Most Genteel Residences in the City,'" The Metropolitan Museum of Art *Bulletin*, XXV (April 1967), 283–291.

85. See "99. To Prepare an Imitation of Gold Bronze," in Rufus Porter, *A Select Collection of Valuable and Curious Arts, and Interesting Experiments* (Concord, New Hampshire: Rufus Porter, 1825), p. 81. Also see "1. Water-proof Gilding and Silvering," pp. 9, 10; "2. The Art of Burnish Gilding," pp. 11, 12; and "3. Ornamental Bronze Gilding," pp. 12, 13.

86. See Tracy, *Classical America 1815–1845*, pp. 55, 77: fig. 38. Also see J. Stewart Johnson, "The Egyptian Revival in the Decorative Arts," *Antiques*, XC (October 1966), 489–494.

87. Advertisement of Joseph Adam Fleming, *New-York Independent Journal . . .*, February 2, 1785; in Gottesman, *The Arts and Crafts in New York 1777–1799*, pp. 117, 118.

88. Advertisement of Thomas & Caldcleugh, *Federal Gazette* (Baltimore), January 20, 1808.

In Ebenezer Tracy's inventory (1803), stone yellow and lampblack are listed, as is a "Marble paint Vat & Grinder."

89. For figures 265 and 266, see David B. Warren, "The Empire Style at Bayou Bend: New Period Rooms in Houston," *Antiques*, XCVII (January 1970), 122–127.

90. Sheraton, *The Cabinet Dictionary*, II, 299. For information on Buttre, see Montgomery, *American Furniture: The Federal Period*, pp. 459, 479. The 1829–1830 Albany directory does not list Buttre. Two earlier advertisements from his New York City period, showing single-cross-back fancy chairs, are in Esther Stevens Fraser [Brazer], "Painted Furniture in America. I. The Sheraton Fancy Chair 1790–1817," *Antiques*, V (June 1924), 302.

91. See Walter Muir Whitehill, *George Crowninshield's Yacht Cleopatra's Barge and a Catalogue of the Francis B. Crowninshield Gallery* (Salem, Massachusetts: The Peabody Museum, 1959).

92. Information kindly supplied by Kenneth D. Roberts, Curator, American Clock & Watch Museum, Bristol, Connecticut.

93. See John Ware Willard, *A History of Simon Willard, Inventor and Clockmaker* (Boston, 1911; retitled *Simon Willard and His Clocks* and reprinted Mamaroneck, New York: Paul P. Appel, 1962; also reprinted New York: Dover Publications, Inc., 1968), pp. 63, 64. Other comments on painting are on pp. 48, 62. Information kindly supplied by Charles S. Parsons.

94. See Brooks Palmer, "Acorn Clocks," *Antiques*, LV (March 1949), 192–194.

95. Sarah Anna Emery, *Reminiscences of a Nonagenarian* (Newburyport, Massachusetts: William H. Huse & Co., 1879), p. 222.

96. The box (fig. 289) is shown in color in Nina Fletcher Little, *The Abby Aldrich Rockefeller Folk Art Collection* (Boston and Toronto: Little, Brown and Company, for Colonial Williamsburg, 1957), p. 215.

97. Emery, *Reminiscences*, p. 233. She repeats this in *My Generation* (Newburyport, Massachusetts: Moses H. Sargent, 1893), p. 56. See also John J. Currier, *History of Newburyport, Mass., 1764–1909*, II (Newburyport, Massachusetts: Privately printed, 1909), 294–295.

98. Information kindly supplied by owner. See Gertrude J. Taylor, "Mrs. Susanna Rowson, 1762–1824; An Early English-American Career-Woman," *Old-Time New England*, XXXV (April 1945), 71–74. Also see Jane C. Giffen, "Susanna Rowson and Her Academy," *Antiques*, XCVIII (September 1970), 436–440. Other known academy worktables were decorated in Portsmouth, New Hampshire, and in Newbury, Northampton, and Salem, Massachusetts.

99. The writings on Hitchcock chairs are nearly as voluminous as the marked chairs themselves. See Esther Stevens Fraser [Brazer], "Random Notes on Hitchcock and His Competitors," *Antiques*, XXX (August 1936), 63–67; and Alice Winchester, "The ABC's of Hitchcock Chairs," *Antiques*, XLI (June 1942), 369–370: reprinted *Antiques*, LXI (March 1952), 256–257.

100. *A List of Patents Granted by the United States from April 10, 1790 to December 31, 1836* (Washington, 1872).

For the techniques of stenciling, see Janet Waring, *Early American Stencils on Walls and Furniture* (New York: Dover Publications, Inc., 1968; reprint of 1937 edition), pp. 87–135; and L. M. A. Roy, "Redecorating a Hitchcock Chair," *Antiques*, LVI (August 1949), 110–112.

101. Eaton's stencils and tools are at The Society for the Preservation of New England Antiquities in Boston, with many other stencils and tools used by wall and furniture decorators. See Marjorie W. von Suck, "The Janet Waring Collection of Stencils," *Old-Time New England*, XLIV (Spring 1954), 100–102. See also Little, *American Decorative Wall Painting*, pp. 99–106; and Waring, *Early American Stencils*, pp. 19–86.

102. Advertisement reproduced in Waring, *Early American Stencils*, p. 108.

103. See Montgomery, *American Furniture: The Federal Period*, p. 456.

104. See Waring, *Early American Stencils*, figs. 126, 153; and Shirley DeVoe, "Hudson River Scene Cornices," *The Decorator Digest*, ed. Natalie Allen Ramsey (Rutland, Vermont: Charles E. Tuttle Co., Inc., for the Historical Society of Early American Decoration, Inc., 1965), pp. 192–196.

105. Nathaniel Whittock, *The Decorative Painters' and Glaziers' Guide* (London: Isaac Taylor Hinton, 1828), p. 72.

106. See Frank O. Spinney, "Joseph H. Davis," in *Primitive Painters in America 1750–1950*, ed. Jean Lipman and Alice Winchester (New York: Dodd Mead & Company, 1950), pp. 97–105; and Nina Fletcher Little, "New Light on Joseph H. Davis, 'Left Hand Painter,'" *Antiques*, XCVIII (November 1970), 754–757.

107. Waldo Tucker, *The Mechanic's Assistant* (Windsor, Vermont, 1837), p. 29. In his instructions for mahogany graining (pp. 156–157) he recommends "strong beer" be used for the grinding of pigments.

108. *Kennebunk Gazette*, January 5 and July 7, 1832.

109. From Mrs. Ellen Hobbs Robbins, "My Grandfather's House," in *New England Bygones* (Philadelphia, 1883), quoted in *Old-Time New England*, XV (October 1924), 79.

110. London, 1828, p. 48.

111. Advertisement of Malcolm & Palmer, *Newbern Spectator*, March 21, 1829, in Craig, *The Arts and Crafts in North Carolina 1699–1840*, p. 100.

112. Craig, p. 103.

113. For a further discussion of this technique, see Esther Stevens Brazer, *Early American Decoration* (Springfield, Massachusetts: The Pond–Elsberg Company, 1940), p. 131.

114. P. 31. Another painted Sheraton New Hampshire card table, probably made by John Wilder of Keene, is illustrated in *Antiques*, XCIX (March 1971), 348.

115. Information kindly supplied by Philip F. Purrington, Curator of the Old Dartmouth Historical Society Whaling Museum, New Bedford, Massachusetts.

116. White MS., Old Sturbridge Village.

117. Porter, *A Select Collection of Valuable and Curious Arts*, p. 31.

118. From *Western Carolinian* (Salisbury), May 13, 1828, in Craig, *The Arts and Crafts in North Carolina 1699–1840*, p. 100.

119. See Little, *American Decorative Wall Painting 1700–1850*, pp. 66–79. The Custis letter, April 10, 1723, is quoted on p. 66.

120. Another tall clock with imaginative painted graining and inlay from Massachusetts is at Old Sturbridge Village. See *Antiques*, XCIII (March 1968), 326.

121. See *Bulletin*, The Connecticut Historical Society, IX (January 1943), 12. On page 13, instructions are given "to gain the Colour of Cherry wood the appearance of mahogany"—a practice done frequently in the early periods. All[e] wine advertisements are in Prime, *The Arts & Crafts in Philadelphia . . .* Series Two, pp. 165–166.

122. For a study of a turn-of-the-century rural craftsman who made Windsors, see Henry J. Harlow, "The Shop of Samuel Wing, Craftsman of Sandwich, Massachusetts," *Antiques*, XCIII (March 1968), 372–377.

123. From reminiscences written by Mary Angeline (Walkley) Beach (1824–1897) about her childhood in the Stephen Walkley house, Southington, Connecticut. See "Notes on Furnishing a Small New England Farmhouse," *Old-Time New England*, XLVIII (Winter 1958), 79.

124. Beekman inventory in Joseph Downs Manuscript and Microfilm Library, Winterthur Museum. Also see Sarah Anna Emery, *My Generation*, p. 116. A Boston armchair with yellow ground is illustrated in *Antiques*, LXXXIII (January 1963), 70. Figure 422 was restored about 1925 by Helen C. Hagar of Salem. Raymond also made arrow-back Windsors.

125. Gottesman, *The Arts and Crafts in New York 1800–1804*, pp. 141–142.

126. From Craig, *The Arts and Crafts in North Carolina 1699–1840*, p. 226. Thumb-back and children's Windsors are known by Brown. For chairs by Joel Pratt, Jr., see Celia Jackson Otto, *American Furniture of the Nineteenth Century* (New York: The Viking Press, 1965), fig. 118 (arrow-back armchair); *The Ornamented Chair*, ed. Zilla Rider Lea, p. 125 (rocking armchair); and *Antiques*, C (July 1971), 74 (arrow-back side chair).

127. See E. Boyd, "Antiques in New Mexico," *Antiques*, XLIV (August 1943), 58–62; and Alan C. Vedder, "New Mexico Spanish Colonial Art for Britain," *Antiques*, LXXXIII (May 1963), 553–556.

For other painted pieces from the Midwest, see *Antiques*, LXXXVII (March 1965), 314–315.

128. See Edward Deming Andrews, *The People Called Shakers* (New York: Oxford University Press, 1953).

129. Quotation in John Joseph Stoudt, *Early Pennsylvania Arts and Crafts* (New York: A. S. Barnes and Company, Inc., 1964), p. 26. See also Clarence W. Brazer, "Pennsylvania German Decorations," in *The Decorator Digest*, Ramsey, ed., pp. 214–221.

130. Jedidiah Morse, *The American Universal Geography* (Boston, 1805), I, 548.

131. Another "Maser" chest is illustrated in *Antiques*, LXXI (June 1957), 545. A cupboard is in *Antiques*, LX (July 1951), 16.

132. The clock (fig. 473) is shown in color in Davidson, *Colonial Antiques*, p. 318.

133. The dough trough (fig. 489) is shown in color in Davidson, *Colonial Antiques*, p. 323. For information on Lehn, see Earl L. Poole, "Joseph Lehn, Driven to Design," in *The Decorator Digest*, Ramsey, ed., pp. 209–213. (Reprinted from *The American German Review;* also appeared as *Bulletin* No. 20, School District of Reading, Pennsylvania, Museum and Art Gallery.)

134. Information kindly supplied by Harley J. McKee. See also *APT—Newsletter of the Association for Preservation Technology*, I (August 1969), 18.

135. See Shirley Spaulding DeVoe, "The Litchfield Manufacturing Company, Makers of Japanned Papier Mâché," *Antiques*, LXXVIII (August 1960), 150–153.

136. Tenth ed. (Philadelphia: Henry Carey Baird, 1869), pp. 162–164. Published in 1850, this book was in its sixteenth revised edition by 1889. It owes a great deal to Nathaniel Whittock's work.

137. The first stanza of the poem reads:

Oh! the firm rock, the wave-worn rock,
That braved the blast and the billows' shock;
It was born with time on a barren shore,
And it laughed with scorn at the ocean's roar.
'T was here that the first Pilgrim band,
Came weary up to the foaming strand;
And the tree they reared in the days gone by,
It lives, it lives, it lives, and ne'er shall die.

138. *The Architecture of Country Houses* (New York: D. Appleton & Company, 1850; reprinted New York: Dover Publications, Inc., 1969), p. 415.

139. See Joseph S. Van Why, "The Harriet Beecher Stowe House in Nook Farm," *Antiques*, XCIV (September 1968), 376–381.

140. From Henry W. Cleaveland and Samuel D. Backus, *Village and Farm Cottages* (New York, 1855), p. 126, quoted in *APT—Newsletter of the Association for Preservation Technology*, I (August 1969), 13–14. For Salem Charitable Mechanics Association awards, see Essex Institute *Historical Collections*, LXXXVIII (July 1952), 276.

141. The sofa is illustrated in Comstock, *American Furniture*, fig. 630. See also Comstock, figs. 604, 617, 631, and 632.

142. Downing, *The Architecture of Country Houses*, p. 429.

143. See John Ramsay, "Zoar and Its Industries," *Antiques*, XLVI (December 1944), 333–335; and *Antiques*, LXXXVII (March 1965), 315.

144. In 1830 young Jefferson Davis had made some furniture himself. See *Antiques*, XCIX (March 1971), 432, 434.

A pine wardrobe with painted graining made about 1865 by Jacob Pfeil of New Braunfels, Texas, is illustrated in *Antiques*, C (July 1971), 76.

145. Tenth ed. (Philadelphia, 1869), pp. 183–184.

146. Elizabeth A. Ingerman, "Personal Experiences of an Old New York Cabinetmaker," *Antiques*, LXXXIV (November 1963), 579–580. See also *19th-Century America* (New York: The Metropolitan Museum of Art, 1970), figs. 166, 168, 176, 177, and 179.

BIBLIOGRAPHY

NOTE: *The listings in this bibliography are selective and have bearing on painted furniture.*

I. GENERAL

A. Books and Catalogues

American Naïve Painting of the 18th and 19th Centuries. New York: The American Federation of Arts, 1969.

America's Arts and Skills. New York: E. P. Dutton & Co., Inc., 1957.

Andrews, Edward Deming. *The People Called Shakers.* New York: Oxford University Press, 1953.

——, and Andrews, Faith. *Shaker Furniture—the Craftsmanship of an American Communal Sect.* New Haven, Connecticut: Yale University Press, 1937; reprinted New York: Dover Publications, Inc., 1950.

Barker, Virgil. *American Painting: History and Interpretation.* New York: The Macmillan Company, 1950.

Bell, J. Munro (ed.). *The Furniture Designs of Chippendale, Hepplewhite and Sheraton.* New York: Robert M. McBride & Company, 1938; reprinted New York: Tudor Publishing Company, 1940.

Bentley, William. *The Diary of William Bentley, D.D.* 4 vols. Salem, Massachusetts: Essex Institute, 1905–1914.

Bjerkoe, Ethel Hall. *The Cabinetmakers of America.* New York: Doubleday & Company, Inc., 1957.

Brazer, Esther Stevens. *Early American Decoration.* Springfield, Massachusetts: The Pond–Ekberg Company, 1940; reprinted 1961.

Butler, Joseph T. *American Antiques: 1800–1900.* New York: The Odyssey Press, 1965.

Candee, Richard M. *Housepaints in Colonial America–Their Materials, Manufacture, and Application.* New York: Chromatic Publishing Company, 1967.

Comstock, Helen. *American Furniture: Seventeenth, Eighteenth, and Nineteenth Century Styles.* New York: The Viking Press, 1962.

——. *The Looking Glass in America 1700–1825.* New York: The Viking Press, 1964, 1968.

Cummings, Abbott Lowell. "Decorative Painters and House Painting at Massachusetts Bay in the First Period (1630–1725)," unpublished MS. from the author's forthcoming study on the seventeenth-century architecture of Massachusetts.

Davidson, Marshall B. *The American Heritage History of American Antiques from the Revolution to the Civil War.* [New York]: American Heritage Publishing Co., Inc., 1968.

——. *The American Heritage History of Antiques from the Civil War to World War I.* [New York]: American Heritage Publishing Co., Inc., 1969.

——. *The American Heritage History of Colonial Antiques.* [New York]: American Heritage Publishing Co., Inc., 1967.

Downing, Andrew Jackson. *The Architecture of Country Houses.* New York: D. Appleton & Company, 1850; reprinted New York: Dover Publications, Inc., 1969.

Downs, Joseph. *American Furniture: Queen Anne and Chippendale Periods.* New York: The Macmillan Company, 1952.

Eberlein, Harold Donaldson, and McClure, Abbot. *The Practical Book of Period Furniture.* Philadelphia and London: J. B. Lippincott Company, 1914.

Edwards, Ralph. *The Shorter Dictionary of English Furniture.* London: Country Life Limited, 1964.

Englefield, W. A. D. *The History of the Painter-Stainers Company of London.* London: Chapman and Dodd, 1923.

Fede, Helen Maggs. *Washington Furniture at Mount Vernon.* Mount Vernon, Virginia: The Mount Vernon Ladies' Association of the Union, 1966.

Gettens, Rutherford J., and Stout, George L. *Painting Materials.* New York: Van Nostrand, 1942.

Gould, Mary Earle. *Early American Wooden Ware.* Springfield, Massachusetts: The Pond–Ekberg Company, 1942. (Chapter 11 deals with paints.)

Groce, George C., and Wallace, David H. *The New-York Historical Society's Dictionary of Artists in America, 1564–1860.* New Haven, Connecticut: Yale University Press, 1957.

Hallett, Charles. *Furniture Decoration Made Easy.* Boston: C. T. Branford Company, 1952.

Hansen, H. J. (ed.). *European Folk Art in Europe and the Americas.* New York and Toronto: McGraw-Hill Book Company, 1968.

Hipkiss, Edwin J. *Eighteenth-Century American Arts: The M. and M. Karolik Collection.* Cambridge, Massachusetts: Harvard University Press, for the Museum of Fine Arts, Boston, 1941.

Hogarth, William. *The Analysis of Beauty.* London, 1753; reprinted London: R. Scholey, 1810.

Honour, Hugh. *Chinoiserie: The Vision of Cathay.* London: John Murray, 1961.

Kirk, John T. *Early American Furniture.* New York: Alfred A. Knopf, 1970.

Lea, Zilla Rider (ed.). *The Ornamented Chair: Its Development in America (1700–1890).* Rutland, Vermont: Charles E. Tuttle Company, for the Esther Stevens Brazer Guild of the Historical Society of Early American Decoration, Inc., 1960.

Lipman, Jean, and Meulendyke, Eve. *American Folk Decoration.* New York: Oxford University Press, 1951.

——, and Winchester, Alice (eds.). *Primitive Painters in America 1750–1950.* New York: Dodd Mead & Company, 1950.

Little, Nina Fletcher. *The Abby Aldrich Rockefeller Folk Art Collection.* Boston and Toronto: Little, Brown and Company, for Colonial Williamsburg, 1957.

——. *American Decorative Wall Painting 1700–1850.* Sturbridge, Massachusetts: Old Sturbridge Village, 1952; reprinted New York: Dutton Paperbacks, 1972.

——. *Land and Seascape as Observed by the Folk Artist.* Williamsburg, Virginia: Colonial Williamsburg, Inc., 1969.

Metropolitan Museum of Art, The. *19th-Century America: Furniture and Other Decorative Arts.* New York: The Metropolitan Museum of Art, 1970.

Montgomery, Charles F. *American Furniture: The Federal Period.* New York: The Viking Press, A Winterthur Book, 1966.

Morse, John D. (ed.). *Country Cabinetwork and Simple City Furniture.* Charlottesville, Virginia: The University Press of Virginia, for The Henry Francis du Pont Winterthur Museum, 1970.

Nutting, Wallace. *Furniture of the Pilgrim Century.* Framingham, Massachusetts: Old America Company, 1921, 1924; reprinted New York: Dover Publications, Inc., 1965.

——. *Furniture Treasury.* Framingham, Massachusetts: Old America Company, 1928–1933; reprinted New York: The Macmillan Company, 1948, 1954.

Otto, Celia Jackson. *American Furniture of the Nineteenth Century.* New York: The Viking Press, 1965.

Palmer, Brooks. *The Book of American Clocks.* New York: The Macmillan Company, 1950.

Porter, Arthur L. *The Chemistry of the Arts.* Philadelphia: Carey & Lea, 1830.

Ramsey, Natalie Allen (ed.). *The Decorator Digest.* Rutland, Vermont: Charles E. Tuttle Co., Inc., for the Historical Society of Early American Decoration, Inc., 1965.

Randall, Richard H., Jr. *American Furniture in the Museum of Fine Arts, Boston.* Boston: Museum of Fine Arts, 1965.

Sack, Albert. *Fine Points of Furniture: Early American.* New York: Crown Publishers, Inc., 1950.

Schwartz, Marvin D. *Country Style.* Brooklyn, New York: The Brooklyn Museum, 1956.

Sweeney, John A. H. *Winterthur Illustrated.* New York: Chanticleer Press, for The Henry Francis du Pont Winterthur Museum, 1963.

Toller, Jane. *Papier-Mâché in Great Britain and America.* Newton, Massachusetts: Charles T. Branford Company, 1962.

Tracy, Berry B. "The Decorative Arts," in *Classical America 1815–1845.* Newark, New Jersey: The Newark Museum, 1963.

Ward-Jackson, Peter. *English Furniture Designs of the Eighteenth Century.* London: Her Majesty's Stationery Office, 1958.

Waring, Janet. *Early American Stencils on Walls and Furniture.* New York: William R. Scott, Inc., 1937; reprinted New York: Dover Publications, Inc., 1968.

Winchester, Alice (ed.). *The Antiques Treasury.* New York: E. P. Dutton & Company, Inc., 1959.

Wright, Florence E. *How to Stencil Chairs.* Penn Yan, New York, 1949. Fifth printing, 1966.

B. Articles

[Brazer], Esther Stevens Fraser. "The Golden Age of Stencilling," *Antiques,* I (April 1922), 162–166.

——. "Painted Furniture in America. I. The Sheraton Fancy Chair 1790–1817," *Antiques,* V (June 1924), 302–306; "II. The Period of Stencilling 1817–1835," *Antiques,* VI (September 1924), 141–146; "III. The Decadent Period 1835–1845," *Antiques,* VII (January 1925), 15–17.

——. "Some Decorated Woodenware of the 1830's," *Antiques,* XIII (April 1928), 289.

Candee, Richard M. "The Rediscovery of Milk-based House Paints and the Myth of 'Brickdust and Buttermilk' Paints," *Old-Time New England,* LVIII (Winter 1968), 79–81.

Carson, Marian Sadtler. "Early American Water Color Painting," *Antiques,* LIX (January 1951), 54–56.

Copeland, Charles H. P. "Japanese Export Furniture," *Antiques,* LXVI (July 1954), 50–51.

"Country Furniture: A Symposium," *Antiques,* XCIII (March 1968), 342–371.

Downs, Joseph. "American Japanned Furniture," *Old-Time New England,* XXVIII (October 1937), 61–67. Reprinted from *Bulletin of the Metropolitan Museum of Art,* March 1933.

[Evans], Nancy A. Goyne. "American Windsor Chairs: A Style Survey," *Antiques,* XCV (April 1969), 538–543.

Fales, Martha Gandy. "Looking Glasses Used in America," *The Concise Encyclopedia of American Antiques,* Helen Comstock (ed.). New York: Hawthorn Books, Inc. [1958], I, 72–78.

Halm, Philipp Maria. "The Peasant Furniture of Southern Germany," *Antiques,* XV (January 1929), 34–39.

Johnson, J. Stewart. "The Egyptian Revival in the Decorative Arts," *Antiques,* XC (October 1966), 489–494.

Keyes, Homer Eaton. "Introducing Stencilled Furniture," *Antiques,* I (April 1922), 154–155.

Kindig, Joe, III. "The Perspective Glass," *Antiques,* LXV (June 1954), 466–468.

———. "Upholstered Windsors," *Antiques*, LXII (July 1952), 52–53.

Kirk, John T. "Sources of Some American Regional Furniture," *Antiques*, LXXXVIII (December 1965), 790–798.

Lehmann, Hans. "The Painted Peasant Furniture of Switzerland," *Antiques*, XIII (April and June 1928), 282–284 and 486–489.

Little, Nina Fletcher. "Coach, Sign and Fancy Painting," *Old-Time New England*, XLV (April–June 1955), 83–87. From *Art in America*, May 1945.

———. "'Deception Pieces' in Architectural Painting," *Antiques*, LXII (October 1952), 304–307.

———. "Picture Frames with Painted Decoration, 1775–1850," *Antiques*, LXXIV (September 1958), 242–245.

"More About Upholstered Windsors," *Antiques*, LXIII (June 1953), 526–527.

"Paint Color Research and House Painting Practices," *APT—Newsletter of the Association for Preservation Technology*, I (August 1969), 5–20. See also I (December 1969), 21–24.

Price, E. L. "The Art of Lacquering," *Antiques*, XXII (November 1932), 183–185.

Raley, Robert L. "Irish Influences in Baltimore Decorative Arts, 1785–1815," *Antiques*, LXXIX (March 1961), 276–279.

Ralston, Ruth. "The Style Antique in Furniture, I. Its Sources and Its Creators," *Antiques*, XLVII (May 1945), 278–281 and 288–289; "II. Its American Manifestations and Their Prototypes," *Antiques*, XLVIII (October 1945), 206–209 and 220–223.

Riff, Adolphe. "Old Alsatian Marriage Chests," *Antiques*, XII (July 1927), 36–38.

Roy, L. M. A. "Paint Grinding and Decorating," *Antiques*, LIII (January 1948), 62–63.

Schwartz, Marvin D. "American Painted Furniture Before the Classic Revival," *Antiques*, LXIX (April 1956), 342–345.

Selden, Marjorie Ward. "Colors Used in Early Wall Painting," *Antiques*, LV (May 1949), 354.

Spinney, Frank O. "Country Furniture," *Antiques*, LXIV (August 1953), 114–117.

Thomas, Gertrude Z. "Lacquer: Chinese, Indian, 'right' Japan, and American," *Antiques*, LXXIX (June 1961), 572–575.

Tolman, Ruel Pardee. "Human Hair as a Pigment," *Antiques*, VIII (December 1925), 353.

Von Suck, Marjorie W. "The Janet Waring Collection of Stencils," *Old-Time New England*, XLIV (Spring 1954), 100–102.

"The Windsors in the Washingtons' Parlor," *Antiques*, LXXXIV (December 1963), 725, 731.

II. REGIONAL

A. Books and Catalogues

Baltimore Furniture: The Work of Baltimore and Annapolis Cabinetmakers from 1760 to 1810. Baltimore: The Baltimore Museum of Art, 1947.

Belknap, Henry Wyckoff. *Artists and Craftsmen of Essex County, Massachusetts*. Salem, Massachusetts: Essex Institute, 1927.

Bulkeley, Houghton. *Contributions to Connecticut Cabinet Making*. Bloomfield, Connecticut: The Connecticut Historical Society, 1967.

Corbett, Michael S. "Variegated Architectural Painting in Otsego County, New York" (unpublished master's thesis, Cooperstown Graduate Programs, 1968).

Craig, James H. *The Arts and Crafts in North Carolina 1699–1840*. Winston-Salem, North Carolina: The Museum of Early Southern Decorative Arts, Old Salem, Inc., 1965.

Cummings, Abbott Lowell. *Rural Household Inventories*. Boston: The Society for the Preservation of New England Antiquities, 1964.

Dow, George Francis. *The Arts & Crafts in New England 1704–1775*. Topsfield, Massachusetts: The Wayside Press, 1927.

———. *Every Day Life in the Massachusetts Bay Colony*. Boston: The Society for the Preservation of New England Antiquities, 1935.

Downs, Joseph. *Pennsylvania German Arts and Crafts: A Picture Book*. New York: The Metropolitan Museum of Art, 1949.

Fales, Dean A., Jr. *Essex County Furniture: Documented Treasures from Local Collections 1660–1860*. Salem, Massachusetts: Essex Institute, 1965.

Gottesman, Rita Susswein (comp.). *The Arts and Crafts in New York 1726–1776*. New York: The New[-]York Historical Society, 1938.

———. *The Arts and Crafts in New York 1777–1799*. New York: The New-York Historical Society, 1954.

———. *The Arts and Crafts in New York 1800–1804*. New York: The New-York Historical Society, 1965.

Hornor, William Macpherson, Jr. *Blue Book, Philadelphia Furniture, William Penn to George Washington*. Philadelphia: Privately printed, 1935.

Kettell, Russell Hawes. *The Pine Furniture of Early New England*. New York: Doubleday, Doran & Co., Inc., 1929; reprinted New York: Dover Publications, Inc., n.d.

[Kirk, John T.]. *Connecticut Furniture: Seventeenth and Eighteenth Centuries*. Hartford, Connecticut: Wadsworth Atheneum, 1967.

Luther, Clair Franklin. *The Hadley Chest*. Hartford, Connecticut: The Case, Lockwood & Brainard Company, 1935.

Lyon, Irving W. *The Colonial Furniture of New England*. Boston and New York:

Houghton, Mifflin and Company, 1891.

[Page, John]. *Litchfield County Furniture 1730–1850*. Litchfield, Connecticut: Litchfield Historical Society, 1969.

Prime, Alfred Coxe (comp.). *The Arts & Crafts in Philadelphia, Maryland, and South Carolina, 1721–1785*. Series One. Topsfield, Massachusetts: The Wayside Press, for the Walpole Society, 1929.

———. *The Arts & Crafts in Philadelphia, Maryland, and South Carolina, 1786–1800*. Series Two. Topsfield, Massachusetts: The Wayside Press, for the Walpole Society, 1932.

[Randall, Richard H., Jr.]. *The Decorative Arts of New Hampshire 1725–1825*. Manchester, New Hampshire: The Currier Gallery of Art, 1964.

Rice, Norman S. *New York Furniture Before 1840*. Albany, New York: Albany Institute of History and Art, 1962.

Schiffer, Margaret Berwind. *Furniture and Its Makers of Chester County, Pennsylvania*. Philadelphia: University of Pennsylvania Press, 1966.

Selden, Marjorie Ward. *The Interior Paint of the Campbell–Whittlesey House 1835–1836*. Rochester, New York: The Society for the Preservation of Landmarks in Western New York, 1949.

Stoudt, John Joseph. *Early Pennsylvania Arts and Crafts*. New York: A. S. Barnes and Company, Inc., 1964.

Wainwright, Nicholas B. *Colonial Grandeur in Philadelphia: The House and Furniture of General John Cadwalader*. Philadelphia: The Historical Society of Pennsylvania, 1964.

B. Articles

Baker, Muriel L. "Decorated Furniture and Furnishings," *Bulletin*, The Connecticut Historical Society, XXV (July 1960), 65–73.

Bassett, Preston R. "An Unrecorded Hadley Chest," *Antiques*, LXXV (May 1959), 450, 460–461.

Berkley, Henry J. "Early Maryland Furniture," *Antiques*, XVIII (September 1930), 209–211.

Boyd, E. "Antiques in New Mexico," *Antiques*, XLIV (August 1943), 58–62.

Brazer, Esther Stevens Fraser. "The Early Boston Japanners," *Antiques*, XLIII (May 1943), 208–211.

———. "A Pedigreed Lacquered Highboy," *Antiques*, XV (May 1929), 398–401.

———. "Pennsylvania Bride Boxes and Dower Chests," *Antiques*, VIII (July and August 1925), 20–23 and 79–84.

———. "Pennsylvania German Dower Chests . . . ," *Antiques*, XI (February, April, June 1927), 119–123, 280–283, and 474–476.

———. "Pioneer Furniture from Hampton, New Hampshire," *Antiques*, XVII (April 1930), 312–316.

———. "The Tantalizing Chests of Taunton," *Antiques*, XXIII (April 1933), 135–138.

Butler, Joseph T. "A Case Study in Nineteenth-Century Color: Redecoration at Sunnyside," *Antiques*, LXXVIII (July 1960), 54–56.

Claiborne, Herbert A. "Some Colonial Virginia Paint Colors," *The Walpole Society Note Book*. Portland, Maine: The Walpole Society, 1951, 33–56.

——. "Some Paint Colors from Four Eighteenth-Century Virginia Houses," *The Walpole Society Note Book*. Portland, Maine: The Walpole Society, 1948, 57–81.

Cornell, Edna. "Smoky Gold," *Old-Time New England*, XXXI (October 1940), 41–43.

Deane, Samuel. "An Account of Yellow and Red Pigments, Found at Norton . . . ," *Memoir of the American Academy of Arts and Sciences*. Boston, 1785, I, 378–379.

Dyer, Walter A. "Connecticut Valley Craftsmen Produced Painted Chests," *American Collector*, III (March 21, 1935), 1, 7.

Garrett, Wendell D. "Living with Antiques: The Connecticut Home of Mary Allis," *Antiques*, XCVI (November 1969), 754–762.

Giffen, Jane C. "New Hampshire Cabinetmakers and Allied Craftsmen, 1790–1850," *Antiques*, XCIV (July 1968), 78–87.

Gillingham, Harold E. "The Philadelphia Windsor Chair and Its Journeyings," *Pennsylvania Magazine of History and Biography*, LV (1931), 301–332.

"Hadley and Connecticut Chests," *Antiques*, XLIX (February 1946), 132–133.

Harlow, Thompson R. (comp.). "Connecticut Cabinetmakers," *Bulletin*, The Connecticut Historical Society, XXXII (October 1967), 97–144 and XXXIII (January 1968), 1–40.

Kane, Patricia E. "The Joiners of Seventeenth Century Hartford County," *Bulletin*, The Connecticut Historical Society, XXXV (July 1970), 65–85.

Little, Nina Fletcher. "The Painted Decoration" (New York State Historical Association), *Antiques*, LXXV (February 1959), 182–185.

"Living with Antiques: The Cannondale, Connecticut, Home of Mr. and Mrs. Howard Lipman," *Antiques*, LXXI (June 1957), 542–546.

Lyon, Irving W. "The Oak Furniture of Ipswich, Massachusetts. I. Florid Type. Dennis Family Furniture," *Antiques*, XXXII (November 1937), 230–233; "II. Florid Type. Miscellaneous Examples," *Antiques*, XXXII (December 1937), 298–301; "III. Florid Type. Scroll Detail," *Antiques*, XXXIII (February 1938), 73–75; "IV. The Small-Panel Type," *Antiques*, XXXIII (April 1938), 198–203; "V. Small-Panel Type Affiliates," *Antiques*, XXXIII (June 1938), 322–325; "VI. Other Affiliates: A Group Characterized by

Geometrical Panels," *Antiques*, XXXIV (August 1938), 79–81.

——. "Pedigreed Early Furniture," *Old-Time New England*, XXIX (October 1938), 55–61.

Marvin, G. R. "'Painters Arms' Signs in the Society's Collections," *Proceedings*, The Bostonian Society (1934), 39–45.

Nickerson, C. H. "Robertsville and Its Chair Makers," *Antiques*, VIII (September 1925), 147.

Norman-Wilcox, Gregor. "Is It Pennsylvania Dutch?" *Antiques*, XLV (March 1944), 127–130.

Park, Helen. "The Seventeenth-Century Furniture of Essex County and Its Makers," *Antiques*, LXXVIII (October 1960), 350–355.

"The Pennsylvania German Arts" (The Philadelphia Museum of Art), *Antiques*, LXXV (March 1959), 264–271.

Ramsey, John. "Zoar and Its Industries," *Antiques*, XLVI (December 1944), 333–335.

Randall, Richard H., Jr. "Works of Boston Cabinetmakers, 1795–1825," *Antiques*, LXXXI (February and April 1962), 186–189 and 412–415.

Robacker, Earl F. "Wooden Boxes of German Pennsylvania," *Antiques*, LXI (February 1952), 171–173.

Roth, Rodris. "Interior Decoration of City Houses in Baltimore: The Federal Period," *Winterthur Portfolio 5* (1969), 59–86.

Stockwell, David. "Windsors in Independence Hall," *Antiques*, LXII (September 1952), 214–215.

Vedder, Alan C. "New Mexico Spanish Colonial Art for Britain," *Antiques*, LXXXIII (May 1963), 553–556.

Warren, William L. "More About Painted Chests," *Bulletin*, The Connecticut Historical Society, XXIII (April 1958), 50–60.

——. "Were the Guilford Painted Chests Made in Saybrook?," *Bulletin*, The Connecticut Historical Society, XXIII (January 1958), 1–10.

Whitmore, Eleanore M. "Origins of Pennsylvania Folk Art," *Antiques*, XXXVIII (September 1940), 106–110.

Winchester, Alice. "Living with Antiques: Cogswell's Grant, the Essex County Home of Mr. and Mrs. Bertram K. Little," *Antiques*, XCV (February 1969), 242–251.

III. INDIVIDUALS

[Brazer], Esther Stevens Fraser. "The Elimination of Hotchkiss," *Antiques*, XVI (October 1929), 303–306. (Hitchcock.)

——. "Random Notes on Hitchcock and His Competitors," *Antiques*, XXX (August 1936), 63–67.

Burton, E. Milby. *Thomas Elfe, Charleston Cabinet-Maker*. Charleston, South Carolina: The Charleston Museum, 1952.

Comstock, Helen. "An Ipswich Account Book 1707–1762," *Antiques*, LXVI (September 1954), 188–192. (John and Thomas Gaines.)

Davidson, George. MS. Waste Book, Boston, 1793–?. Old Sturbridge Village.

DeVoe, Shirley Spaulding. "The Litchfield Manufacturing Company, Makers of Japanned Papier Mâché," *Antiques*, LXXVIII (August 1960), 150–153.

[Evans], Nancy A. Goyne. "Francis Trumble of Philadelphia—Windsor Chair and Cabinetmaker," *Winterthur Portfolio One* (1964), 221–241.

Giffen, Jane C. "Susanna Rowson and Her Academy," *Antiques*, XCVIII (September 1970), 436–440.

Gray, William. MS. Account Book, Salem, Massachusetts and Portsmouth, New Hampshire, 1774–1814. Essex Institute.

Hansen, David. "Gawen Brown, Soldier and Clockmaker," *Old-Time New England*, XXX (July 1939), 1–9.

Harlow, Henry J. "The Shop of Samuel Wing, Craftsman of Sandwich, Massachusetts," *Antiques*, XCIII (March 1968), 372–377.

Hipkiss, Edwin J. "A Seymour Bill Discovered," *Antiques*, LI (April 1947), 244–245.

Hoopes, Penrose R. *Shop Records of Daniel Burnap Clockmaker*. Hartford, Connecticut: The Connecticut Historical Society, 1958.

Kimball, Fiske. *Mr. Samuel McIntire, Carver: The Architect of Salem*. Portland, Maine: Southworth–Anthoensen Press, for the Essex Institute, 1940.

Lipman, Jean. "Asahel Powers, Painter," *Antiques*, LXXV (June 1959), 558–559.

——. *Rufus Porter, Yankee Pioneer*. New York: Clarkson N. Potter, Inc., 1968.

Little, Nina Fletcher. "New Light on Joseph H. Davis, 'Left Hand Painter,'" *Antiques*, XCVIII (November 1970), 754–757.

Longcope, Henry. "Some Rescued Stencils of Earlier Days," *Antiques*, I (April 1922), 159–161.

McClelland, Nancy. *Duncan Phyfe and the English Regency 1795–1830*. New York: William R. Scott, Inc., 1939.

McClinton, Katherine M. "Ezra Ames, Ornamental Painter," *Antiques*, LX (September 1951), 194.

Moore, Mabel Roberts. *Hitchcock Chairs*. New Haven, Connecticut: Yale University Press, for The Tercentenary Commission of the State of Connecticut, 1933; reprinted Southampton, New York: Cracker Barrel Press, n.d.

"Paints and Receipts for Wooden Work," *Bulletin*, The Connecticut Historical Society, IX (January 1943), 9–16. (Unidentified painter, c. 1801.)

Park, Helen. "Thomas Dennis, Ipswich Joiner: A Re-examination," *Antiques*, LXXVIII (July 1960), 40–44.

Parsons, Charles S. *The Dunlaps & Their Furniture*. Manchester, New

Hampshire: The Currier Gallery of Art, 1970.

Poole, Earl L. "Joseph Lehn, Driven to Design," reprinted in Ramsay (ed.), *The Decorator Digest*, pp. 209–213. From *The American German Review*; also *Bulletin* No. 20, School District of Reading, Pennsylvania, Museum and Art Gallery.

Priest, Elizabeth. "The Hitchcock Chair," *Old-Time New England*, XLII (Summer 1951), 14–17.

Raley, Robert L. "Interior Designs by Benjamin Henry Latrobe for the President's House," *Antiques*, LXXV (June 1959), 568–571.

Rea, Daniel and Johns(t)on, John, etc. MS. Account Books, Boston, 1764–1802. 10 vols. Daybook of Samuel Perkins, 1811–1824, included. 10 vols. Baker Library, Harvard University School of Business Administration.

Robinson, Olive Crittenden. "Signed Stenciled Chairs of W. P. Eaton," *Antiques*, LVI (August 1949), 112–113.

Roy, L. M. A. "Redecorating a Hitchcock Chair," *Antiques*, LVI (August 1949), 110–112.

Stoneman, Vernon C. *John and Thomas Seymour: Cabinetmakers in Boston 1794–1816*. Boston: Special Publications, 1959.

——. *A Supplement to John and Thomas Seymour: Cabinetmakers in Boston 1794–1816*. Boston: Special Publications, 1965.

Swan, Mabel Munson. "John Ritto Penniman," *Antiques*, XXXIX (May 1941), 246–248.

——. "The Johnstons and the Reas—Japanners," *Antiques*, XLIII (May 1943), 211–213.

——. "The Man Who Made Simon Willard's Clocks," *Antiques*, XV (March 1929), 196–200 (John Doggett.)

——. *Samuel McIntire, Carver, and the Sandersons, Early Salem Cabinet Makers*. Salem, Massachusetts: The Essex Institute, 1934.

——. "Where Elias Hasket Derby Bought His Furniture," *Antiques*, XX (November 1931), 280–282.

Taylor, Gertrude J. "Mrs. Susanna Rowson, 1762–1824; An Early English-American Career-Woman," *Old-Time New England*, XXXV (April 1945), 71–74.

Thompson, Mrs. Guion. "Hitchcock of Hitchcocks-ville," *Antiques*, IV (August 1923), 74–77.

Watkins, Walter Kendall. "John Coles, Heraldry Painter," *Old-Time New England*, XXI (January 1931), 129–143.

Willard, John Ware. *A History of Simon Willard, Inventor and Clockmaker*. Boston, 1911. Retitled *Simon Willard and His Clocks* and reprinted Mamaroneck, New York: Paul P. Appel, 1962; also reprinted New York: Dover Publications, Inc., 1968.

Winchester, Alice. "The ABC's of Hitchcock Chairs," *Antiques*, XLI (June 1942), 369–370; reprinted *Antiques*, LXI (March 1952), 256–257.

Wolf, Edwin, 2nd, and Smith, Robert C. "A Press for Penn's Pump," *Art Quarterly*, XXIV (Autumn 1961), 227–248.

Wood, Charles B., III. "Mr. Cram's Fan Chair," *Antiques*, LXXXIX (February 1966), 262–264.

[Wood], Elizabeth A. Ingerman. "Personal Experiences of an Old New York Cabinetmaker," *Antiques*, LXXXIV (November 1963), 576–580.

IV. MANUALS AND EARLY WORKS WITH SECTIONS ON PAINTS

The American Grainers' Hand-Book. New York, 1872.

Arrowsmith, H. W. and A. *The House Decorator and Painter's Guide*. London, 1840.

The Artist's Assistant. London: Laurie & Whittle, 1806.

The Artist's Companion and Manufacturer's Guide. Boston, 1814.

Bate, John. *The Excellent Arts and Sciences of Drawing, Colouring, Limning, Paynting, Graving, and Etching*. In *The Mysteries of Nature and Art*. London: Andrew Crook, 1654.

Cooley, Arnold James. *A Cyclopædia of Six Thousand Practical Receipts.* New York: Appleton, 1854.

[Dobson, Thomas (comp.)]. *Encyclopædia; Or A Dictionary of Arts, Sciences, and Miscellaneous Literature*. 18 vols. Philadelphia: Thomas Dobson, 1798. And *Supplement*. 3 vols. Philadelphia: Thomas Dobson, 1803. (See Japanning, IX; and Painting, XII, especially.)

The Domestic Encyclopedia. 3 vols. Philadelphia, 1821 (2nd ed.).

Dossie, Robert. *Handmaid to the Arts.* London, 1758 (2nd ed., 1764).

Edwards, George, and Darly, Mathias. *New Book of Chinese Designs*. London, 1754.

Enfield, William. *Young Artist's Assistant*. London: Simpkin and Marshall, 1822 (3rd ed.).

Gandee, B. F. *The Artist, or Young Ladies' Instructor in Ornamental Painting, Drawing, &c.* London: Chapman and Hall, 1835.

Gardner, Franklin B. *Everybody's Paint Book.* New York: M. T. Richardson, 1885.

The Gilder's, Grainer's and Varnisher's Manual. London: M. Taylor, 1838.

The Golden Cabinet; Being the Laboratory, or Handmaid to the Arts. Philadelphia, 1793.

Hay, D. R. *The Laws of Harmonious Colouring Adapted to Interior Decorations, Manufactures, and Other Useful Purposes.* Edinburgh, 1828.

The Household Cyclopædia of Practical Receipts and Daily Wants. Springfield, Massachusetts, 1874.

The Ladies' Amusement, or Whole Art of Japanning Made Easy. London, n.d. (c. 1760).

Mackenzie's Five Thousand Receipts in All the Useful and Domestic Arts. Philadelphia, 1829.

The Method of Learning to Draw in Perspective. . . . Likewise a New and Curious Method of Japanning. London, 1732.

Moore, R. *The Artizan's Guide and Everybody's Assistant* Montreal, 1873.

The Painter, Gilder, and Varnisher's Companion. Philadelphia, 1850 (8th ed., 1866; 10th ed., 1869; 16th rev. ed., 1889).

Porter, Rufus. *A Select Collection of Valuable and Curious Arts, and Interesting Experiments.* Concord, New Hampshire: Rufus Porter, 1825.

Rees, Abraham (comp.). *The Cyclopædia: Or, Universal Dictionary of Arts, Sciences, and Literature.* 41 vols., plus 6 vols. plates. Philadelphia: Samuel F. Bradford, n.d. (c. 1821). (See Painting, XXVII, especially.)

Salmon, William. *Polygraphice.* London, 1685.

The School of Miniature. London: S. Harding, 1733.

Sheraton, Thomas. *The Cabinet Dictionary.* London: W. Smith, 1803; reprinted New York: Praeger Publishers, 1970.

Smith, George. *The Cabinet-Maker and Upholsterer's Guide: Being a Complete Drawing Book.* London: Jones and Co., 1826.

Smith, John. *The Art of Painting in Oyl.* London, 1701 (5th ed., 1723).

Stalker, John, and Parker, George. *A Treatise of Japaning and Varnishing.* Oxford, 1688; reprinted London: Alec Tiranti, 1960.

Tingry, P. F. *The Painter and Varnisher's Guide.* London, 1804 (2nd ed., 1816; 3rd ed., 1829); also Philadelphia, 1831. Title here is from 2nd edition.

Tucker, Waldo. *The Mechanic's Assistant.* Windsor, Vermont, 1837.

Valuable Secrets Concerning Arts and Trades. London, 1775; Dublin, 1778. American editions published in Norwich, Connecticut, 1795; Boston, 1798; and New York, 1809 and 1816.

Wheeler, Gervase. *Homes for the People.* New York, 1855.

White, J. *Arts Treasury of Rarities and Curious Inventions.* London, 1770 (5th ed.).

Whittock, Nathaniel. *The Decorative Painters' and Glaziers' Guide.* London: Isaac Taylor Hinton, 1828.

——. *The Oxford Drawing Book; Or, The Art of Drawing.* London: Edward Lacey, 1825.

CREDITS

INDEX

INDEX OF OWNERS OF
FURNITURE ILLUSTRATED